AN UNKNOWN GOD

*Essays in Pursuit
of the Sacred*

AN UNKNOWN GOD
Essays in Pursuit of the Sacred

An ex-priest reflects on priestly formation, the crisis in Catholicism, and the past and future of faith.

TONY EQUALE

The Institute for Economic Democracy
Sun City, Arizona

An Unknown God
Essays in Pursuit of the Sacred,
Tony Equale

Published by the Institute for Economic Democracy (IED) Press

The Institute for Economic Democracy
(Sustainable World Developnment ... Elimination of Poverty and Wars)
13851 N 103 Ave
Sun City, AZ 85351 USA
ied@ied.info
1-888-533-1020

© copyright 2008, Tony Equale. All rights reserved.

Bowkerlink categories: (1) Religion (2) Spirituality

Library of Congress Cataloging-in-Publication Data

Equale, Tony.
  An unknown God : essays in pursuit of the sacred : an ex-priest reflects on priestly formation, the crisis in Catholicism, and the past and future of faith / Tony Equale.
     p. cm.
ISBN 978-1-933567-26-6 (pbk.: alk. paper) --
ISBN 978-1-933567-27-3 (hardback)
 1. Spirituality. 2. Catholic Church. 3. Christianity--21st century.
4. Faith. I. Title.
  BL624.E68 2009   202--dc22
   2009011680

To the Memory of Mary Perkins Risacher
compañera, presente!

So Paul, standing in the middle of the Areopagus, said: "Men of Athens, ... as I passed along I found an altar with this inscription, 'To an unknown god.' What therefore you worship as unknown ... gives to all men life and breath and everything. ... he is not far from each one of us, for 'In him we live and move and have our being.' ... 'We are indeed his offspring.'

The Acts of the Apostles, 17:22 - 28 (RSV)

CONTENTS

PROLOGUE … 1

CHAPTER I *Is Reform Possible?* … 7

CHAPTER II *The Doctrine of the Soul* … 58

CHAPTER III *The Doctrine of God* … 118

CHAPTER IV *Toward a Metaphysics of Process* … 203

CHAPTER V *Testimony of the Mystics I: Meister Eckhart* … 240

CHAPTER VI *Testimony of the Mystics II: Overview* … 273

ACKNOWLEDGEMENTS

I would like to express my deep gratitude especially to Zenya Wild who read the whole manuscript and made many valuable suggestions to improve readability.

Likewise my thanks go to Sheyla Hirshon who brought a critical eye to key sections

... and to those whose constant encouragement over the course of years moved me finally to complete this project, Ann Pat Ware, Vera and Barney Rooney, Dorothy Semple, Paul Knitter, Bill Duncan, Vic DeVita, John and Patty Hyland, Pat and Maureen Kenny, Tom and Eileen McCabe.

... and to my late spouse Mary Risacher whose insight and spirit permeate these pages.

AN UNKNOWN GOD

Prologue

There is a time to tear down, says Qoheleth the Teacher. But he never said there was a time when it would be convenient. Nor did he assure us that the result would leave intact our cherished institutions. I refer to Christianity in general and for sure, Roman Catholicism. It may be that any time is as good as any other for this most distasteful of tasks: tearing down what needs to be torn down ... not repairing, not tinkering, not hedging ... and accepting the possibility that what gets torn down may be replaced by something very different.

In my opinion it has to be done. The sooner we get it over with, the sooner the next step can begin. That's what these essays are about: renewal — renewal of our relationship to the Sacred. That's the priority and that's what I think this book accomplishes. Then ... only maybe ... voluntary renewal of the institution that has claimed the exclusive rights to broker the Sacred ... and even *to be* the Sacred.

Tearing down and rebuilding, uprooting and planting, separating the baby from the bathwater. Pick your metaphor. The image that defines the terms of my personal search is bonded to my psyche, welded there from years of reciting the psalms at the traditional hours. Tuesday at midday we say:

> *My soul thirsts for God*
> *for the living God*
> *When will I come and behold the face of God?*[1]

The face of this "God" is unknown. My question since I was very young has always been, "what is 'God' like?" I've decided, at

---
[1] *Holy Bible,* Revised Standard Version New York: Thomas Nelson 1953, Psalm 42: vs 2

this point in my travels, that "God" may not be the best word for what I'm looking for ... and finding. So I keep it in quotes.

My background may help explain this obsession: I was a Roman Catholic priest. Catholic Christianity forms the background of my formation and hence for me "the Sacred," past and future, is focused through those lenses. These reflections, however, will take us well beyond what have been traditionally considered the Christian answers. The Christian institutions may not have the flexibility to absorb them. We have to anticipate that. If you are not mainstream Christian, it may be easier for you to consider my suggestions.

In any case, you may not be familiar with the elements of Catholic Christian formation. Don't worry. I explain things as I go. You won't get lost. I suspect that we share an obsession with the Sacred, you and I. It's what brought you to this book. That's all you need.

The Essays

The chapters in this set of reflections are separate essays. Each could stand on its own. But, there is an intrinsic relatedness among them that justifies their being gathered as a collection. Together they cover the territory that, I believe, will at least get us started on this daunting undertaking.

I wrote these essays as a stimulus to dialog. They are unavoidably controversial and challenging for traditional Christians. Writing can be robust or conciliatory depending on the level of polemics one is willing to sustain. I have chosen robust, and I expect a robust response from my readers. This is not an academic exercise. I write these as letters to unknown friends, and I invite your correspondence.

The first essay is autobiographical and stands out from the others because of its personal character and the criticism it levels at the operations of the institutional Catholic Christian Church. All the other chapters are of a more topical nature. The second reviews the concept of the immortal soul; the third examines the traditional doctrine of God. The fourth is philosophical and challenges the traditional understanding of "God" as *esse in se subsis-*

tens, "Being itself." The last two essays attempt to recapitulate the entire discussion by examining the remarkable and at times entirely unexpected ideas of the mystics, Christian and other.

A *caveat*: some of this material reads quickly, some does not. If the waters get turbid and unfamiliar, slow down. The theological and philosophical thinking that was the core of my formation, had to be confronted. There was no other way for me. It's thick, but navigable.

The occasion of writing Chapter I in 2002 was the emerging news of the pedophile phenomenon within the Catholic clergy. While the prurient fascination with the issue has since subsided, it remains unresolved, an open wound, a standing indictment against the moral credibility of the Catholic Christian Church. In tandem with the decrease in popular interest, media coverage has waned even though evidence of equally appalling events and an even wider cover-up involving the Vatican itself, have been revealed.[2] So, from a superficial point of view, some may consider that first essay *passé*. But Catholic priests and ex-priests that I know are still tearing themselves apart over the issue, not to mention those people who were abused and now abandoned. In fact, it is perhaps only at this remove, as we begin to reflect on these revelations with some distance, that we can discern the depth of the foundational fractures they reveal. The phenomenon of pervasive pedophilia speaks to root flaws in denominational Roman Catholic Ideology that must be unearthed and dealt with — radically. There is bathwater here that needs to be flushed away.

Mary

Most of these essays were written between 2002 and 2004, a period of extreme emotional intensity in my personal life. Mary Risacher, my wife of 29 years, was diagnosed with lymphatic cancer early in 2002. She died on the 5th of December 2005 after four years of a roller-coaster of hope and despair, short term victories and ultimate defeat, which I shared intimately with her. In keeping

---

[2] Cf. articles May-June 2006 in NCR on Marcial Maciel Degollado of the "Legionaires of Christ" in Mexico. Also Jason Berry and Gerald Renner, *Vows of Silence*, Free Press, NY, 2004.

with our practice of sharing everything, we spent her last year preparing for death. When she died that Monday morning — alone — I felt unexpectedly abandoned ... somehow I had never prepared myself to be left behind.

A companion is like a part of yourself. When she dies, that part of you dies, too. But the other part lives on to howl in the night. For me it is even more complex than that. This intensity, this symbiosis, this expanded "self," as well as this loss would have been denied me by the celibate vow. This reflection was not included in that first Chapter which focuses on the issue of mandatory celibacy for the Catholic clergy. It's an important omission, but there was no way around it. Because partners tend to take one another for granted, the extent of the ingrafting — the personal expansion — is never realized until a loss of this magnitude actually occurs. Sickness didn't even come close; diminishment, no matter how severe, was not loss. Loss is beyond imagining. When I originally wrote Chapter I, I had no idea.

Mary treated everything as if divine. People first, and then nature. She loved everybody and everything. Her "social work" practice was to have relationships, not clients. On the farm we lived on for her last 15 years, it was the same. She cherished the animals, the chickens, the goats, the dogs, not for what they did for us; she made them part of our family. She marveled at the songs and plumage of the birds, she was fascinated by the life that abounded in our forest, the wildflowers, the trees. She worked the land, relished the simple tasks that attended producing our own food and taking care of ourselves. She was very conscious of living on Sacred Ground, and it was infectious. All these things built between us a vision of life on this earth that evoked the embrace of Transcendent Love. Understanding how the flesh we shared with the world around us, unveiled in evolution, was our genetic inheritance, our family name, brought us to our knees. We are sacred in a sacred world.

It was the beginnings of a new spirituality for us that demanded the articulation that are these reflections. They come out of our common life, our shared discoveries, our mutual love and the awe that was born in us. There is nothing here that is *mine* alone. The fact that one person writes down, or in some other way makes real, what both have discussed, analyzed, wrestled with over years and years renders the notion of authorship almost a fiction. In the deepest sense, the material in this book is as much hers as mine.

One element in particular stands out in this regard. When we were first married almost 30 years ago she told me she didn't believe in Providence — that "God" personally micro-managed our lives. I was surprised. After all, she had been a Catholic nun. A belief in that kind of hovering divine presence is one of the bedrock notions of religious life, the focus of a great deal of faith and passionate prayer. To challenge it was huge.

The idea that "God" does not act in any way outside the natural order, obvious as it was, was foundational for me, altering my image of "the face of God." I realized that once you question the naïve, popular and anthropomorphic view of Providence, an entire "theological" world view is also challenged, and that includes a great deal of traditional Church practice. I remembered reading the *Summa Contra Gentiles* of Thomas Aquinas, and realizing from what he said there, that he must have come to the same awareness. Providence, he said, is fulfilled in the natural order. Aquinas repeatedly warned against anthropomorphism. I use a *reductio* analysis on anthropomorphic providence at the start of Chapter III in order to sketch out the conventional, entirely dysfunctional imagery of the popular theist "God."

It may not emerge explicitly in any of these reflections, but the entire world-view being proposed in this book, which includes a reinterpretation of the traditional notion of "God," was an elaboration of that fundamental readjustment to which I was led by Mary.

I hope that by saying this now, it puts these essays in the context from which they emerged. I hope the voice you hear in these words is the collectivity that was really responsible for them: our relationship, nourished and sustained by everyone and everything around us, including yourselves, the readers whom I always had in my mind as I wrote.

Letters

And so, my sacred friends, I am writing you a series of letters around a central theme in an attempt to understand, with concepts and categories that speak to us in our times, that all of reality is Sacred, not only ourselves. I can guarantee that letting you in on the secret, the end of the story, will not in any way eliminate the drama and adventure, the suspense and the anguish that attends arriving there. There is much to be done in separating the baby from the bathwater, reflecting on the past, contemplating the future. The journey from where the Christian Churches have left us, into the new territory that I believe we have all begun to adumbrate in the darkness, is difficult. And the Churches we have come from may not be able to follow us there. It will challenge us to the core. It will question all of the equipment — footwear, vehicles, crutches — we have up to now used for our travels. It will tear down and it will pull up. But I would add that it can't be avoided, especially now when our traditional foundations do not seem strong enough to support the weight of what the centuries have accumulated.

There is no "dogma" here. Nothing finished or definitive. Work with me in this straightforward attempt at an open analysis and re-interpretation of our traditions, — bring your tools and your lunch pail, dig, tunnel, burrow, participate, contribute. Don't be afraid, the task is yours by birth. And don't be afraid of me, I'm only your foil. What's on the table and under the knife is nothing less than our collective tradition. What we wrestle with are the very foundation stones of our common life. If, as I suggest, they must be radically renewed, it will take a community to do it. And at the very end, what will be accomplished in the doing, is nothing other than the community we seek.

There's a time for everything under the sun. And for this hard and dirty work, there's no better time than now.

Tony Equale
Willis, Virginia
September 2008

CHAPTER I:
Is Reform Possible?

The recent pedophile disclosures have wracked the Roman Catholic Church with one of the worst scandals of modern times. The Church has weathered many crises in its two thousand year history; what makes this situation so unusually bad is not only the revelation that many priests have preyed sexually on children, but that it went on for years, known by the bishops who protected the priests and kept it hidden from the public. The authorities showed a callous disregard for the welfare of the people. Catholics reacted with shock and revulsion at these disclosures. It has passed well beyond a scandal; it has become a crisis of survival.

Of all the effects of this disaster, the looming financial bankruptcy of the Church, certainly not beyond the realm of possibility,[3] may in the long run turn out to be the least damaging. What's on the block and could be lost forever is the Church's moral credibility.

I would like to address the issue of the sexual misdeeds of priests and the charges of "cover-up." I offer as credentials for the reflections that follow, two intimate facts about myself: I was a priest and I stopped attempting to be celibate while I was still a priest. I believe that the details of what I call my ordeal, some of which will be forthcoming in this chapter, are relevant and illuminating for the current crisis. I would not bring them forward otherwise. This is not easy for me to write. It may not be easy for you to read.

But I want to say from the start, if I speak about myself and my life, the things that I did, and the things that others did to me, it's not out of a desire to exonerate or condemn any individual, no matter how high or low a status, including myself. I have only one

---

[3] As of 2005, estimates run close to a billion dollars paid out in settlements to victims.

intention in all of this. And that is to provide a *structural critique* of what has made the Catholic Church — which calls itself "the expert in humanity"[4] — a dysfunctional caricature of what it claims to be. The present difficulties are only symptoms, as I will try to show, of transcendent factors that have under girded Western Christianity for millennia, considered bedrock absolutes. If they don't change, you can expect more of the same. This is not a condemnation of individuals; it is the condemnation of *an ideology*.

There's more: The foundational tenets I accuse and attack have done more than define the Catholic Church; they have created Western culture as we know it, with its affects and defects, in the ascendancy in our times, admired and imitated by non-Western people the world over. I say this with deep chagrin. I'm not convinced that the admiration for Western civilization that I've seen coming from other cultures amounts to much more than the inevitable adulation of wealth and power. We must be frank: Western colonial hegemony was gained by the genocidal exploitation of primitive, defenseless people. I am convinced imitating us is not good for our species or our planet. I believe Catholic Christian dogmatic religious absolutes and the Western Culture they have spawned have distorted the humanity of everyone unfortunate enough to have been drawn into their orbit, and the closer to the center, the more distorted.

Harsh? Yes, indeed. But even as we see unfolding before our eyes the characteristic efforts to lay blame on one or another player involved in the drama — the "Cover-Up Cardinal," the serial pedophile or sex abuser, or "the permissive society" — I intend to direct my aim squarely at what I consider to lie at the core of the problem, hidden and protected as always: *the doctrines, ideological assumptions, authority structures and dubious religious practices that we call Western Christianity.* This cult of piety, now diffused throughout the world, has been promoted through the millennia principally by the dogma and discipline of the Roman

---

[4] Instruction On Christian Freedom and Liberation, March 22, 1986, Joseph Card. Ratzinger; Address Of John Paul II To The Commission Of Episcopates Of The European Union (Comece), 30 March 2001. And many more.

Catholic Church. On the altar of this self-divinizing human construct, untold numbers of victims have been sacrificed through the centuries — not least of all its true believers, priests, nuns, dedicated laity — who have been willing to offer themselves for its survival. The Catholic Church is the Sacred Cow of Western Civilization, and some would say it's time it was slaughtered. Protestant and other reformers' attempts to mollify the deleterious effects of traditional Catholic teaching through the restructuring of Christian doctrine and practice in the 16th century have been at best partial and therefore, of less overall consequence than the inheritors of these traditions would like to believe.

Jesus the Nazarene

Through the assistance of those who have spent a generation in search of the historical Jesus,[5] I emphatically contrast Catholic Christian dogma with what I discern to be the simple message of the Nazarene, a first century Palestinian Jew, who remains for me religious guide and paradigm, spiritual father and compassionate companion. I believe Jesus, like the rest of us, is a victim of this Imperial Christian travesty. It is from here that my critique takes flesh. I enlist this Jewish Jesus himself, my brother human being, assassinated as a subversive by the Empire of his time, in the assault on the Catholic Christian absolutist construct.

There are people who welcome the fact that the Church has never been so discredited. They believe it forecasts Catholicism's imminent collapse. But criticism always carries the possibility of reform, and reform may breathe life into a moribund monstrosity. Their formula is simple: DNR, "Do Not Resuscitate," a modification of Voltaire's bitter cry: *"Écrasez l'infame."* "Crush the Beast." I can understand the sentiment, but it is not my intention.

I prefer to work with a different dynamic, harnessing my anger to a different, self-correcting, hermeneutic. It works like this: If

---

[5] Cf. Robert W. Funk, *Honest to Jesus,* Harper Collins, 1996; Marcus Borg et al. *The Search for Jesus,* Bib.Arch.Soc. 1994, Borg, "Portraits of Jesus" p.87. Marcus Borg, *Jesus,* HarperCollins, NY, 2006.

everything I say about Catholicism is true, there is no worry. It will not, it cannot, reform itself — and it will die.

I. The Seminary

I wanted to be a priest for as long as I can remember. No doubt that desire was born of the awe that my Catholic family held for the Church and the dedicated, celibate men who ran it and the women who taught in the schools. Parochial elementary school, taught entirely by nuns, confirmed and intensified my intentions. If my people had any misgivings about the life I said I wanted, it rarely reached the point of discussion much less discouragement. I applied and was accepted into the seminary system which began at high school. It was 1953. I had just turned 14.

Because I was a diocesan seminarian, I was able to live at home and commute to school daily rather than board at some far off rural location, as was generally the case with those who entered the religious orders like the Franciscans or the Jesuits. But for all of us, New Yorkers of ethnic Catholic ancestry, mostly working class and middle class sons and grandsons of immigrants, the minor seminary immediately involved the beginnings of bearing the burden of celibacy.

Given the life we aspired to, this was not unexpected. There would be no dating, no attending even Church-sponsored dances, no "girls" in our life. We were to live as if we had taken a vow. In that first year of high school, we were just kids, in some cases our voices hadn't yet changed, we weren't even shaving. Our ideas about girls, sex, marriage, companionship, family were prepubescent: typically terrified, misogynistic, and dominated by fantasies of the paladin warrior. At that point it was easy to make us willing participants in our own arrested formation. I can't emphasize this fact too strongly. It's important in understanding what happened later in my life, and in the lives of many of us.

We were given Thursdays off and obliged to attend classes on Saturdays to discourage us from developing friendships not in keeping with our "vocation." That meant girls, of course, and other boys who freely related to girls. We were prevented from having those experiences that normally accompany the transition to manhood in our society. That would have involved knowing girls, women, and discovering through those relationships who we were. This was expressly forbidden by the rules, and young as we were, we took those rules very seriously. It was, after all, a seminary. We wanted to be priests. This is what you were supposed to do, so we did it.

A deprivation such as this is central. You can't skip this stage. For maturity, the ground between childhood and adulthood must be traversed sooner or later. If these transitions are postponed forever, the personality remains distorted, immature, infantile. These are key words; we should remember them. They will return to haunt us later in the story. They help explain the ordeals some of us went through and put others through.

In the current welter of recriminations, admissions, confessions and apologies forthcoming from all the principals in the seamy pedophile drama that unfolded to the delight of the press, I have not heard one word of recognition or apology for what in my clear understanding, was the primordial injustice, the root-flaw of the problem. The Church, in the inflexible conviction of its own ideological constructions, persisted in depriving young adolescent aspirants to priesthood of the fundamental building blocks of gender-maturity. The relevance of this fact for understanding the present problems should hardly need elaboration. Pedophilia, minimally, suggests immaturity and sexual repression.

Preparation for a *voluntary* rather than an obligatory celibacy could have easily included the inter-gender contact of adolescence as an essential ingredient for a mature and informed decision to live that life. But in our case there was nothing voluntary being offered; the celibacy of the priesthood was *mandatory* and we were asked to live it in high school. The theory was, if you couldn't handle celibacy, you would know it in adolescence. There was no recognition that social and career pressure on insecure young men could actually repress needs that would only surface later, when the pressure was off. The obligation of celibacy would not tolerate allowing young candidates to go through the processes of normal development.

We should have known, you say? How could we have known? Who were we? None of us, not our families, nor any of our people would have dared sit in judgment on the Church. My father had his reservations at the time, but he was quickly dismissed as "unfamiliar with traditional ecclesiastical practice." He put up no fight. Would it have mattered if we had come from more sophisticated stock? Not according to the evidence. Catholics across the board, no matter how educated, had been conditioned to defer to the "wisdom" of the Church in such important matters.

I began this section by relating that I was only 14 years old. Not everyone started that early. Others entered later, but I want to keep our youth in focus: there were very few who came in after adolescence. Those that joined after high school were still in their late teens and while they were somewhat more experienced, their development was similarly arrested at a pre-adult level. As time went on, of course, the differences between us leveled out. We all developed into adults, but not in sexual maturity.

Of course there were some of my school companions who "broke the rules" and dated. Would I say most? Probably not. I never did. There was an intensity to our seminary *ethos*. And the ones who dated were often careful not to advertise the fact to the rest of us, so serious was the atmosphere for learning to handle the celibate life.

We were like marine recruits; we knew celibacy was a near impossible work of utmost self-discipline. It was our major challenge. Ironically, you have to understand, it was a *macho* thing. Caving in to girls and sex was considered weakness, a lack of dedication, "going soft," a betrayal of our God-given vocation. The battle-plans were drawn along very simple, clear lines. We were fed stories of the great celibate warriors like the many saints — all males of course — who threw themselves into flesh-tearing briers in order to quell sexual temptation. Great efforts went into developing and protecting this fidelity. We were teen-age boys. Nobody knew better than we did what volcanic forces we had to contend with.

Sexual Repression, Moral Inversion

None of this, I'm sure, is news to anyone reading this, but its very obviousness may cause us to lose focus on how devastating it would be for an adolescent's development. I ask you to allow the implications of this simple anti-sexuality and gender separation to sink into your own imagination. And I insist that you understand the dead seriousness that we brought to it. You may laugh at us, at our people and our times; but no one is laughing now at the tawdry results thirty and forty years later. And it was no laughing matter to us and to those who were guiding us.

I'd like to explain a little more how this early-on and sustained repression functioned, and therefore what it did to us psychologically. The most salient feature of the prohibitions was the avoidance of contact with girls. "Don't let skirts stand in your way," was a classic remark that came from one of the more gung-ho priests who were our teachers and models in high school.

"Skirts" were a problem, but not so much for being direct competitors for the priestly aspirant's attentions, as for another more important reason. Sex. Sex was sin. Fundamentally we understood that we were in a promethean struggle with our sexuality itself. "Zero-tolerance" was the goal. No sexual thoughts, no sexual feelings, no sexual experience of any kind. In theory, this applied not only to seminarians but to everyone. The only sexual experience, mental or physical permitted to a Catholic Christian was in marriage and related directly or indirectly to the procreation of the species. Anything else was *mortal sin*. Sexual fantasies were "impure thoughts" and if indulged in, accepted willfully, were labeled in ecclesiastical latinese, "morbose delectation." These were mortal sins. In the scheme of salvation that was taught to us, nothing less was at stake than the very integrity of creation and one's own eternal punishment.

Mortal sin was no laughing matter, not only because you might go to hell for all eternity, though obviously such a threat got your attention. For some of the more serious and sensitive among us, other consequences were more dire. For once you had committed a mortal sin you were in a condition of absolute alienation from

God, you were the possession of Satan, you had forfeited your place in creation. You had destroyed the delicate filaments of harmony that bound the universe together, and you to it, and to the Creator. You were "spiritually dead." You had perpetrated the moral equivalent of taking all the oxygen out of the atmosphere. You suffocated everything you touched. You were a burden on the earth. Everything you did and every word you spoke during that time was rendered meaningless, separated, out of harmony with God and God's world — dead. You could not receive communion (the sacrament of the body and blood of Christ), and you remained in that situation until absolved, in practice always by a priest in the confessional. The psychological effects on those who took all this seriously were devastating.

For some of us, it was worse than hell.

Girls (women) were to be avoided because they were the very objects that your sex drive was all about. Sex was sin; and *therefore* girls were mortally dangerous. Girls might also be *persons* under all that feminine flesh, but it was of much less moment. It always had to be taken as secondary to their potential for being an "occasion of sin" even if that only meant the fantasies generated about them. Please observe. The basic healthy subordination of sexuality to personal relationships, and the inclusion of sexuality within the category of human tenderness, is completely inverted in this scheme of things. Sex, not person, was the central issue; and negatively, at that. Sex was not "good," it was almost always bad, and therefore destructive, alienating, dehumanizing and inimical to the purpose of creation. And for young candidates to the priesthood it also meant personal derailment, failure, career suicide. "Skirts!"

How did teen-aged boys deal with their emerging sexuality in this kind of atmosphere? In my case, the catastrophic significance of sin and betrayal of vocation evoked in me a sufficient horror and hatred of my fantasies, my bodily functions and my meaning as a gendered individual — and most important, of the other gender — that it made me terrified of what stood in the way of my deepest aspirations and most cherished loyalties. Adolescent fear of the opposite sex was compounded exponentially by these influences and for many it turned to repulsion and disgust. What was the result of all that? Ultimately, the efforts to "neutralize" the proper object of our sex drive *actually worked*. It froze our sexual development at the point of neutralization. In my case and many others,' that was in full blown raging adolescence. And when we later decided to de-neutralize, we found ourselves where the time-machine had left us.

For others, neutralization was the psychological equivalent of castration. Shocked? Don't be. It was quite traditional. Origen of Alexandria, the great third century Christian philosopher and theologian, under the pressure of the same horror of sexual sin, actually castrated himself in a literal reading of a statement of Jesus' recorded in the gospels that "if your hand scandalizes you, cut it off." (It's noteworthy that after that unfortunate event, Origen's exegesis became famous for its emphasis on allegory.) But 1700 years later, many of us felt we were faced with the same dilemma as Origen. Mutilation or damnation. Some, it seems, psychologically speaking, did not hesitate. What it did to them, psychologically, only God knows.

Or perhaps we all know ... now.

Who's to Blame?

It serves no purpose to blame the individuals who administered the system in those years. I refer to our teachers and counselors and later the priest-professors in the Major Seminary. They were as much victims of it as we were. They were true believers. We looked up to them, as well we should have. They were vowed celibates who had achieved what we aspired to. They were the hardened soldiers, the disciplined troops in the service of the Divine Master — at least so we thought. And I would venture to say, that in those days most of them really were. You might legitimately criticize some of them for being automatons, self-righteous, judgmental, lacking a human dimension, but not for hypocrisy, and not for weakness. If there was something else going on, we didn't know about it; and in that small religious village, very few secrets were well kept.

In the minor seminary, the equivalent of high school, there was a priest, the one who had made the "skirt" comment I referred to earlier, who would often regale us with stories of his own disciplined accomplishments and conquest of weakness and laziness. He was put there by the Church to be our guide. I felt it was my duty to be impressed by his good example — and so I was. Many were not. To this day I wonder where they got their sense of independent humanity. Many years after I had left the priesthood (itself considered an act of betrayal) he came to my father's funeral, not on my account, but for the sake of my mother who had given his parish financial support. He wouldn't even speak to me. When I recounted this to an ex-priest classmate he said, "Some people never learn what it's all about." I'm not trying to blame anyone; I consider this man a victim like the rest of us. But I do want to emphasize that "learning what it's all about" is ultimately what these reflections are all about.

The Major Seminary

The last six years of training were spent in a monastic environment known as the Major Seminary. It was located in a remote rural area. We were boarded there with no visitors and only two short furloughs for the months of the academic year, September to June. We wore cassocks all day and surplices to chapel, and spent all but 2 hours of most days in silence. Our meals were taken together in silence. We carried about 30 hours of class per week. Each had his own room and bathroom. We were roughly 250 students ranging from about 19 to 25 years of age.

By this time, we were no longer adolescent and most of us had achieved the neutralization that I spoke of earlier. Those who still had questions about their ability to handle celibacy would have left or would shortly leave. I can't speak with numbers, but it seemed to me that the great majority of us were of heterosexual orientation and had reached a certain quiescence of the volatile hormonal assaults of our younger years. Six years without the distraction of "sexual objects," actually made for a relatively peaceful and intellectually stimulating environment. Libido became sublimated, I guess Freud would say, and its energies channeled for many of us into academic areas.

II. Bodies and Souls, Sex and Sin

It was in the Major Seminary with its contemplative environment, however mediaeval, that I became aware of the theoretical background of Catholic doctrine. Much of what I was taught were the traditional conclusions of ancient philosophies that in the time of Christianity's formative period had been accepted virtually as "scientific" fact. And that included the anti-sexuality and gender suppression that were part of the rationale for celibacy.

Some of the seminary courses were being taught in the early sixties by professors — themselves all diocesan priests — who brought an unofficial academic criticism to these attitudes. Their perspectives reinforced an avalanche of progressive theological literature that was emerging at the same time, associated with the "modernization" of the Second Vatican Council, then in session. This was a new perspective for me. My own mentality began to modulate with these new attitudes. These openings seemed to portend future reforms. But Church law and discipline remained the same. They have not changed to this day, and after forty years, my suspicion is they will never change. The virtual absence of any talk about rescinding the requirement of mandatory clerical celibacy after all this time and tragedy is a clear indicator how impervious the Church is to change.

It's not irrelevant that some of the professors who offered those courses were among the many priests who later left the priesthood and married when it became clear that no modifications were forthcoming.

What follows here is a thumbnail sketch of what I was learning. It is central to these reflections for it is the historical and theological background to the sexual issues that have created the crisis in Catholicism at the present time.

1. Early Christianity and the "Immortal Soul"

Fear, if not disdain, has dominated traditional Christian attitudes toward the body from early on. This negativity was born of an ancient Greek belief that the human person was in reality a *disembodied spirit* residing like a prisoner captive in corrupt flesh. To all extents and purposes, the Western imagination was formed by this Platonic mental picture of the soul as a spiritual Charioteer that inhabited and directed the material body as if the latter were a chariot and horses.[6]

Plato was convinced of the utter corruption of matter. Having a body was humankind's punishment for an imagined sin.[7] In this view of things, the human person is really *only spirit*, and is fully existent and functional even in the absence of the organic structures that support human life. Hence, the soul is immortal.

The Resurrection of the Body

It was not always this way. Jewish Christianity's earliest attempt at translation into Greco-Roman terms was patterned on the Mediterranean Mystery cults. The body-spirit split was not a major focus for them. These ritualistic mystery religions — the cults of resurrected god-men like Mithra, Osiris, Tammuz — popular with the lower classes, taught that ritual immersion (baptism) in the "mystery" of the saving god in question achieved for the initiate, participation in the god's conquest of death. This provided an interpretation of the significance of Jesus' resurrection. *Early Christians did not believe the soul was naturally immortal.*[8] For them, immortality was a divine attribute given as a free gift, first to Jesus as a reward for his labors and then to those initiated into his Mysteries.[9] A key phrase inherited from those early days, the

---

[6] Fredrick Copleston, *A History of Philosophy,* Newman Press, Westminster MD, 1962, vol II, p.78. Augustine also held this view.

[7] Plato, *Timaeus, Phaedo*

[8] Jaroslav Pelican, *The Emergence of the Catholic Tradition,* U. of Chicago Press, 1971, p.30 quotes Tatian (d. late 2nd century). The immortality of the soul was considered a *pagan doctrine* that was originally attacked by the early Christian apologists. cf Adolph Harnack, *The History of Dogma,* tr. Buchanan, Dover, NY 1904, vol II p.191,fn.4; p.213, fn.1 "Most of the Apologists argue against the conception of the natural immortality of the human soul." Tatian 13; Justin, Dial. 5; Theoph. II.27

"resurrection of the body" identifies the focus of this faith and is cemented into the earliest Christian Creeds.

But the trend in Mediterranean Greco-Roman religious philosophy, a project of the upper-classes, was toward the *body-spirit dualism* represented by Plato's image of the Charioteer. As the centuries passed and Christianity attracted more upper class members, it embraced Platonism, whose vision and imagery came to displace those of the Mystery cults. In the dualistic Platonic view, the soul is *naturally immortal*; death is entirely due to matter, and a "consequence of sin." The "resurrection of the body" was put on the back burner as it became clear that Jesus' return was not imminent as first believed, and now increasingly irrelevant to an ideology that had no need and little regard for the body. The "afterlife" lived by the disembodied spirit in a "world" other-than-this-one came to dominate the Christian imagination.

Constantine's Word

Parallel with these developments, there was a decisive political shift in the 4th century that had a fatal impact on Christianity's view of itself. Constantine made it the Religion of the Roman Empire, effecting a conversion from "Christianity" to Catholicism. This solidified the Church's transformation from a salvation-cult of the lower classes to an upper-class ritual counterpart to Greek philosophical speculations. The dominant partner in this unfortunate relationship, I hardly need to point out, was the Roman Empire. This partnership of the Church and the Empire had far reaching effects, religious and political.

The very first ecumenical Council, held at Nicea in 325, convoked and directed by the Emperor Constantine himself and held at one of his villas, displays the controlling presence of Greek philosophy, as well as Roman Imperial Politics. It was at this Council, acceding to the personal wishes of the Emperor,[10] that Jesus

---

[9] Cf the many places in the NT where the language about the resurrection of Jesus evokes the "donation of immortality" to him by God: e.g. **Rom. 8:11**, 8:34, 10:9; Gal 1:1

[10] A.H.M.Jones, *Constantine and the Conversion of Europe*, Collier, NY 1962, p.135. "... Constantine ... suggested the relation of the Son to the Father might **be expressed by**

was declared for the first time not only of divine quality but *God-in-person*, of the same "substance" as God the Father. Thus there came into being, a full three hundred years after Christianity's inception, the *dogma* of the Three Persons in God, a blasphemy to monotheistic Jews and later Muslims, and an incomprehensible mystery to everyone else. The many Christians who dared to claim that these declarations about Jesus were an innovation *not* faithful to ancient tradition, were branded "heretics," and persecuted by the Roman State apparatus until they were completely exterminated.[11] I leave to your political imagination the reasons why the now-Catholic Roman Empire found it in its best interests to promote the icon of Jesus as Almighty God, the *Pantocrator*, the All-Ruler, instead of "the first-born of the dead," the oppressed victim of state brutality.[12]

2. Augustine of Hippo — the Architect of the New Rome

The man historically known as "St. Augustine" was an upper class Roman philosopher from North Africa who lived in the first generation after Constantine. Aurelius Augustinus came to Christianity as an adult by way of Manichaeism and neo-Platonism.

The Manichees condemned the human body which they thought to be a creation of the God of Evil.[13] They also prohibited procreation.[14] Neo-Platonism, for its part, shared the Persian Mani's negative view about the body but based its reasoning on the more sophisticated grounds established by Plato — body-spirit dualism. These ancient attitudes towards matter, the body and sex were given a definitive Christian interpretation by Augustine. After his conversion to the religion of the Roman Emperor, Augustine moved to a thoroughly Christian explanation for the evil of the body — namely that it had *originally* been created good by God

---

the word *'homoousios'* ... Eusebius is explicit that the Emperor himself proposed this term, ...;" Cf Pelikan, *op.cit* pp.202f.,207, 210

[11] These heretics were called "Arians" after the name of their spokesperson, Arius, a priest of Alexandria. Cf Pelikan, *op.cit.*, pp. 172-225; also Adolph Harnack, *History of Dogma*, tr Buchanan, Dover, NY 1961 vol IV pp 1-107.

[12] Col 1:18

[13] Copleston, *op.cit*, p.41

[14] Gary Wills, *Papal Sin*, Image Doubleday, NY, 2000, p.166

but that Adam's sin had corrupted it to the core. In spite of the divergent explanations, in all three cases the moral assessment and practical effect were the same. The human body was matter. Matter was corrupt. The body's desires and drives were therefore similarly corrupt and dehumanizing, requiring corrective suppression. This prejudice is undeniably present throughout the writings of Augustine whose thought dominated Christian theology and practice in Western Europe for the next thousand years and beyond.

Original Sin

Augustine's whole era was negative toward sexuality. But he gave it a new twist. Capitulating to sexual desire meant copulation, and coitus was the act, according to him, that was specifically responsible for the transmission of Original Sin — literally passed on in the male seed.[15]

The idea that some great sin lay behind the human condition was a theory of Plato's stemming from at least the 4th century b.c.e. and universally shared by pagans and Christians in late antiquity.[16] Augustine has done the most to elaborate the Christian doctrine of Original Sin as an unpardonable insult to God. In his interpretation, the entire human race was not only affected by Adam's sin, but *was damned* as a result. It was only by incorporation into the *sacrificial death* (note the shift away from the resurrection) of Jesus through Christian baptism that the individual can be saved from eternal punishment. For Augustine, Original Sin was congenital; that meant babies were born with it, and if they died unbaptized, they went to hell for all eternity.[17] This provided the ultimate rationale for infant baptism.

This outrageous position drove the Celtic monk Pelagius and his followers to take Augustine's entire theological construct to task. The Pelagians rejected Augustine's version of Original Sin;

---

[15] This is really only a variation of the prevalent Christian belief in the physical transmission of original sin through the father. Cf Pelikan, *op.cit.*p.289. The insistence on the virginity of Mary was due in great measure to the need to assert the absolute sinlessness of Jesus. This was guaranteed because he had no human father.

[16] Peter Brown, *Augustine of Hippo*, U.of CA. Press, rev.ed 2000, p.390

[17] *Ibid.*,p.401

they denied that babies were damned and people corrupt. Human beings, they said, were naturally capable of living a good human life on their own. In the ensuing polemics, Rome decided that Augustine was right. Pelagius and his followers were declared heretics.

Now that the Empire had become "Christian," being labeled a "heretic" was not an enviable position to be in. Augustine considered the coercive use of state power an indispensable tool for the promotion of God's Kingdom. The Pelagians narrowly escaped the fate of their contemporary Donatists who were suppressed by the Legions of Rome sent by the Emperor Honorius at Augustine's personal request. State power was called the "secular arm" of the Church. Thus were the grounds laid for the Christian persecution of others.

Augustine's interpretations served as a justification for the dictum *extra ecclesiam nulla salus,* "outside the Church there is no salvation." In Augustine's time and on into the future, this "doctrine" came to be applied to the condemnation and periodic slaughter of Jews, Moslems, heretics and "heathen" of all kinds, to the deep shame of all Christians throughout history.

Augustine's "doctrines" were part of an interlocked system that stands at the core of Catholic self-identity to this day. That volatile concoction of premises — an angry warden "God" monitoring a prison full of congenital sexual deviants — supported a conclusion of unparalleled arrogance, as lethal as it was totalitarian: *outside the Church there is no salvation.* It was an assertion that resonated well with the goals and purposes of the Empire.

Christian Mysticism, Concupiscence and Voluntary Virginity

The traditional Christian attitude toward sex was set in stone by Augustine's work. Sexual desire, an ecstatic "loss of reason," was called *concupiscence* and was the special object of Augustine's hostility. In his neo-Platonic world, reason, believed to be a purely "spiritual" operation, was the only *truly human* activity; the movements of the body were either *in se* evil or led eventually to sin. He speculates in his *De Civitate Dei,* written in his mature years, that had Adam not sinned, seminal transfer for the purpose of human procreation would have proceeded as a tranquil act of pure undistracted reason, entirely "without carnal lust."[18] The problem with sex, by Augustine's standards, is its attendant concupiscence, lust, emotional disorder, the palpable result of the fall. It is inordinate, unnatural and inhuman.[19]

We must understand this. Augustine believed we *personally experienced* the effects of Original Sin. It was clearly identified: *lust* with its consequent guilt and shame. And conversely, he believed the action of God — grace, redemption and healing — was *actually experienced* in the quiescence of those bodily upheavals. *The struggle for that quiescence was religion, and the permanent achievement of that quiescence was Christian perfection.* He identified it with the experience of union with God. This was the heart of his theology and spirituality, just as it was the core experience of his life.[20]

Contemplative tranquility, freed from the nagging demands of sin-corrupted flesh, represented a return to original goodness. It was Augustine's quest because it was the quest of the ancient world, and it became the goal of Christian perfection. That quest took concrete form in the monastic life.

Augustine's era saw the rise of small monastic Christian communities that were engaged in the pursuit of the contemplative life and a personal union with God. Virginity was a central feature of the monastic life-style. The ultimate psychological motivation for this virginity was the sublimating absorption of a personal intimacy with God — a *marriage*, in other words, that required, as do all marriages, absolute sexual fidelity. It was a *psycho-erotic* relationship that was supposed to eclipse the need for an erotic relationship with a human being. The Manichaean element — the radical interpretation of procreation as a kind of unnatural karmic re-incarnation — disappeared from the horizon. But the aspect of "mystical marriage" remained throughout Christian history, and continues to function even in our times.

---

[18] St. Augustine, *The City of God,* tr. Walsh et al, Image / Doubleday, Garden City NY, 1958 Bk XIV, Ch 26, p.318
[19] Brown, *op.cit.*p.391
[20] *Ibid.*

3. Mandatory Celibacy

It should be pointed out, however, that the Church never *required* celibacy of the clergy until the 12th century,[21] by Catholic standards a very late development indeed. A forced virginity would have run counter to the very inner dynamic of the mystic's quest — the free self-donation of the human being in expectation of the free self-revelation of God.

Obviously unsuitable as a program for the whole Church, virginity became confined to the monasteries. This monastic virginity was one of the building blocks used for the later erection of celibacy into a *required condition* for Holy Orders and the exercise of ritual priesthood. There were more. Economic and practical matters, like the inheritance of benefices,[22] conflated to produce what is an old[23] but by no means traditional *obligatory* mandate for the clerical state. I want to emphasize the word *obligatory*. Celibacy as an *obligation* for the clergy did not go back to the apostolic era. Even in Augustine's time, despite his denigration of human sexuality, and for another 700 years, celibacy was still a voluntary option for the clergy.

The unprecedented *prohibition of marriage* for the clergy, not imposed for more than a thousand years after the birth of Christianity, is really a remarkable innovation, and a most salient feature for our discussion. Given the continuous tradition from the earliest days emphasizing the *voluntary* nature of celibacy,[24] it would seem that the *prohibition* of marriage, *which was expressly forbidden in*

---

[21] Paul in 1Cor7, *passim* but especially 25-38

[22] "Benefices" were Church offices or appointments that were given to clergy as "in kind" payment. They were meant to guarantee a livelihood to the recipient, and therefore had all the protections of ownership. A parish community or a diocese thus became as someone's "private property." That was considered tolerable during the recipient's lifetime since he had to be supported anyway. But it was not tolerable that the benefice, as private property, should pass as an inheritance to the cleric's son — even though the priest's son may himself become a priest as they often did.

The earliest canons did not prohibit marriage, but prohibited sex and procreation of offspring to the clergy. This would have prevented the conflict of interest anticipated from the possession of the benefice. See fn#18.

[23] First Lateran Council, 1123, Can.3

[24] 1Cor 7

Paul's letter to Timothy [25] can only be attributable to the ultimate ascendancy of the Platonic spirit-flesh dualism. Those ancient prejudices, expressed in Christian terms by Augustine, as we've seen, defined sex as irrational, unnatural, dehumanizing and un-Christian, a necessary evil tolerated only for the reproduction of the species, and an unseemly activity for the sacred hands that touched the body and blood of Christ.[26] These are what decided that marriage, a natural right of the human person, should be forbidden to the Catholic Christian clergy in utter disregard of clearly expressed injunctions of the New Testament — and we might add, the demands of common sense.

A major chapter of this story ended in our times. Near universal recommendations, made in the aftermath of Vatican II, to return to the *traditional voluntary* nature of priestly celibacy were summarily rejected by the Vatican. In any assessment of subsequent clerical life and practice, it is impossible to omit or exaggerate the importance of this rejection.

4. Sex in Marriage

Sexuality "tolerated" for the sake of procreation, an attitude inherited from that ancient Greco-Roman era, was a general principle of Catholic morality that prevailed into our times. It defined marriage exclusively as a contract about sex for reproduction. But by the 1950's and '60's, that ancient perspective had begun to change. In the official seminary courses in my student years, sexuality was beginning to be defined under the category of love and mutual support in marriage. This "theological" shift, minimal and long-overdue as it may appear, in fact represented a major alteration in the Catholic doctrines surrounding sex. It seemed great revisions were underway. For once it was admitted in principle that sex is legitimately performed for purposes *other* than procreation, its morality fundamentally changes. Why, for example, under these new

---

[25] 1 Tim, 4:3
[26] Many statements of the official *magisterium* make exactly that point. Cf Gary Wills, *op.cit.*, pp 132-133. But it seems that the earliest recorded laws that pre-dated the prohibition of marriage, were demands for *ritual abstinence from sex and the reproduction of offspring* for priests and bishops. Cf Denzinger-Schoenmetzer: (ind. syst. K6bg) p.875. esp.## 119 & 185.

principles should contraception continue to be considered morally wrong? There was a momentum underway then that would have radically modified Catholic moral doctrine in the practical order. This went further than the Vatican leadership was willing go. For it would have called for a modification of the "absolute and immutable" claims made for the Church's *magisterium,* its teaching authority. This is the general infallibility that the Church says is guaranteed to function whenever it speaks on faith and morals.

An adjustment to the policy on birth control was so obviously called for that even a Panel made up of bishops and theologians, chosen by the Pope himself and commissioned after the close of Vatican II, returned a recommendation that the prohibition be lifted. As in the case of celibacy, however, it was unilaterally rejected by the Vatican in a famous Encyclical issued in 1968, *Humanae Vitae.* The encyclical amended the update to say that the exercise of sex, in spite of being an expression of mutual love, must *always be open to the possibility of procreation.* Thus "moral consistency" was narrowly interpreted to mean absolute radical immutability, and contraception remained banned.[27]

This turn of events was so irrational that even a few national bishops' conferences, in an unheard of disregard for Rome, advised their people to follow their own conscience in the matter.[28] (Most, however, went along in silence.) And whether advised so or not, most Catholics decided for themselves.

I would like to draw your attention to the way events developed in this case. It exactly parallels the issue of priests' celibacy. There was a responsibly recommended change in traditional teaching and practice, offered by respectable mainstream experts, inspired by the deliberations of the 2nd Vatican Council, rooted in the researched reassessment of the historical factors, that was summarily rejected by a unilateral action of the Pope, citing as justification the consistency of Catholic Doctrine and practice.

The Church's obsession with an inflexibly conceived *consistency* in this area reveals itself for the insanity that it is when you

---

[27] Gary Wills, *op cit,* p 87ff
[28] Ibid.,p.90

realize that the Vatican continues to prohibit condom use in marriage even in the case where one of the partners has HIV-AIDS.[29]

5. Divorce and Annulment

Consistency is a characteristic that has taken on altogether irrational proportions in the post Vatican II Catholic Church. But as we will see, it derives from other doctrinal foundations that seem to leave little room for flexibility. It's illustrative to watch this obsession with doctrinal consistency functioning in the Catholic "solution" to another important marital issue that we learned about in the Seminary: divorce.

"What God has joined together, let no man put asunder," (Mt 19:6) has been cited since the earliest days as gospel proof that divorce was forbidden by God. Prior to the ecclesiastical solution that I will shortly describe, Catholics who divorced and remarried committed "mortal sin;" they were forbidden to receive communion, and would not be granted absolution unless they left their new partners. (Their new union was referred to as "adultery," and "concubinage.") But surprisingly in this case, for a number of reasons, the Church seemed amenable to certain quiet, legally justified adjustments for people who wanted to remain in the Catholic Church, but who also wanted a divorce.

The "way out" was to exploit a loophole in Canon Law. There was a Catholic legal category affecting marriage called "annulment." Most civil codes follow this terminology. Annulment means simply that, upon review, it becomes clear that there was "no valid marriage contract from the very start." In other words, with an annulment, there was no disobedience to the "divine prohibition" against divorce. There was no divorce because there had never been a marriage.

---

[29] In April 2000, Monsignor Jacques Suaudeau of the Pontifical Council for the Family published a little-noticed article in the Vatican's official newspaper *L'Osservatore Romano* entitled, "Prophylactics or Family Values? Stopping the Spread of HIV/AIDS." In it he said that Jon D. Fuller, S.J., M.D., and James F. Keenan, S.J. had distorted church positions in their September 23, 1999 *America* article by suggesting that the Vatican had become "more tolerant" about the distribution of condoms to fight AIDS. He said the Vatican stance hasn't changed. "This is a manipulation. It is blown up and exaggerated," he told The Associated Press.

When you consider the traditional conditions for invalidating (annulling) a marriage contract, the hypocrisy functioning under the surface in this purely verbal solution becomes clear. We had been taught that the marriage contract would be invalid *only* if there was a significant "defect in either matter or form." The "form" of the sacrament was the free mutual consent of the partners, and the "matter" about which the mutual consent was expressed was sex, for the purpose of the procreation of children.[30] Consummation was *prima facie* evidence of consent. Consequently, we were taught that an annulment was not even a remote possibility unless there was some indication that the marriage had *never been consummated*. At any rate, with some creative thinking on the part of astute Canon lawyers, all kinds of marriages were annulled — many of which had existed for years and had produced multiple offspring. What kind of "defect" could you claim for them?

The argumentation brought forward was that there was a "defect in form" because there had been no fully free mutual consent due to *unforeseen and unembraced incompatibilities*. Apparently "for better or worse," did not apply across the board. The newly-expanded definition of the "purposes" of sex within marriage to include mutual support, created a corresponding expansion of the bases for a "defect of form" and therefore annulment.

So divorce became acceptable by *calling it* annulment. On the surface one may commend the flexibility on display here. But note: the operating principle in this verbal sleight-of-hand was to maintain the fiction of the Church's "infallible" magisterium and its juridical control. It could not allow itself to be seen disobeying a divine ordinance and changing its position on divorce.[31]

In this particular matter, which many hailed as "progressive," we can see functioning the dynamic that rules the decision-making process in the Church. An inner logic makes the Church's "image"

---

[30] This requirement simply reproduced the obligatory contract form required by the Roman Imperial government. This was, in turn, derived from Augustus Caesar's policy of discouraging childlessness which was becoming a serious trend among ruling class Romans.

[31] Wills, *op.cit*, pp 170-172

(regardless of the reality) as the bearer of unchangeable infallible divine truth, *a higher moral priority* than anything else on God's good earth — including, as we have all come to realize, the protection of children and their normal, healthy development.

6. The Sexual Revolution

America in the sixties and seventies went through a sexual revolution of major proportions. Society virtually reversed itself on what had been an American reticence about sexual matters in general.

Attitudes changed radically. Sex, after being taboo for so long, came to be accepted as a natural part of the human make-up. The availability of new methods of birth control took much of the fear of pregnancy out of sex, and its casual use became more common. Pre-marital sex became almost routine. Couples regularly "lived together." This was unheard of in prior years.

Religious people expressed themselves with a new-found respect for sex. Denigration of the body and condemnation of the sexual drive as a corruption resulting from Original Sin was no longer considered an acceptable attitude at the practical, pastoral level, even though official Church doctrine remained unchanged. In the psychological realm, there was emphasis on recognizing the unnecessary damage caused by sexual guilt and healing oneself from the repressive past. This "liberated" atmosphere pervaded the Church. The intense fear of sin that had been associated with every sexual thought and feeling was no longer the majority perspective.

Those who disagreed with these developments called them "permissive," and refused to go along. Excesses that were spawned in the wake of those new attitudes confirmed traditionalists in their condemnations. But conservative efforts were rarely strong enough to deter the great transformations underway in moral opinion and behavior.

Excesses

Some discussion of the excesses that attended the sexual revolution will help elucidate the context of the times, and explain some of the accusations that are just now coming to the surface after 30 years. Those excesses, involving unprecedented sexual experimentation, were all part of the developments in larger society.

Some experimentation from those days had to do with behavior that was and clearly remains *unacceptable* in our society. I believe, for example, attempting to return to the *paedo-homosexuality* recorded in Plato's *Symposium*, apparently the motivation behind one of the more infamous cases of the recent pedophile scandals, was of this type.[32] That it recalled a once-acceptable ancient Greek practice is not an excuse; but it is a factor. It was an anachronistic anomaly with no public support that has since disappeared as an open movement, though one may suspect its erstwhile proponents have not abandoned their beliefs.

Then, there was behavior once considered unacceptable but which is proving itself more acceptable as time passes. An example *is homosexual marriage* which is gaining support in our society; and if present trends continue can be expected to achieve eventual approval.

Homosexuality was nothing new. What came in new with the sexual revolution was that it was considered "natural" for some people, and therefore its associated behavior not immoral or prohibited. A new boldness entered with these reassessments. Homosexuals demanded a respect for their committed relationships. That would not have been possible at an earlier time. And today, outside of fundamentalist religious circles, there is a tendency to agree that this is a mature and positive development, liberating homosexuals from the dark and sleazy world of obligatory promiscuity to which a condemnatory society had consigned them. A Church-centered movement toward this end developed, supported by progressive Catholics but quickly condemned by the Vatican.[33]

---

[32] I'm referring to Fr Paul Shanley of Boston whose open support in the late seventies for organizations like "The North American Man-Boy Love Association" was one of the more notorious revelations of 2002. Cf Jason Berry and Gerald Renner, *Vows of Silence*, Free Press, NY 2004, p.65.

[33] "The Archdiocese should withdraw all support from any group which does not unequivocally accept the teaching of the Magisterium concerning the intrinsic evil of homosexual activity. ... A compassionate ministry to homosexual persons must be developed that has as its clear goal the promotion of a chaste lifestyle." From **Ratzinger's Report**

Rome often retaliated on religious personnel who supported gay marriage with punitive measures of various kinds. Bishops like Hunthausen in Washington and Mugavero in Brooklyn who promoted such pastoral efforts were quietly derogated from their positions as ordinary, being supplanted by co-adjutors assigned by the Pope.[34]

Communitarian experiments, discredited as "hippie", which involved multiple simultaneous intimate relationships, either in the context of a "communal household" or not, recall now-forgotten ancient patristic hypotheses which defined the perfection of "Christian Love" as egalitarian inter-personal intimacy, *without sex*. It was the original basis for celibacy. The radical Christian commitment to virginity was, in the minds of some Church Fathers, supposed to create a new universal family, replacing the old one born of blood for a new one born of "water" — the water of baptism. Origen of Alexandria, who died a martyr in prison, in 256 CE, was the most articulate spokesperson for this theory.

In Origen's spirituality, virginity was not a program only for the monk or the hermit, but for the entire Christian community. He saw virginity as the basis of a new level of spiritual intimacy between the genders which would transform all of society, bringing on the full and definitive redemption of all humankind. This inter-personal intimacy — "platonic relationships" — functioned to transcend and replace the constrictive obligations imposed by the traditional family relationships which derived from procreative sexuality. Coming as it did from a radical Platonism that considered the cycle of procreation and death as the *unnatural result* of our fallen condition, Origen's virginity claimed to achieve the reversal of the fall and the return of human society to its original "spiritual" residence in the Spirit World of the "One". Virginity, in this view, was redemption itself. Apparently he believed the universal acceptance of the virginal state would bring on the *parousía*

---

on Seattle Archbishop Raymond Hunthausen, September 30, 1985, Sacra Congregatio Pro Doctrina Fidei, reprinted in the *Seattle Catholic,* Jan 5, 2004.

[34] *Wikipedia*, "Hunthausen"

(the Final Coming of Christ).[35] Augustine would have found most of these ideas germane to his own thinking.

In the context of the 1960's and 70's, however, experiments based on these premises all disappeared, universally abandoned by their participants. The *mystique* of a Christian social transformation achieved by rising above the nuclear family was not capable of withstanding the traditional cultural prohibitions against polygamy on the one hand, and the de-mystification of celibacy on the other. The point here, nevertheless, is that those experiments shared features with a vision that was ancient, and rooted in the common ideology of the Hellenic world. While they are now discredited, it must be recognized that they represented an attempt to re-structure human relationships along the lines suggested by perennial Christian ideals.

All this was part of the atmosphere of those times.

Clerical double-speak

Roman Catholic priests were also impacted by these events. Not only the pedophile phenomena but other unprecedented but less notorious sexual behavior can be traced to this atmosphere and these explorations. The realization, however, that the Official Church was not going to alter its rule of priests' celibacy in any way, even for the most socially acceptable — marriage — entailed a number of problematic consequences.

First of all, after the mass exodus of clergy in the early '70's, the incidence of "vocations" fell sharply. Annual ordinations dropped by as much as 90% in many instances. There are some observers who assert that the Roman Catholic clergy have become predominantly homosexual because of this conjunction of factors.[36]

Secondly, and more to the point, those who were priests stopped being preoccupied with absolute sexual purity. Some even appeared no longer to be particularly concerned about living a life of

---

[35] Peter Brown, *The Body and Society,* Columbia U.Press, 1988 pp.160-177
[36] cf. Donald Cozzens, *The Changing Face of the Priesthood,* Collegeville, MN: Liturgical Press, 2000. It hardly needs to be pointed out that as heterosexuals left the priesthood in order to lead socially acceptable lives as married men, homosexuals were offered no such alternative. There was little incentive to do anything but stay in the priesthood and "make do."

sexual abstinence. For many within the profession, celibacy came to mean *not being married*, rather than abstaining from sexual activity. This was true of both heterosexuals and homosexuals. It was not universal but it was a significant phenomenon. It was known and reluctantly tolerated by the hierarchy, so long as it was accompanied by due discretion.

Given the climate of opinion and the refusal of the Vatican to reconsider the celibate requirement, few would deny that the sexual revolution within the ranks of the clergy was inevitable. But whatever your opinion, please focus on this: *it institutionalized an hypocrisy*. It created a situation where it was quietly understood that if you were a priest *you preserved appearances* but as far as sex was concerned you pretty much did whatever you decided was right.

In a real sense, the entire Catholic presbyterate was drawn into an atmosphere of double-speak on this issue. Many lay people who discovered the naughty little secret may have understood it perfectly, winked knowingly and not been scandalized; but others were very disturbed indeed. In any case, it was a massive exercise in *institutional cover-up* in which most priests, if only to protect the reputation of their profession, were made complicit.

It was also the pre-condition for what followed.

III. The Cardinal And The Cover-Up

Perhaps now is a good time to refocus. My central argument is that the foundational sources that lie at the root of the current problems are *doctrinal*. But the Church habitually diverts criticism from its dogmatic substructure by placing the blame on "sinful individuals."

Deflective scapegoating is an old story. All institutions do it. And it's often tolerated because larger society feels dependent on these institutions; it cannot afford to have them go belly-up. This was the mechanism functioning, I believe, in the case of the Cardinal of Boston who was forced to resign early in 2003 in the wake of the scandals. The alacrity of everyone including the press to accept his resignation as if it were a significant change, somehow inexplicably guaranteeing reform, strikes me as so naïve as to be unbelievable. All public outrage is now declared officially satisfied by this resignation and the assignment of a new bishop. One suspects that the media, like the general public, are embarrassed for the Church and just want the whole damn thing to go away. But the problems will not go away with the departure of a Cardinal, or a flock of them; because the problem does not reside in the men or (future) women who might manage the Church, but in the authority structures themselves and the doctrines that justify them.

Democracy

"A Prince Has Fallen," keened a half-page headline in a New York paper the day after the announcement of Cardinal Law's resignation. Such public grieving illustrates the attachment that our society has for the ancient forms of governance that still exist and function within the Catholic Church. This unexpected pathos might seem surprising in a society that defines itself by the revolutionary overthrow of exactly such antiquated forms of political authority more than two centuries ago. The American rebellion of 1776 not only dismissed the king of England, it did so on the basis of a deliberate rejection of the principle of "divine right" as the philosophical ground for the legitimacy of authoritarian government. Democracy, in theory, is the absolute antithesis of autocratic authoritarianism. The Roman Catholic Church is one of the few institutions in the Western European societal complex that has remained impervious to these profound changes — by which I mean *democracy* — accepted the world over as essential to just government.

Revolutionary democracy was more than the aesthetic preference of a handful of 18th century French intellectuals and their American admirers. It was chosen for the supremely practical purpose of preventing the heinous abuses that are characteristic of, and some might say endemic to, paternalistic authoritarian autocracy. It is unnecessary to point out that the abuses of the current Catholic crisis fall squarely within that category. So besides the inconsistency of having a warm nostalgia for these long-repudiated forms of government, this strange affinity for antiquated authority patterns implies something far worse; it precludes the possibility of the reforms that our present situation requires. The Catholic hierarchy's adamant refusal to allow lay people (i.e. Catholics who are *not* vowed celibates) any but the most superficial advisory role in the resolution of the present problems is not the product of selfish arrogant men; it is the unalloyed, organically consistent expression of the Church's self-definition and doctrinal ground.

Ecclesiastical Authority

The Church is not a democracy and states that fact "definitively." To clarify: the Church defines itself as a "hierarchy."[37] That word, in spite of its sound-similarity to "higher" is actually derived from the Greek word for "holy" or "sacred," and thus means "sacred rule" or "sacred authority." If we took it to mean "divine right" it would not be an inaccurate translation.

The word nearest "democracy" that the official Church has been willing to allow in its self-description is "collegiality"[38] which, in fact, refers only to a certain acceptable interchange among the hierarchy, the Bishops themselves and then, patronizingly, with their associated clergy; it does not include the laity except by the gratuitous invitation of the bishops or pope.

Catholic hierarchical authority is not a quaint, harmless tradition, like the blowing of the shofar on the Jewish Yom Kippur, or the robed rituals of England's symbolic Queen. It is the living, breathing instrument of Catholic social power vigorously and astutely employed in the detailed management of an enormous transnational empire of people, infrastructure and invested wealth. The Pope and Bishops are not impotent figureheads; they have and they exercise absolute unconditional power over the religious lives of a billion people.

But we know the Church is not only the hierarchy. It is a living convocation of human beings who have every right to be governed as justly and fairly in their religious lives as in their political com-

---

[37] Vatican II, *Lumen Gentium* [LG] ch III passim
[38] *LG* ch III, 21

munities. If real participatory democracy is a critically important feature of the exercise of just government, it must apply to the church as well. But it must be recognized that there is no democracy in the Church. And I claim there never will be. Why is that?

Church hierarchical authority is defined in Catholic doctrine and rooted in its core belief; it is *immutable*; it is not open to change, modification, reinterpretation or revision, much less abrogation or removal. There are two classic doctrinal components of Catholic authority. They are "Apostolic Succession" which I combine as one with the Petrine primacy (and papal infallibility), and the other, no less central, the *"ex opere operato"* function of the Catholic Sacraments which works together with the doctrine of the "indelible seal of the priesthood." Both of these, while born in the mists of the past, are fully alive and functioning even "as we speak."

Apostolic Succession

There is hardly anything we could imagine that speaks more to the heart of Catholic self-identity than Apostolic Succession. This doctrine refers to the alleged "fact" that Jesus chose twelve associates not only as friends and followers, but as "apostles," missionaries to the world and future wielders of absolute authority in a powerful Organization that would serve *all humankind* as an exclusive reservoir of divine truth and salvation. The doctrine further declares that Jesus intended that these specific men should choose and empower their own successors, to begin an unbroken chain of inheritance that will continue forever.[39] As I suggested in the introduction, my sense of who Jesus was serves as a hermeneutical tool here as elsewhere. My perspective, guided and encouraged by Biblical Scholars from many denominations in search of the historical Jesus, makes entirely questionable the official Church interpretation of the relevant gospel dialogs.

The historical facts as proposed by the current biblical analysts differ from the perennial Catholic claims. The scholars say that

---

[39] "forever" i.e. "until the consummation of the world" — a phrase used over and over by the Council; LG III, 20

Jesus was a faithful Jew. He had no intention that he or anyone of his disciples should start a new religion. He empowered no one.[40] His call was to renew fidelity to the universal spirit of traditional monotheistic Judaism. He specifically cited as central to his message, the great command of Deuteronomy known as the *"sh^{e}ma ishrael"*: Love God with all your heart and your neighbor as yourself.[41] He never spoke of Original Sin, or his own role as its expiator, which the Church would later claim was the sole and exclusive reason for his mission and death on the cross — and hence his entire purpose in life. He never claimed to be the messiah,[42] much less God; and on one occasion expressly denied the latter.[43] He defined no dogmas, instituted no sacraments, made no rules. His message, derived from the implications of ancient Judaism, was implicitly universalistic, but, in fact, was directed only to his fellow Jews. By insisting that we were all God's children, he emphasized the intrinsic value of every human being, regardless of nationality or social status. Encouraging self-esteem in the context of Roman repression may have been a fatal decision on his part; for in spite of conspicuously avoiding politics in his discourses, he earned the hostility of the Roman Imperial machine and was executed as a political subversive.

Jesus was a moral Teacher and Jewish reformer in the tradition of the prophets. He transmitted his message to a community of his followers as to faithful companion Jews who would continue his work of Yahwist-universalist renewal. Texts, mainly found in the very late (90 CE) gospel of Matthew granting power and authority to Peter, are universally acknowledged to be the interpolations of the later Church community seeking to justify emerging structures by retrofitting them into the mouth of Jesus.[44]

Does this deny the right of the Church to exist or to have developed forms of governance and discipline of its own choice? Not at all. But it does call into question its claims of divine establish-

---

[40] Stephen Patterson, "Sources for a Life of Jesus," in *The Search for Jesus,* Biblical Archaeology Society, Washington DC, 1994, p.24
[41] Deut 6:5
[42] Albert Nolan O.P., *Jesus Before Christianity,* 1976, Orbis, p.107
[43] Mk 10:18; Lu 18:19
[44] Patterson, *op.cit.* p.24

ment. This is critical. The Church has a right to structure its government as it sees fit. *But it also has the right to change it.* The Church argues, however, that it does *not* have that right. It claims *it cannot change* because it was established by God. If you accept the premises of divine foundation, it's hard to argue. How can a community, whose form of government was chosen by God-in-person, ever change it? It would seem only a new revelation could supersede the first. But the Church declares revelation "closed" with the end of the apostolic age. No new revelation about the divinely established structure of Church Authority can be forthcoming. Even a cursory examination of the behavior of the Church throughout its long history will show that it has always acted in accordance with this belief about itself.

There are corollaries here that cry out for attention. We've already alluded to the principal one: *extra ecclesiam nulla salus,* "outside the Church there is no salvation." Once again, the doctrinal premises lead to an inexorable conclusion: How can a Church that is founded by God-in-Person ever have any rivals? How could it ever consider another tradition or denomination to be anything but benighted and in gross error, no matter how sincere, mystical and ethically refined? The Catholic Church's arrogance is not due to sinful men who have not heard its "message of love;" it is, quite the contrary, due to the disciplined and often outstanding performance of those who have accurately heard and faithfully carry out the implications of its beliefs. *Catholic arrogance is due directly to its doctrinal core which is self-divinizing.* Were it to stop claiming itself to be God's personally chosen, exclusive and necessary vehicle for the salvation of all the people on planet earth (even if they don't know it), it would cease being the Catholic Church as we know it.

Ex Opere Operato and the Seal of Ordination

Ex opere operato. This Latin phrase refers to the Catholic belief that its sacramental rituals, like baptism, the eucharist, confession, when they are performed by the authorized minister and in accord with the proper form, achieve their effect automatically and infallibly, in spite of what may be the sinful condition or intent on the part of the celebrant. "From the work being worked" is the literal translation. This functions in tandem with the doctrine of the *sacramental seal* of priestly ordination. The "seal," conferred by the *sacrament* of Holy Orders, is "indelibly imprinted on the soul" of the priest at ordination and remains there forever. It is the *sine qua non* requirement for the performance of critically important sacramental rituals that work automatically, *ex opere operato* — specifically the Sacrament of Penance, and the Eucharist, or Mass, without which the purpose of the Church disappears.

It's difficult to consider such a perspective to be anything but magical. The religious rituals lose their symbolic dimension and become mechanical formulae for the production of projected effects imagined in almost physical terms. The seal is "imprinted indelibly" on the priest's soul. The sacraments are said to produce an automatic "infusion" of grace (as if "grace" were some substance that is poured or injected), the acquisition of which serves as a kind of accumulated currency (it was called, popularly, "gaining grace") earning entrance into heaven. There has been a great effort made in some circles to de-emphasize these features of Catholic belief, but they remain as ever the official doctrine.

The doctrine of *ex opere operato* is a development of the fifth century and certainly not attributable to the early "mystery" perspective that created the sacraments. That fact might serve someday as a basis for its serious review and renewal. But at the present time there is no trend in this direction, and the impact of the doctrine on Catholic authority structure is determinative. Consider. If there must be an ordained priest for a valid Eucharist to be celebrated, it makes him indispensable. Lay people are eternally dependent. Without priests (ordained exclusively by a "successor of the Apostles"), there is no mass, no confession, no last rites, no "Church" as we know it. Hence the Church is necessarily "hierarchical" by its very inner reality. Priests will always run the Church.

Cover-up or Mystique?

What has been denounced as a "cover-up" and the callous refusal to derogate derelict priests, when seen in the light of Catholic doctrine, can be easily comprehended as the by-product of the central position priests occupy in the Church. From the Catholic point of view, priests are not just monastery-trained church employees. They are sacred entities. They are the signed and "sealed," ontologically transformed instruments of God whose invisible sacred powers are uniquely capable of conjuring into existence the very life-blood of the Church, the divine food on which it feeds. They bring God-in-Person to Earth. These are not just *men*, you must understand, they are *super-men*, the symbols of God's powerful presence among his people. They are Christ-on-earth. The priest is the heart of the Catholic religious *mystique*. These men are sacred realities; they *cannot* be "fired." (And the traditional mythology claims they cannot quit, either.)

I often get the impression that people don't really believe that the Church operates on the basis of its dogmatic assertions because they seem so antiquated. Accustomed as we are to *realpolitik* as a counterpoint to the ideological rhetoric coming from national governments, many feel sure that the same political realism is functioning with the Church. We assume that when horrendous and widespread derelictions take place, like the protection of sexual abusers among the clergy, they must be the result of gross individual human error. In the case of the Church, however, you can't jump to the usual conclusions. The Catholic Church didn't "cover-up" the scandals or shift culprits around out of malice or negligence, ignorance or stupidity, laziness or venality. The Church did it because it was convinced of the absolute truth of the doctrines that have been handed down to it through two millennia of infallible authority — in this case the transcendent sacredness and abiding salvific power of the priesthood, which functions *ex opere operato* in spite of the sinfulness of the priest.

The priest, however imperfect, is the channel of salvation for the world. There is no way the hierarchy would choose the benefit of the "allegedly abused" lay person, especially if it were a possibly confused child, over the welfare and continued functioning of the priest.

The Forgiveness Of Sins

Of course the Church is concerned about scandal and immoral behavior. You must understand, however, "sin" has never been a problem for the Church. Sin is the very object of its work, as disease is for a doctor. Combating sin is what it does. And just as when a doctor's prescriptions don't work, the Church feels perplexed when its ministrations for the rehabilitation of the sinner don't bear results. The Church has the very transformative power of God at its disposal: the sacraments and their "sanctifying" grace. There is no other recourse more powerful and effective than the Church and its God-given tools. To whom shall the Church go to heal the infirm — the Church is the divinely appointed physician. So the physician tries again. And again and again. Always applying the same remedies. Does this sound familiar?

The lawyers for the victims of sexual abuse say the Church just "moved the pedophile priests around, to new locations;" they claim this is culpable negligence, the heartless and uncaring disregard for the sufferings of others. They may have guessed rightly that the Church was trying to preserve its reputation. But they seem not to have realized that the Church was, in fact, also employing its classic medicines, the sacraments, *defined as infallibly effective*, to work in these embarrassing and threatening cases, if not at first, then for sure when applied the second, third or fourth time. It was, after all, only "sin." They were priests. The Church was not willing to have the world think that its elite corps, the very instruments of salvation, were themselves beyond the reach of its healing powers.

Yes, there may be more effective ways of handling these pathologies. But, given the traditional literal understanding of the dogmas involved, if the Church were to face the full extent of the problem it would mean the admission of failure across the board: structural failure, sacramental failure, doctrinal failure. That was not about to happen.

The Church was caught on the horns of a dilemma. From a traditional perspective, if its classic powerful remedies did not work, its doctrine said *it could only be due to the resistance and evil in-*

tent of the sinner "refusing" God's grace. (Hence, the Church *always* blames the individual, by default). Ultimately the sacraments *had* to have their intended effect (*ex opere operato*) where the disposition of the recipient was positive. But these men were clearly penitent and sincere. If the sacraments did not work under these circumstances, it would mean the unthinkable: they *could not* work; they were not the powerful instruments they were said to be. And that meant the Church was not what it claimed to be. Without sacramental power the Church was nothing. This was not thinkable.

To change this self definition, and therefore to stop this protection of priests, was not thinkable.

Vatican II

We were ordained, many of us, at the very end of Vatican II in the full blown hope that there would be radical changes to come. I would probably say now looking back, we should have read the documents more carefully since most of what we expected had never really been offered. The hierarchical structure of the Church,[45] the primacy of the See of Rome interpreted to mean absolute, unaccountable, independent power vested in one man alone, the Pope, who was declared to rule and speak with the very mouth of God,[46] the necessity of the Church for universal salvation,[47] the "slavery of error" from which the Church saves the targets of her necessary missionary work to bring "all nations to Christ"[48] — all this was there still, as it had always been, in black and white. Vatican II effused a spirit of collegiality and community, of openness and ecumenism, of humility and humanity that when committed to the printed page, was carefully worded to maintain strict subordination to the same absolutes that had always defined Church identity since the days of Constantine. Read Vatican II. The spirit of *aggiornamento,* the adjustment to contemporary life,

---

[45] LG III, 18
[46] LG III, 18
[47] LG II, 14
[48] LG II, 17

is unquestionably there, but if read by the letter of the text, it's the "same ol' same ol'".

But in those days, we all read it as "spirit." Was that a mistake on our part? There was a clear desire of the Council Fathers, bishops from all over the world, to adjust to the modern world. It's taken us forty years to realize that virtually the only changes that the Papal executives in the Vatican were willing to permit were the use of the vernacular and mass facing the people. If this is an exaggeration, it's not a gross one.

Naturally, one of the changes that many of the clergy had expected was some modification in the rule of mandatory clerical celibacy, especially since it was, by everyone's admission, not central to the definition of the priesthood nor the mission of the Church. Besides, from the Church's point of view on history, it was a "recent" development, coming a full millennium after the apostolic age.

Discussion of such topics, on the agenda of the National Council of American Bishops in 1969, however, was expressly forbidden by the Vatican. The items were removed without a word of protest from the American bishops; and the trickle of men leaving the priesthood turned into a flood. This was unheard of. But the Pope — and the compliant American bishops — seemed to prefer that to discussing any change in Church practice.

This has implications for the pedophile revelations. Some believe that sexual abuse at the level of the recent revelations has always existed in the Church. But there are others of us who feel that the pedophile phenomenon is exclusively a post-Vatican II affair. And, we would argue, not because of the "permissiveness" of Vatican II but rather for the completely opposite reason: the refusal to deal with the re-assessment of Christianity's historic pathological attitude toward sex, inherited from ancient times, which includes mandatory celibacy. There was a radical change of attitude toward sex. The healthy adjustments that were obviously called for were rejected. There would be no married clergy, said the Vatican. Better to be rid of those who could not be trusted to live the celibate life.

So laicization for priests who desired to be released from their vows was made extremely easy in those days, almost automatic, and many took immediate advantage of it. I took a leave of absence in June of 1969 but, unlike many others, I did not seek laicization. I had taken a principled stand in my own mind. There would be a married priesthood, I was convinced, and I would be one of the first. This never happened, of course. I spent many years clinging to that hope. I should have known better.

Ostracism

Prior to the great exodus around 1970, quitting the Catholic priesthood was very rare and those who did were held in opprobrium by the Catholic Community. Priests who "jumped the league" or went "over the wall" virtually had to move far away from their home localities and adopt another identity to be able to live in peace. That attitude of rejection was often carried over to seminarians. Young men who left the seminary before ordination would typically be referred to as "spoiled priests," and often suffer transitions to lay life as painful and awkward as any that fell upon us who were ordained.

Escape was not easy. We came out of an ancient tradition with historic ethnic roots. We were soon to discover that deep in our connective tissues lived psychic forces as powerful as they were invisible. Immobilized by these subconscious imperatives, some who wanted to leave postponed it for years, and many others tried but could never bring themselves to do it. I knew men in their thirties, priests who had been companions of mine in the seminary, who fled literally in the middle of the night so as to avoid a violent and potentially paralyzing confrontation with their families as they attempted to leave the celibate state and begin life as married men. One married ex-priest confided in me in the '70's, "You know," he said, "if my parents were still alive, I don't know if I would have been able to do this." He also told me that after years of giving sermons and lectures, he temporarily found himself unable to deliver a public speech. Another married ex-priest developed an auto-immune reaction of eczema and boils that rivaled the Book of

Job. He had never even had an allergy in all his life before that. The etiology here, to my mind, was not ever in doubt.

Another of our most talented brother priests who left and married said to me that if he had known how difficult leaving the priesthood would be, he would never have even tried it. This same man tragically developed a condition of pathological lying, got himself into legal and financial trouble and ended up leaving his wife and baby and disappearing entirely. He was gone for a year and a half before anyone knew whether he was dead or alive. He began a new life with a new identity in a city a thousand miles away. We had all known him since we were boys; this behavior was completely out of character for him. I have no doubt whatsoever that it was a catastrophic personality breakdown directly attributable to the phenomenon under discussion here.

We ostracized ourselves. We ran on our swords or disappeared, like Romans sentenced by the Emperor to suicide or exile, like Kafka's bewildered culprit. That shouldn't be a surprise. We were as Catholic as the Pope. We, too, believed in the "indelible seal;" we too had internalized the condemnations of our ancient tradition. And, like Loch Ness monsters, these condemnations arose out of the bottomless depths of our subconscious to shipwreck us when we broke the code.

There are also the horrors that befell those who stayed in. But you already know some of them. They are the occasion for this essay.

Who's to blame? In every one of these cases, what these men went through was chalked up as some kind of just retribution for betrayal, or their personal failure or moral turpitude, rather than impute any flaw to the ideological system that set them up for destruction. There is not a word of recognition from the Church on these matters, much less apology, and nothing analogous was forthcoming from the self-proclaimed investigative press except prurient interest in the next titillating, sales-boosting scandal.

The wonder is that so many of us emerged without more scarring. On one occasion, after some years of being out of the priesthood, I bumped into an old seminary companion in Manhattan near the New School where he was taking courses. Apparently he had also been in psychotherapy and was having difficulties. The first words out of his mouth when he saw me were, "they ruined us, they ruined us!" He laughed it off nervously. That was his way. But he was serious, and there was no doubt about what he meant.

There are many stories. I would generate compassion, if I could, for the older priests I knew, credulous idealistic men who had struggled mightily from the time they were children with forces that grew to demonic proportions, within and without, that ultimately, because they were human beings, had to overwhelm them. Those who were not overwhelmed were successful in conquering their humanity. Imagine! And of what value was that? They won a Pyrrhic victory that left many truncated, pusillanimous, uncompassionate and bitter, and many others cynically focused on money and power. Those whose humanity deepened in these circumstances were few indeed.

I would tell you the stories of gentle old men drinking themselves into oblivion in front of late night television. Oh, yes, I knew them. I can assure you these men kept their hands to themselves. It was their alcoholic mush-for-brains that ultimately exploded in massive cerebral hemorrhages that was the bodily organ that ended their priestly careers. At the time I left in 1969, Roman Catholic priests were the occupational group with the largest percentage of alcoholics in the nation.

But that was all right, I guess. They were priests. They were supposed to know all about sacrifice. They sacrificed themselves on the altar of celibacy, bleeding to death ever so slowly through stomach ulcers and broken hearts. These men were not degenerates. They were committed Catholics whose principal fault was to believe what their Church had told them. They were also human beings to whom the normal supports of family life were denied. And when they proved unable to sustain themselves without those supports, they were condemned as traitors and weaklings.

And they were my brothers.

Orthodoxy

I'm trying to build a picture of the internal anatomy of the Church as formed by its traditional theological configurations.

Once the Church's millennial orthodox view of itself is understood, its apparently bizarre behavior becomes much more intelligible. I emphasize "traditional and orthodox" because there are many in the Church, lay and clergy alike, who have passed well beyond the literal understanding of the ancient doctrines that I've outlined here. By official standards, however, you must realize these people are *crypto-heretics*. In an earlier age, they would be in deep trouble indeed. But of these non-traditional believers, very few are bishops. At the highest level of ecclesiastical power, conservative men of unassailable orthodoxy, whose appointments as Bishops were multiplied astronomically by the last Pope, John Paul II, are in complete, almost universal control. And from the cloning achieved in the College of Cardinals by this same pope, his successor is, not surprisingly, of the same ilk as he.

The structural elements I've highlighted logically engender certain practices. It should surprise no one that the Church would maintain these practices. Take the question of democracy. If an ideological foundation for democracy doesn't exist, you cannot *legislate* the participation of lay people. Clerical privilege and oversight can never ultimately be suppressed while the doctrines of Apostolic Succession, the seal of Holy Orders and *ex opere operato* are *taken literally* in the way they've come down to us. With these ideological bases intact, sooner or later the corresponding behavior will reassert itself. Doctrine implies practice. You can't change practice without changing doctrine.

With regard to Christianity's historic intolerance, a traditionally orthodox Catholic must believe that Jews, Moslems and other "heathen" are *religiously inferior* to Christians because they are in *gross error* about God's will and plan of salvation. Error, says Vatican II, is "slavery." (A variation on the old canon of the inquisition, "error has no rights.") Christians alone have the "whole truth" and therefore the mission to "liberate" the unbelievers.[49] Thank God, many Catholics do not believe this any longer. But, historically we all did and many still do. It is official Church doctrine, and proselytizing mission is still the practice. In the past, we

---
[49] LG Ch II, 17

recall, "mission" was not the only response to the "heathen." Other responses, like the atrocities recounted by Bartolomé de las Casas, and perpetrated by the "Holy" Inquisition, were less benign. The effect of this doctrine on Jews, Moslems, heretics and primitives throughout Catholic history at times reached genocidal proportions.

The claim to absolute truth is characteristic of Christian denominations across the board. In the cacophony of Christian voices all declaring they speak for God, however, the Catholic assertions not only antedated the others by many, many centuries, but also served as their paradigm and model in every case. Christianity has always been intolerant of other religions. It is sheer blindness to believe that the erstwhile practices of intolerance, like the "Holy Inquisition," will not reassert themselves once the necessary conditions are again present, unless *extra ecclesiam nulla salus* ("outside the Church there is no salvation") along with its doctrinal justifications are publicly repudiated.

Conversely, religious unity and mutual respect among traditions pursued as a moral imperative of the highest priority, would provide both incentive and illumination for the difficult work of restructuring Christian Doctrine. Were there such a program sincerely in place, the Church would instantly be less damaging to humanity, and in time, perhaps, might even become the expert in humanity it claims to be.

The subject, after all, is *humanity*.

IV. Rediscovering Humanity

She was the love of my life. And as these first overwhelming experiences of love can never be repeated, they tend to cauterize the psyche in irreversible ways; so in a sense that we all know about, she still is. When we started, I was 28, she was much younger. Our star-crossed on-again off-again relationship went on for five years and provided what could easily have been the material for that many years of high-end soaps. We suffered through dramatic intensities that only the young could survive. Thank God, we were young.

In a very real sense, I was younger than she was, for up to that point I had had no experience whatsoever in relating amorously to the opposite sex. She was, literally, the first girl I had ever kissed. It seems to me now, as I look back, that I picked up my life as a gendered individual exactly where I had left it off in high school. The problem was, I was no longer a kid. I was a Roman Catholic priest.

The relationship had an explosive effect on my life. The finger was out of the dike, and in what seemed an instant I was in a sanity-threatening process attempting to cross no-man's land from the stalled trenches of adolescence to the dizzying heights of triumphant manhood, under circumstances that rendered most observers — including myself — uncomprehending and unsympathetic. As that sentence shows, I still don't even know what metaphor to choose to express that vertiginous, guilt-ridden, anguished process that, if it happened to me now, thirty five years later and in my aging sixth decade of life, I would surely die. Thank God, I was young.

In the beginning, my strange behavior was so different from who I thought I was that I seriously wondered if I wasn't completely insane — schizophrenic or psychotic in some other way. I feared others must think the same thing. For one thing, I was overwhelmed with guilt. I began to understand the immobilization I had seen in others who had abandoned the celibate state. The sources of social ostracism were hard at work. Yet, in spite of my anguish, I instinctively knew that I had to move forward with integrating this part of me that I had never seen before. The attempt to identify what might be good and important in a grab-bag of sex-related activities that had heretofore *all* been considered mortally sinful, or forbidden by the vow, was beyond me and I realized it. After 12 years of seminary preparation, I was totally unprepared for this. In order to avoid further scandal and a possible breakdown I took a leave of absence. That was 1969.

That relationship meant a great deal to me. I might have been immature in matters of love, but in other ways I was no longer a child. I had a deep sense of paternal care and protective responsibility toward my partner. But I had a great deal to learn in this regard. I didn't realize that in a love relationship paternalism is counter-indicated.

I also felt committed to an attempt to change church policy. I believed a married priesthood was possible; and I was convinced the priests of my generation could make it happen, if necessary by stonewalling. We were strong and clear on the issue. I wanted to be in the thick of that fight. But I didn't realize how relentlessly effective Catholic ostracism would be in immobilizing the young clergy as a group, and that included me. The issue of course, for all of us, was guilt. With guilt came a feeling of an impending punishment resulting in a psychological paralysis.

But there were other issues. After a while, it began to appear that, even though the two of us, my friend and I, may have shared adolescence, there seemed much else we didn't share; I began to have doubts about the relationship.

That was unfortunate. Because not only was I in love, but she represented everything I loved in the people that I was committed to serve. She was black, and she was Puerto Rican, I was white. I had dedicated my life to these people. They had become my people, my new family. Romantic? Adolescent? In those days of incipient racial integration, those issues were important for me as they were for many people. Today I would like to think I would simply relate to the person without regard to such questions; but in those days it mattered. The relationship on my part was loving and committed; but it still included that residual racism and paternalism, however benevolent. These youthful fidelities, such as they were, were braided into the interstices of my situation and my sense of commitment did not allow me to accept the evidence of our incompatibility.

It was another piece of my immaturity. The mix of loving the people I served *as a priest* and loving the person who was my friend, in my case proved catastrophic. I couldn't separate these things in my own head. I was unable to identify for myself those necessary factors — like shared values — that would have insured that the personal relationship would be mutually sustaining and therefore enduring. In loving her, I was loving my people, I was reforming my Church, I was battling racism and I was building a new world. It seemed simple enough. What the hell was there to think about?

I refuse to let hindsight trivialize the idealism and perceived potential of those days, however tragically or fruitlessly they may have ended. These multiple loyalties put me in what I saw as a titanic struggle with overwhelming forces like the racism of our society. At a second level, I was battling a hidebound Church that I felt committed to reform but which offered me nothing but resistance and hostility. But I was immature, and a fatal component of immaturity is that you don't realize it.

Initially I felt abandoned by my brothers-in-rebellion whom I saw defeated by the forces of ostracism and professional pressure. As time went on I realized from my own crippling experience what these men were up against. At first I was appalled that cherished possibilities were being jettisoned for career and the middle-class life-style. Later I finally understood that they were responding to intense guilt and the fears that resulted from social judgment and rejection. As I saw my own middle-class upbringing inject a galling ambivalence into every alternative I put my hand to, I knew that they were surviving in the only way they knew how. But at the time, the clear, possible goal of "forcing" the Church to accept a married priesthood, by simply refusing to accept laicization and continuing to function as priests while married, evaporated as quickly, it seemed, as it was conceived.

And in the midst of all this, could it be possible that my partner could not travel with me on this great quest? I refused to believe that this relationship would not work out. I couldn't have made a mistake of such magnitude. What I didn't recognize at the time was that I was making the priesthood — or an idealized version of it — the priority. I was trying to bend the relationship to serve these purposes. They were my goals, not hers.

As time went by it became clearer to me that I could not suppress my priorities — and they were not something we shared. I would decide to split, and of course, I would reconsider, repent and persuade myself that I could make it work, that I could try this or that, that she would grow to want the same things I did. She would take me back. We would start up again, always with great hope. I desperately wanted it to work; and I saw in retrospect that in my guilt I was also trying to protect her from the break-up. It took a long time for me to learn that you just can't do that. You can't protect someone from yourself without leaving that person . . . or leaving yourself.

It was a circus of immaturity. And I was the clown.

This went on for five years, until finally, exhausted from driving us both crazy, I left for good. She married some years afterward. I'm definitely in a different place now, almost forty years later, but looking back I still don't know if, at the time, it was the right thing for me to have done. . . .

. . . as I write these words, it's hard to hear myself say that. . . .

I thought it would kill me. Part of me did die with it. . . . I dated some after that, but in spite of a few passing relationships that were temporarily very intense, I had no other serious partner for many years. Eventually I met a wonderful woman with whom I could share my life, such as it had become after years of solitary and ambivalent struggle with alternatives. As I write this at this point in time, I have been married for 26 years to that same marvelous person. My marital life has been a joy and an adventure for me. When my ordeal began as a priest in my 28th year of life, and for some time after, I never thought I would be able to say that. I believed I was cursed, a "vessel of wrath," an Ethan Frome crippled forever by the eternal chains of the celibate vow.

By the time I finally entered into a mutually sustaining and balanced relationship I was almost forty years old.

Immaturity and Immobility

Many of the difficulties in my case had to do with immaturity, and ultimately resolved themselves over time. Meanwhile, however, they continued to create suffering for the people around me. They are matters we all have to go through and the process of maturation is rarely a tranquil one. It's been suggested that it would have been no easier if it had taken place in adolescence.

Perhaps. But when you go through adolescence at the proper time, however miserable you feel and make others, it's at least taken in context. People understand. This is important for future integration. In my case, I offered myself no such excuse nor was there any forthcoming from those privileged to witness my pathetic flailings. My immobilization lasted for many years.

Even while accepting blame, the attempt to identify the *structural factors* — unnecessary and humanly debilitating — that set the conditions for events that need not have happened, must *not* be allowed, once again, to be denied and dismissed. The defects in the Catholic system that collaborated in producing my minor tragedy were the same that were guaranteed to precipitate major tragedies in others, like the pedophiles perhaps, whose internal problems were different, deeper, and for which their position as priests left no room for maturation. The phenomenon, I believe, was analogously the same for all of us: immaturity and sexual repression. Yes we all had personal blame. But personal blame should not be used to "cover-up" the grave distortions of Catholic institutional and doctrinal inhumanity, excused many thousands of times during a thousand years, always concealed from public view, *which played an indispensable role* in these affairs. If these structural flaws remain in place, they will play a similar role in the future, perhaps in ways that we may not now be able to anticipate.

The Church and Reform

If the priority of dynamic moral responsibility over dead mechanical righteousness is a principle of authentic humanity, it is applicable to the Church that claims to guide humanity. But for far too long the Church has escaped the human criterion suggested by Jesus himself to his friends and followers as the universal test of human truth, *"By their fruits you will know them."* Jesus was not encouraging us to judge other people here; we already know how to do that. He was teaching us how to judge the truth.

The inquisitors are supposed to have asked only one question that gave Luther pause, "Are you alone, wise?" Who would dare answer "yes"? How could he respond? Who among us, without Jesus' bold insistence would have the audacity to use our unadorned humanity as the standard to judge this millennial institution — and hence every other institution — that claims the divine right to rule over us? We may begin to discern here the true subversiveness of this God-shaken Palestinian workman that so threatened the Roman war machine that it had to stop, wheel about and crush him and those of his "way." For the Roman Empire was exactly such an institution and it reared its daughter, the Roman Catholic Church, in those very same values.

On the dead mechanical face of it, who will claim that a Church that says to a totally trusting 14 year old, "it is God's will that you live the rest of your life without exercising one of your core human functions," should be blamed for a pathological "blow-back" of the very same prohibited function? What law was broken? Perhaps, at the time, no one knew; by its fruits, however, now we all know. You cannot separate clerical sexual abuse from the system of sexual repression from which it emerged.

Sexual misconduct has apparently been part of the regular experience of Catholic Christians at the hands of their priests, always hidden, always covered-up, lest the Church be forced to re-think its priorities. This intolerable behavior, only some of which is crime punishable by law, cannot be laid at the feet of a few sick individuals to be eliminated by more effective psychological screening. I am clearly suggesting that these men's problems, not entirely unlike my own, were forged and set in motion by a Church wed to a doctrinal complex that exercised a deforming influence on their personalities, rendering them infantile and dysfunctional. These men are still accountable for their conduct, yes; but if larger society is to get beyond the forbidden pleasure of throwing the first stone and is interested in seeing real reform, it must look elsewhere. It must look at the traditional practice of the Church and its archaic doctrinal premises.

If the Church had changed, or even *was trying to* change the obsolete value system that was responsible for these mutilations, I would have no reason to be writing this denunciation. My private ordeal would have been one with the ordeal of so many others and one with the Church itself. Together, we were *all* the victims of the same historical forces over which we had no control. We all came to the same realizations at the same time. We all made painful and damaging mistakes. If we admitted it and tried to undo the damage, helping one another to make healthy transitions, the ordeal for all of us would now be over, except for the healing. You would expect nothing less from an "expert in humanity."

But no, that's not what happened. The hierarchy abandoned the attempt at real reform. They betrayed the spirit of the Council. There was no rejection of the past nor condemnation of its premises. What they condemned and rejected were those of us Catholics who chose to move beyond the discredited past. The Vatican retrenched and re-affirmed Catholic Christianity's most questionable traditions making the Church culpable in a way now that before, perhaps, it was not. At this remove, a full forty years later, not only does the Church carry the same sickness at a worse stage of morbidity, but there is still the same refusal of treatment, the same denial of responsibility. We are asked to believe that these pedophile priests are *solely* to blame for what happened, and that the Cardinal is personally to blame for not declaring it to the world and turning them over to the secular arm. But we know better.

Public Opinion it seems, has been all too willing to accept the Church's persistent habit of assigning blame everywhere except in her own millennial sexual immaturity. But the public must beware. Mandatory clerical celibacy, still in force, is no more a harmless museum artifact than the absolute autocratic authority of the hierarchy. Both these ancient invalidated social forms are currently being actively maintained; and they will continue to cripple the people they touch.

Calls for change fall on deaf ears. The Catholic Church claims that it *cannot* change its teachings and practices — not even ultimately for the reason that they were commanded by scripture, *for in the case of priests' celibacy, the Church admits they were not* — but rather because it must maintain its status: that the Church is the very mouth of God, that the Church alone is wise.

The Catholic Church feels it must present to the world an unchanging face or the authenticity of its "divine foundation" will be compromised. What might be good for people — in Christian terms, what God might actually want — is always secondary.

Perhaps we can begin to see patterns in the way the Church responds. What's the issue? Celibacy? Divorce? Birth Control? Democracy? Gender equality? Respect for other traditions? Take a step back and things begin to merge. There are two constants always in operation in the Church's stance toward these issues: 1) the doctrine and practice of absolute hierarchical power 2) in the defense of the infallible magisterium and traditional discipline. Take one more step back and you will see these two items themselves are only facets of the one single overriding assertion of *divine establishment*. The Catholic Church resists change because it believes it is *not* human, *it is divine*, that's why it *must* say, "outside the Church there is no salvation."

Make no mistake. The Church holds to this with unrepentant tenacity. Read the most current documents, like the Catechism promulgated by the Vatican in 1992 and the teaching of the Holy Office of September 2000,[50] and re-read history. This is the very reason the Church launched the crusading slaughter of the Cathari and the Moslems in the 12th century; it is the same reason it permitted the genocide and enslavement of the primitive peoples of Africa, Asia and the Americas in the 16th and following centuries; it is the same reason it has tolerated the recurrent holocausts of Jews in all centuries. In this matter the Church has been hideously consistent.

It believes it is *not* human, *it is divine*. This is the issue.

Personally, I do not believe the Catholic Church can reform itself. Vatican II was not a minor event. It is hard to imagine a more revealing expression of the Church's true priorities than the rejection of an ecumenical Council. The Church is so invested in its own immutable self-definition that it has lost the capacity to change. It has systematically eliminated all vestiges of its fallible humanity and now it has nothing left to fall back on as the basis of a new identity. It has burned all its bridges. It has locked itself in the dungeon of its own divinity.

---

[50] The teaching is entitled *Dominus Jesus,* and was issued by Joseph CardinalRatzinger, Sept.15, 2000

Reform at the depth I believe is called for, requires a new beginning, a new life, and great humility. Only human beings can do this. *It is beyond the reach of the gods.* Those who have passed this way know that there has to be something small and vulnerable left from the early days before self-projection was cemented into self-definition, something poor and perishing, the way God made us. There is no reform without conversion, no change without repentance. If the Church can rediscover itself not as "God's partner," but as one small part of God's needy people, perhaps it can re-join the great pilgrimage from all over the world of those hungry and thirsty for the creative love that comes to us like dew from the night sky, the same untamed pathway as our splendid and improbable humanity.

The reappropriation of humanity — to be born again as *human beings* — is the issue. We cannot escape it It's not optional. It's not a matter of preference or predilection. If the Church cannot lead us there, we will have to find a way to get there by ourselves.

CHAPTER II
The Immortal Soul

INTRODUCTION

The Catholic Church, I believe, is perishing; and I'm not referring to bankruptcy. The Church has lost contact with its own humanity and ours. And while it may continue, maybe even for more millennia, as a propertied institution with its accustomed commercial functions — schools, church services, funerals, marriages, social clubs, perhaps even participation in debate over public policy — it has become increasingly irrelevant to issues of faith. The unfortunate fact is that no one seems to notice or care. Most people are so concerned with the Church's corporate existence, or its consoling traditions, or its political clout, or even its moral credibility as to have little interest in its real reason for being.

The reason for the existence of the Church is faith; and the need for faith will not disappear, not even with the disappearance of the Church. The greater problem is that if the Church becomes dysfunctional for faith while still continuing its institutional existence, it then becomes an obstacle to faith. It confuses believers and discourages them from searching for faith elsewhere.

My criticism is not limited to the list of grievances that we usually call "the issues," like celibacy, democracy, the role of women or even the divinity of Jesus. In the first chapter, I proposed that, well beyond the issues, there is a *self-divinization* in place by which the Catholic Church consciously and purposely sets itself apart from all other human institutions. I identified the problem to be the Church's claim to have been founded and structured *as she is* directly by Jesus taken as God-in-Person. By insisting on its own divine establishment, the Church effectively claims it does not have to respond to the imperatives that affect other human societies. That fantasy inhibits clarity of conscience and commitment to reform. The "issues" merge into a *single profound and intrinsic defect* which I called the escape from humanity. Our humanity is the issue. But what does it mean to be human?

Not surprisingly, the very notion of what a human being is has been dominated by the Church's *insistence upon antiquated hypotheses of human nature.* The effect of this is dehumanizing.

We are human beings. What we think it means to be a human being will determine how we live: what we expect of ourselves and how we will treat others. Just who do we think we are ... anyway?

That is the principal focus of this chapter.

I. The Legacy of Greece: The Immortal Soul

Religious faith is *relationship*. Raimundo Panikkar assigns the term "beliefs" to the so-called "facts" of religion, for instance that Jesus is God, or that the human condition is due to Original Sin. "Faith," on the other hand is a word he reserves for the *relationship* of trust — surrender to the demands and the protections of the Sacred. I follow this terminology. Please take note of it. It is somewhat different from our ordinary usage in which "faith" and "belief" mean the same thing. Here they do not.

Faith is not "beliefs," nor "scientific truth" and yet we realize faith always functions within the world that knowledge perceives to be the real one, the world of the facts. Knowledge in our world is mediated by science. Faith is a grateful, familial *relationship* that accepts reality as sacred. That "reality," however, is always the "scientific" world-view, the world as people believe it really is.

I want to emphasize that for any given time and place, there is no other world than the real world. This may seem an empty redundancy, but as we will see, it needs to be said. The scientific world-view is the way the Cosmos and everything in it is conceived by people. Its imagery determines how the *faith* relationship to that world must be explored and expressed. Faith, the perception that reality is sacred, must take *reality* seriously.

Christianity consolidated its message in ancient times, in the terms of the world-view then considered scientific truth. The conclusions of Greek philosophy were taken as *rationally proven fact*. Christianity's unmistakable consonance with the Platonic world-view aligned the Church with what was then, without a doubt, the science of the times. It was this association that helps explain the peculiar characteristic that is so central to Christianity's self-definition: it claims its doctrines are *literal truth*. Christianity denies the symbolic nature of its stories and its statements, rendering itself unique among the religions of the world. Others admit their teachings are metaphors, the poor and limping symbols that speak of unknowable, ineffable realities. Christianity alone claims to be a religion of facts, science, truth. It derives from Christianity's original association with Platonism in the ancient Greco-Roman world. It is no surprise that these values are also characteristic of the culture that Christianity created ... what we call "the West."

1. Platonic Theory and the Christian Doctrine of the Soul

When Christianity first crossed over from being a heterodox Jewish sect and became one of the many mystery cults recently introduced into Greco-Roman culture at the beginning of the Common Era, the "immortality of the soul" was not an article of Christian faith. Most people today are unaware of this historical fact.

Christianity had originally clothed itself in the "mystery" genre as the clearest way to express its belief in the fully human immortality — the resurrection of the body — which Christians believed was offered to them by Jesus' redemption. This was accompanied by the anticipation of an imminent, apocalyptic end-of-time. At that terminal moment, Christians believed, immortality would be given to the whole person as a physical organism in its integrity. Immortality belonged only to the gods. For humans, it was a *free gift* that came with the special "divinization" conferred on the

Christian *mystēs*[51] by Baptism and the Sacred Meal. The "resurrection of the body" was an article of Christian belief, as the ancient creeds attest; the "immortality of the soul" was not. In fact, the earliest Christian apologists, like Tatian, felt they had to counter such a "pagan doctrine" because it was an obstacle to Christian belief in the real significance of the resurrection of Jesus. A natural immortality would have made us gods by birth, rendering the resurrection superfluous.[52]

The natural immortality of the soul seems not to have been declared *de fide* by the Church until the 5th Lateran Council, 1513.[53] The doctrine, at first, was not even an assumption of popular culture. In the beliefs about the "soul" reflected in literature throughout the Mediterranean region in pre-Christian times, death was thought to cause people to change into lifeless forms, "shades" or shadows. In some of the more egregious cases of bad behavior in this life — where insult to the gods had been committed, for instance — a highly imaginative punishment was meted out after death, but otherwise there was none. In Egypt it was different. The hieroglyphs record belief in a divine judgment of the recently deceased whose sins were weighed in a balance ... against a feather. Plato, in what was an innovation for Greek tradition and consistent with his doctrine of the soul, espoused a theory of judgment followed by consignment to locations of bliss or punishment.[54]

---

[51] *Mystés* is a Greek term identifying the initiate and believing participant in a Mystery Religion.

[52] Adolph Harnack, *The History of Dogma,* tr. Buchanan, Dover, NY 1904, vol II p.191, fn.4; p.213, fn.1 "Most of the Apologists argue against the conception of the natural immortality of the human soul." Tatian 13; Justin, Dial. 5; Theoph. II.27.
Joroslav Pelikan, *The Christian Tradition* U. of Chicago Press, 1971 Vol 1, "The Emergence of the Catholic Tradition," p.30, referring to the polemics of Christian theologians against the pagan doctrine of the immortal soul, quotes Tatian: "The soul is not in itself immortal, O Greeks, but mortal." (Tat. *Or,* 13 [TU 4-I:14])

[53] Karl Rahner *On the Theology of Death,* Herder, NY 1961, tr Charles Henkey p 24. He also notes that "death as the separation of body and soul" is not explicitly found anywhere in the Bible.

[54] EB 1979, Vol 8, p 409a. Cf *Phaedo,* passim. This dialog focuses principally on the immortality of the soul, its pre-existence, its re-incarnation and deals with judgment, reward and punishment after death.

In the course of the Church's formative centuries under the "scientific" influence of Greek philosophy, most especially from the Academy of Plato, the Christian "doctrine of the soul" changed radically. It took on the features of Plato's theory of the fully functional *disembodied spirit*, which ultimately became an unchallenged fact of the Greek world-view. It was accepted by Christianity as a scientific conclusion rigorously deduced from the available evidence. It was in this form that it was handed on in the traditional Christian belief system.

Plato's Universe — a World of Spirit and Ideas

The Christian view of the World inherited from ancient Greco-Roman Culture was *thoroughly Platonic*, and later, neo-Platonic; it was centered on the concept of "Spirit." "Spirit" may be considered a foundational idea which underwent its most refined development first with the Pythagoreans and then under Plato and his school. These Greeks believed that "Spirit" was a genus of being, intelligent, invisible and in all other ways untrammeled by materiality and its requirements. The category of *spirit* was populated mainly by two groups of beings: the "gods," including all major and minor deities (the "One," the Demiurge, Logos, Nous or World Soul, angels and demons, and the "gods" of mythology), and the personalities of deceased humans who were believed to dwell in the world of spirits, in some cases of mixed (divine / human) parentage and therefore with divine powers.

But alongside the divine and deceased strata, the Greeks of the Academy made a key extrapolation in the definition of spirit that became constitutive of the foundational ideology of Christianity. For these people, the notion of *spirit* not only recapitulated belief about ghosts and gods, it also defined the essence of the living, breathing, flesh and blood human being, the individual "soul," popularly assumed to be identified as this or that particular person, the *self*. The theory of the "spiritual soul" was offered as a refined and sophisticated conclusion of logical reasoning. It was considered indisputable *science* — a fact necessary to explain the phenomena of human consciousness that otherwise remained a mystery: human beings had the ability to form concepts, to reason, to communicate through language and to yearn for immortality. The animals could do none of these things. They were not like us, argued the Greeks. They were mere "matter" and had only "material forms," animal souls that dissolved at death. The Platonists believed our souls made us virtually a different kind of being from every other living or non-living thing on the planet; and that had the effect of taking us out of this world of material things.

Ideas

Of all the "spiritual" activities of consciousness, it was perhaps the ability to *form concepts* that most captivated the imagination of the philosophers of the Platonic and neo-Platonic tradition. They held that concepts were generic or "universal" mental phenomena that stripped the realties of everyday life of their deceptive and perishing individuality. This or that man or woman, like Molly Malone, worked hard selling fish, got sick with the fever and died. But "humanity" or "human nature" of which Molly was only an evanescent example, had none of those defects. *Humanity* was universal, not individual. It was the essence of what resided in each and every human being, and we were able to capture it in a universal concept free of limiting materiality. "Humanity" could not die. It was an *idea*; an idea was spiritual.

The Greeks called the universal idea the "form" of the entity in question; in the case of Molly Malone "humanity" existed individuated in the human person making her what she was. The concept thus allowed us to "know" people we had never met. With the concept of humanity, the human mind, in fact, "knew" everyone who ever lived or ever would live, no matter who. This was true of every known entity. By forming the concept "chair," we know every chair that will ever exist.

It was not surprising that a vision with such awesome scope would evoke the very Mind of God. Humanity, after all, was *God's idea*, according to the Platonic vision, thought of by God and implanted in our perishing bodies. It was that divine idea that was captured in the concept. Concepts, in other words, not only connected our minds with *all* the individuals of a given species, concepts also put us into immediate contact with the Mind of God.

By knowing things in their very essences, the Greeks believed we knew them intimately and thoroughly; and on the basis of this direct contact with transcendence, they also believed we knew "God."

Therefore, in their view, since ideas were the reflections of the very Divine Intelligence that is the source of all things, those ideas were considered *more real* than the individual limited perishing substances that they enliven in our world. Reversing the older belief and common sense, they said that this world where we live was the *shadow world*, a pale and distant imitation of the real, the World of Ideas.

So the universal concept embodied the three major facets of the Greek understanding of "spirit": scientific knowledge of genera, the spiritual capacity of the human mind, and the supra-real immortal forms residing in the Mind of God, the World of Ideas.

Matter

The Greeks claimed "matter" was the cause of death in our world. It was matter that created the individuation, hence the limitation, the imperfection, the mortality found in things. Matter was the source of everything that cramped and stifled the *forms*, the ideas, preventing them from being all they could be. Matter without form would de-compose. Matter neutralized the natural immortality of the ideas, forms — except in the one case of the human person, whose independently subsisting *spiritual form* (the soul) was not limited to the material body, survived its death and lived forever.

These Platonic notions constituted the scientific "facts" of Greek times. Platonic philosophy was wholly embraced by Christianity and helped form its doctrinal base. Eventually Platonism was promoted by the Church as essential to the Christian view of the world. That world-view remained essentially intact until the beginning of our modern era, yielding progressively to a new "science" only in the last few centuries.

2. The Mediaeval "Doctrine of the Soul"

Plato did not go unchallenged, even in the ancient world. Aristotle, his student at the Academy, criticized Plato's world-view, probably even within the lifetime of his teacher. He ridiculed the theory of subsistent forms,[55] and the World of Ideas where they were said to reside. Specifically, in the case of humankind, he defined the soul as "the form of the body," and gave it existence as a "principle" of being like the form of any other living thing. He did not assign to the human "soul" separate and independent metaphysical status. It existed as part of a composite, together with matter. The "soul" may have been comprised of "immateriality" for Aristotle, but it was not clear that it was either immortal or personal.[56]

But Aristotle was not to have the great influence history has associated with his name until the middle ages, when Islamic scholars discovered his works in the Arabic domains where Greek culture once flourished. The Caliphate of Cordova in Southern Spain, a crossroads of Mediterranean culture, quickly became a hotbed of intellectual ferment where all the "Religions of the Book" — Islam, Judaism and Christianity — vied to understand and then to harness this newly discovered "pagan scientist" to their systems. The competition was fierce. Thomas Aquinas' first *Summa Contra Gentiles* was written specifically as an alternative to the earlier Arabic interpretation of Aristotle done by Islamic commentators. Moses Maimonides an Arabic-speaking Spanish Jew who wrote in the last decades of the 12th century, published his *Guide for the Perplexed* in order to prove to Jews whose faith had been shaken, that Aristotle's philosophy did not contradict the Torah and the Talmud. Christians were also deeply disturbed by this new thinking that contradicted Plato and the Christian Universe. Their transcendent theological achievements, the *summas* of the 13th century were in large measure also "Guides for the Perplexed" as Christian intellectuals attempted to neutralize a dissenting Aristotle by integrating him into their Platonic spiritual view of the World.

The existence of the immortal soul, and the transformation of Jesus into the Roman *Pantocrator,* the "Judge of the ("souls" of the) Living and the Dead," were inheritances of the ancient world.

---

[55] Aristotle, *Metaphysics* Ch 9, ¶ 990, 20 and *passim*.
[56] Aristotle, *On the Soul,* Bk 2, ch 1; Bk 3, ch5

These beliefs came to be re-examined and re-stated in the light of Aristotle's challenge.

In the 13th century, Thomas Aquinas, attempting to reconcile Plato and Aristotle came up with a very strange amalgam. For him, as for Aristotle, the body and the soul co-exist as matter and form, but unlike Aristotle and just like Plato, he calls the soul a "subsistent form" (SCG, II, 51,1); and "self-subsistent" (51,4). This meant, of course, that the soul was capable of existing apart from the body, a position that was not integral to the Aristotelian system. But the belief had become a fixed and immutable element of Christianity's millennial inheritance, and its philosophical justification had to be retained.

I believe there are great difficulties in the position as articulated by Thomas. For by his own standards, the qualities of the soul that he brings forward — immateriality, incorruptibility, non-quantity, non-extension, universality, infinity, etc (SCG, 49,7) — which supposedly prove that the soul is not commensurate with, and therefore capable of subsisting apart from, the body, would also render the soul *equivalent to God.* Without the presence of the body, Thomas' definition of spirit has no principle of limitation whatsoever.

These platonic features necessary to support traditional Christian imagery, leave Aquinas open to other difficulties as well. In particular, if the "soul" is an entity separate from the body and of a different genus entirely, how does it come to be? "Spirit" could not possibly be produced by mere "matter," and so the human sperm and egg could hardly be considered capable of generating "spirit" on their own. Therefore the scholastics had to say that each and every human soul is specially created and infused by God in a miraculous act *by-passing the laws of nature*. These opinions are welded in steel in the *de fide* definitions of the Church.

Thus the theologians were forced into the anomalous position of claiming that in the case of all life-forms, biological reproduction is entirely responsible for the procreation of the new individuals, generating both matter and form, *except in one case* and one case only: humankind, where the reproductive process, in spite of being specifically designed for its purpose by God and virtually the same as for all the higher animals, was judged inadequate to the task assigned to it — requiring, as it were, a *"deus" ex machina* to provide an immortal spiritual soul.

Many have found this "explanation" an awkward contortion and a transparent rationalization. Certain of its implications are clearly preposterous. For example, God's personal creative action becomes mechanically captive to the sperm penetrating the egg in every single case. In other words, God is obligated to infuse a "soul" miraculously even in the case of rape, teen-age foolishness, adultery.

This constellation of doctrines, all ancillary to the central belief in the immortal disembodied spirit in human beings, has come down to us virtually unchanged since mediaeval times. In 1992, the *Catholic Catechism* published by the Vatican and promulgated by the Pope himself in an Apostolic Constitution, reiterates them together with their "scientific" Platonic terminology, # 365 & 366:

> *The unity of body and soul is so profound that one has to consider the soul the "form" of the body (C. of Vienne, 1312). It is because of its spiritual soul that the body, made of matter, becomes a living human body; spirit and matter, in man, are not two natures united but rather their union forms a single nature.*
>
> *The Church teaches that every spiritual soul is created immediately by God — it is not "produced" by the parents — and also that it is immortal: it does not perish when it separates from the body at death, and it will be reunited with the body at the final resurrection.*[57]

II. Christianity — Mystery or Philosophy

The original ideological form Christianity took was as a "mystery Religion," the result of a missionary strategy of Jewish-Christians who were determined to communicate their beliefs about a Jewish Jesus in terms understandable to Hellenic people. This "Greek version" was represented in the New Testament writings of "John" and "Paul." Ironically, and certainly to the expressed chagrin of "Paul," relatively few Jews joined "The

---

[57] *Humanae Generis* of Pius XII, the *Credo of the People of God* of Paul VI and the 5th Lateran Council,1513, are cited as sources.

Way" started by Jesus' Jewish followers. But the plan devised for the Greeks was extremely effective. Christianity, in spite of its Jewish origins, within the first century, became and remained an overwhelmingly Greek phenomenon.

Prior to the arrival of Christianity, by the first century of our era the people that shared Hellenic culture had generated certain religious interests that were peculiar to them. For one thing, they needed to fill a gap left by the demise of the fabled gods of Greek mythology. The adolescent antics of Zeus and Apollo, Aphrodite and Athena, with their jealousies and rampant promiscuity — already an abomination to the Jews — had also been rejected as a farce by serious religious thinkers among the Greeks since at least 500 BCE. The twilight of the Greek gods, however, left a vacuum in the religious imagination. Christianity, among other rival religions, responded to this Hellenic need for a morally mature, theologically believable, dramatically human religion.

The Greeks began to ask the questions that created that system of rational enquiry we know as "philosophy" which undermined credibility in their outmoded deities. They called their enquiry "science" and thought of its answers exactly that way. We have to understand that what we now call "science" was born of this phenomenon that submitted "religion" to the light of rational enquiry. Science originally was theology; and so also, and for many, many centuries, theology was considered science.

The speculations of the philosophers reached a point of high religious development with Plato who died around 350 BCE. Plato had come to certain conclusions about the divine that were thought to be true and scientific, in contrast with the mythic fables of the gods. But Plato's "truth" was based on inferences drawn from the human process of knowing, as we've seen. It was very abstract and imageless, the conclusion of pallid syllogisms, cold logic and dry reason. He concluded, for example, that instead of many little gods there was one immense incomprehensible Deity, whom he called the "One." The "One" was Spirit just as we were "spirit," beyond matter, imageless, unchanging, eternal. Unmoved by anything, this God was a Master "Mind" who thought only one eternal thought — a Generative Self Image in Which all things came to be.

The One swept away the petty gods of Olympus with their silly misadventures, substituting instead the bare naked stillness of Absolute Thought.

This may have suited the philosophers quite well, but it did not satisfy everyone. People wanted something "human," like their "gods" that they could imagine, and relate to. To meet those needs people began turning to eastern "mystery religions." The rituals of Osiris of Egypt, Tammuz of Syria, and Mithra from Persia, like those of Demeter near Athens, were different from the sacrifice-religions of the official Olympian gods. These new exotic cults spoke about god-men and god-women who *died* went down to the underworld *and rose again*. They were theologies of personal liberation and especially triumph over death. Their dramatic stories and spellbinding rituals introduced a new dimension into religious life. They were responding to the deeper issues of death and loss that corroded life but seemed of little concern to the happy gods of Olympus or the Platonic "One" lost in the bliss of Self-Love. The mysteries addressed the despair that with increasing bitterness seemed to putrefy the human condition in the Mediterranean World.

The brutal domination over the region that came with Roman Imperial control two centuries before the common era, gave new meaning to the ubiquity of suffering for the Greeks, and it put a political face on the obscenity of death. For the more ancient slave-empires of Egypt and Mesopotamia, exploitation was such a permanent feature of social life that it had become an unquestioned horizon for them. The rituals of Tammuz in Mesopotamia, and Osiris in Egypt had long since been developed to confront the issue and offer an escape. Christianity entered the Greco-Roman world in the guise of one of these eastern mystery religions precisely at the time the peoples of the Mediterranean basin began staggering under the burden of Roman oppression and Empire.

Christianity: Monotheism and Mystery

Christianity came recommended to the Greeks for two reasons. First, it was a sect of *monotheistic Judaism* for which they had developed a high regard. The Greeks realized that the Jews worshipped an imageless "God who paralleled Plato's conclusions about the "One," the immaterial and invisible Source of all things. This feature was central to the appeal of Christianity for the Greeks because Christianity bore the banner of the same Jewish "God."

Secondly, Christianity was a mystery cult. It told the story of the god-man Jesus, who just like Osiris, Tammuz and Mithra, died and came back to life. Followers who had known Jesus in the flesh told a dramatic tale that captured the Mediterranean imagination. Jesus was no ego-obsessed, hormone-driven adolescent, like the fiery Apollo or the lustful Aphrodite. Nor was his a tale full of unimaginable surreality like Osiris of Egypt. The tragic story of this wise and compassionate Palestinian workman executed at the hands of the Roman war-machine paralleled real life all too closely. The myths of the gods were obvious fables; the story of Jesus was not. His senseless execution had the ring of unvarnished truth — familiar to all those conquered peoples who paid a heavy tribute to their Roman overlords. Crucifixion was not an extraordinary event to the Greeks. It was a daily reminder of their subjugation — a punishment reserved for slaves and those who paid tribute to the conquerors, even though mere "barbarians" to the proud Greeks.

The gospel stories were accepted as literal history. Christianity was embraced by the Greco-Roman world as much for its gripping human realism as for its transcendent monotheism. When it was proposed that this man, in all his vulnerable humanity, was also *God's man* and was brought back to life again by the "One," the only God, carrying with him the promise of resurrection for all of perishing humankind, the Greek converts recognized it as the reprise in real time of the ancient mysteries they had been so irresistibly drawn to. But this time It was no fairy-tale. It was real; it was "fact." Their ancient religions and their own yearning hearts had already prophesied the one true response of the one true God.

At first, the upper-class Philosophers ignored the Christian story as mere fable; it was the lower classes who found meaning in Christianity. But the educated established the terms of discourse; and the science now known as philosophy set the standards for the "truth." Christianity responded to the challenge and in so doing reinvented itself within the first two hundred years of its existence. The earliest Christian theologians were Apologists who defended the Christian story on the grounds established by Greek Philosophy. Whatever the Greeks demanded, the apologists showed that Christianity had it all: the truth: science, history, fact — both in the doctrine of the "One" and in the drama of Jesus' death and resurrection. The earliest interpreters of the Christian experience, like Justin, Tatian and Athenagoras, constantly repeat in their writings this central theme: the Christian story was the "truth," the stories of the gods were myth.[58]

Athenagoras, for example, who directed his apologetic "Plea" to the emperor Marcus Aurelius himself, expressed his argument in Greek Philosophical terms. The response to upper-class requirements scored successes and expanded Christianity's constituency base among the educated. This shift eventuated in Christian ideology being dominated by upper-class religious questions answered in upper-class philosophical terms. The original apostolic importance given to the "mystery" genre receded into the background as Christianity shed its "storefront" origins. A more respectable Church used a more respectable Platonism to help explain the Christian vision. The "resurrection of the body" was still vigorously defended in Athenagoras' *apologia* in 176 of the common era, but the theological identification of "matter" with Satan and "spirit" with God was clearly present there as a given; and the message of liberation from death was already being recast in the terms of reward or punishment for the naturally immortal spirit.[59]

Progressively over the first four centuries of its existence, Christianity became the religious expression of aristocratic Hellenistic culture: the ritual embodiment of Platonic and neo-Platonic philosophical "truth," both theoretical and moral, and ultimately, the official religion of the Roman Empire.

---

[58] Athenagoras, *Plea,* ch.20 in Cyril Richardson ed., *Early Christian Fathers,* MacMillan, NY, 1970, p.318.
[59] ibid, ch.36, p.339

III. Consciousness and Spirituality

In one place in the *Summa Contra Gentiles* (II,49,8) in arguing for the existence of the soul as a separate substance, Thomas Aquinas asserts that *self-consciousness* is necessarily an immaterial activity — an operation of which matter is not capable, and therefore a proof of the spirituality of the human species. But by this criterion, recent experimental observations of *individual self-recognition* in chimpanzees would seem to prove the existence of spirit in that species as well. This observed self-consciousness lends credence to a more modern perspective which asserts that what we have called "spirit" is, to different degrees, also present in the animals.

We are talking about the *generic homogeneity of consciousness* in all forms of animal life, and it seems to suggest the existence of a potential that is intrinsic to all the equally homogeneous components of life that we have been calling "matter." These components, the *quanta* packets of matter-energy, are the same not only in all forms of life, but also in all the structures and movements of the Cosmos.

It should be emphasized that there is no intention here to deny the dimension of human life that has traditionally been called "spiritual." The data of experience show that human consciousness is *specifically different* from that of any known animal. But is human consciousness *generically different*? Are the differences such as to demand the existence of another *genus of being* ("spirit") to account for them? We have come to believe that consciousness is a generic phenomenon, shared in proportionate degrees among virtually all forms of animal life that we see. We are inclined to understand this phenomenon in a way that incorporates the discoveries of our time about the *energy* that resides at the core of matter — the bedrock components of all things including ourselves.

Transcendence and Universal Consciousness

Life itself, even in its most primitive manifestations, displays *transcendence* as its most remarkable characteristic. That word means different things to different people, however, and we should clarify what we mean by it here. Some still use the term as an indicator of *supra-natural factors* for the explanation of natural phenomena, like the Greeks who posited "spirit" to explain the human capacity for conceptualization. I don't. By transcendence I mean what biologists call "emergence." It is saying that when these elemental material particles — nitrogen, potassium, carbon, oxygen, etc., the components of all things — are organically woven into complex combinations by the living forces of genetic construction (DNA) as they are in our bodies and in all living things, they manifest *new capabilities* that they did not display in isolation or in the more primitive organisms that directly preceded. I believe the science of our times is convinced that this potential was somehow there to begin with, requiring only the extractive ability of genetic DNA for its full expression. Otherwise we'd have to say, with the ancients, it was somehow "injected" with a specific "form" into each new level of living thing by an outside source. And no one who has accepted evolution is inclined to say that. But in any case, it results in a characteristic phenomenon of life: *emergence,* the whole is greater than the sum of its parts. $2+2 = 5$, not 4. This is what I mean here by "transcendence."

We see this in evidence at all levels of life, even the most primitive. The living functions of the simplest forms, like paramecia and bacteria, display a capacity for focus and self identity, purpose, intention, and survival that were *not* in evidence among the particles of which they are made, even complex self-replicating molecules.

As we move "up" from the more primitive levels we see transcendence functioning in analogous ways. Each form and level of life draws upon the same common pool of elements, either in isolation, like water and air, or in a complex chain of living organisms whose very bodies provide food for one another in the form of organic molecules, proteins, amino acids, carbon compounds. The available elements in whatever form, go beyond what they were doing and in most cases what they *seemed capable of doing* in their prior state, and are drawn into the life patterns of the new individual utilizing them. So, we eat plants and the flesh of animals who do not have our level of conscious awareness; their organic compounds are taken in by our bodies and are integrated into the human organism. What was not capable of "thought" in the barnyard, becomes capable of it when assimilated into our bodies. But in all cases *the substrate remains the same;* a protein is a protein, a carb is a carb. The very same oxygen that powers our brain cells to produce human thought, is also fueling the microbes and cancers that kill us.

We are also aware that higher life forms — animals close to us in the scale of complexity — share with us to a greater degree than we realized, the abilities we have traditionally identified with "consciousness." These abilities in us were termed "spiritual," and in the past, they were assigned to the separate reality, "spirit." Recognition, analysis, experimentation, learning, complex communication, loyalty, loneliness, fear, have been historically interpreted as beyond the capacities of "matter" and therefore impossible to the animals. But there was prejudice functioning here. Manifestations in the animals of most of the items on the list just offered — *generic signs of consciousness* — were denied or ignored. In spite of the evidence, no less available to the ancients than to us, all the operations of consciousness of which human beings were *not* the subject were categorically disparaged in the animals as mere *material mechanisms*. Hence we must say: the ancient doctrine of "spirit" was *not* the result of inescapable logic or painstaking observation. It was the ignorant prejudice of the educated classes of the ancient world, unlikely to have ever set foot in forest or barnyard, who were bound and determined to separate "spirit" from "matter" justifying the superiority of humans over the animals and the domination of the earth by humankind.

This inveterate blindness will be easier to recognize for the arrogance that it really is if we remember that human slaves and women were also assigned by these leisured parasites to "subhuman" categories, and their exploitation was thus similarly justified. Aristotle's argumentation for the necessity of slavery was based on the alleged *sub-humanity* of the slaves and the concomitant obligation of their masters to direct their lives for them. This argument was re-applied as a principle of right conduct two thousand years later when the Spanish and Portuguese conquerors of the "New World" used it to justify the mass enslavement of American and African native peoples.

Pursuing this even further, if we examine the human fossil record we are aware that there were many variations of hominid species that existed before us showing signs of a human "consciousness." No one could ever deny that these pre-historic "people," while they were *specifically inferior* to us, were *generically human*. That all such earlier species of *homo* are extinct, may not be simply attributable to the cruel benevolence of evolutionary selection. It is possible that the prejudices of a species such as modern *homo sapiens*, determined to condemn and destroy as *sub-human* everything that was incapable of defending itself against our superior brain power, may have been the responsible factor there as well.[60]

Evolutionary theorists, like Teilhard de Chardin have enunciated principles of biological etiology which assert that *the appearance of a function at one point in evolutionary development implies its presence, perhaps below the threshold of perceptibility, in earlier forms*.[61] This may be considered an expression of the old axiom, *ex nihilo nihil fit*. They adduce it to justify their claim that *consciousness* did not simply appear for the first time with humankind or even with the higher animals, but is an intrinsic characteristic of all reality, no matter how primitive and uncomposed: a *vital impulse* according to Bergson,[62] or an *interiority* as Teilhard con-

---

[60] Theories on the extinction of the Neanderthals are based on mtDNA evidence that while they co-existed locally with *homo sapiens* there was no genetic exchange. Neandertal disappearance, in other words, *was not due to absorption*. Given the adaptability of all species of *homo*, competition for scarce single-niche food sources can be reasonably ruled out as an explanation. This would leave only extermination. Cf. Ian Tattersall, "Once We Were Not Alone" *Scientific American Special Edition*, June 2003, Volume 13, Number 2, Pages: 20-27

[61] Pierre Teilhard de Chardin, *The Phenomenon of Man*, tr.Wall, Harper & Row, NY, 1959 (1955) pp 53-66. He says on p. 57: *"In a coherent perspective of the world, life inevitably assumes a 'pre-life' for as far back before it as the eye can see."*

[62] Henri Bergson, *Creative Evolution*, Dover, Mineola NY, 1998 (tr Mtichell 1910 from the original published 1907). While Bergson sees "matter" and the Vital Impulse as *opposed* to one another, he claims the latter is primordial. He conjectures that a "vague and formless" vitality constituted the "condition of life in our nebula before the condensation of matter was complete." pp.256-257. Given this statement, to my mind, there should be no reason why he would not be amenable to calling "spirit" an identifiable *property of*

ceives it, or *the very primordial nature of God* proposed by Whitehead,[63] responsible for evolution's "upward" direction. The development of *consciousness*, for these men, represents the *unfolding* of a potential within matter.

So we may permit ourselves to be persuaded that what we have traditionally attributed to "spirit" exists in a myriad of gradations and expressions throughout the world of living things and ultimately resides as an intrinsic property of what was believed to be "inert" matter, which produced our bodies, our *selves*.

The Quanta of the Universe

Where did this "matter," these bits and pieces that form us, come from? As we look back at the origin of the elemental particles which are the building blocks of all molecules and the most complex organic compounds, we realize that they were elaborated in the processes of *star formation* which are now, and always have been continuously occurring throughout the universe. These particles are not unique to our earth except in their particular percentages and quantities.

We have also recently become aware that certain of these elemental building blocks — specifically the heavy elements like

---

matter, as I do, and not a separate kind of being. Yet, to my chagrin, he specifically calls the Vital Impulse "spirit" and states that the phenomena of "spirit" display characteristics that are different from matter in kind and not merely in degree.

I believe that Bergson was still under the influence of the unquestioned assumptions of the Platonic Paradigm. I believe those assumptions formed an invisible horizon for him as they still do for many people. They prejudicially and without justification *define* matter *a priori* as *inert* and thus lock in place an unavoidable metaphysical duality. For if matter is intrinsically inert, then any sign of life must be due to something other than matter. But as we will argue, if matter and energy are convertible, and if we accept the phenomena that have been attributed to life (and spirit) as ultimately derived from that energy, then life may be considered an *intrinsic property of matter itself*. You do not have to posit two realities, two kinds of being, and two worlds where each is said to reside — nor do you have to deny the obvious manifestations of life and spirit.

I believe Bergson's intention was to ground the possibility of the "spiritual" dimension, which was being systematically denied in the name of "inert matter" by the mechanists. It was not his main focus to insist on the existence of two kinds of being. The convertibility of matter and energy was only proposed by Einstein for the first time in 1905. Even if Bergson was aware of Einstein's work, it was still in the form an esoteric mathematical theory and not accepted fact as it is for us today

[63] Alfred North Whitehead, *Process and Reality,* (1929, Free Press NY, 1957 pp. 405-416

iron, which is an essential constituent of our blood — are formed *exclusively* in cataclysmic sidereal explosions called supernovas, that were also responsible for those elements' dispersion throughout vast distances of interstellar space. The only sequence of events that can account for the presence of atoms of *iron* in our blood is that after their formation in the violent disintegration of a nearby star, iron atoms were diffused in enormous clouds of material through space, gathered into our Earth as our sun and its planets congealed out of those clouds of particles, was drawn up out of the earth into living things, and finally through evolution and the food chain taken in by us to become an essential constituent of our blood. This is what we are.

Astonishing! Primordial convulsive cosmic events, so far from us in space, time and enormity of scale that our minds stagger in the attempt to imagine them, produced the elements that at this exact instant are coursing through our veins, carrying oxygen to feed the tiny fire of our life. When we think of evolution, we should include an awareness of the material that was used to make us. This incomprehensible process, knitting with a patience as eternal as the threads it finds at hand, is the Cosmos that we live in; it is our Mother and Father. It is ourselves.

What Is This Life?

What is this Life, this *vital impulse,* this *interiority,* this *primordial divinity* embedded in the quarks and muons, the *quanta,* the energy packets that form the nuclei of atoms, that drives so relentlessly toward life, more life, endless life? All life seeks only to live. There is nothing to suggest the fatted calf is any the less intent on staying alive than we who slaughter her. All living things seek immortality. There is nothing unique about our human yearning for eternal life, nor about the unmitigated disaster which is our death. Death is a catastrophe for every living thing, and everything perishes reluctantly. We share that destiny with everything in the Universe. We alone seem to know it beforehand. Perhaps the Universe spawned us so there would be someone to shed a tear.

There is nothing in our experience that demands the existence of a reality — like "spirit" — different from the realities we see functioning all around us, obviously capable of producing "transcendent" effects among organisms heretofore called material. There is nothing to suggest that the *capacity for consciousness,* obviously supported at lower levels by genetically organized matter in the animals, should suddenly cease to function in the case of humankind, which evolved from those same animals, requiring for its explanation *in our case alone* a reality of an altogether different kind. If "matter" is capable of supporting the transcendence we have seen on a myriad of levels right up to the animals directly below us who produced us, there is no reason to assume it is incapable of whatever is necessary to explain every aspect of our humanity as well, including our "spiritual functions." We are, after all, made of exactly the same clay.

So we draw the following conclusion: what we have called "spirit" is a function of matter. This is not in any way meant to deny the existence of the *phenomena* we have traditionally assigned to spirit. What I am saying is that these functions and whatever transcendence they imply *do not demand the existence of realities and entities or worlds, apart from the realities and entities and the world that we experience everyday.* These abilities are the very properties of the component particles of our world.

Our view of the world determines whether we will seek the explanation for the phenomena we've been calling the "experience of spirit" (human consciousness and rationality, morality, the sense of the sacred, the thirst for immortality, mystical experience, etc.) in the things themselves that we see around us, or in other imagined realities we cannot see, like "spirits" or a separate "world of ideas." Clearly, the ancients, *based on their science*, chose the latter. We, on the other hand, confident in our science, do not believe there is any world other than this one.

Many in our times remain unconvinced that "transcendent" human interests like "justice" can be sustained without belief in something like spirit, a separate genus of being, to ground them. I want to include recognition of the depth and intensity of the human moral dimension. But I wouldn't want this recognition to create a misunderstanding. It bears repeating that "the spiritual" is a human phenomenon. It does not exist independently of human organisms nor does it imply the existence of a reality other than our body-persons. I am not denying the existence of "the spiritual" as a metaphor for certain human phenomena. What I am denying is the existence of "spirit" as a cosmo-ontological entity or separate category of being.

This viewpoint has important implications for the way we will view "God," ourselves, and our place in the Whole, from which we derive our morality and "spirituality." In the past, we were ruled by a code of conduct designed and driven by belief in two-worlds — one of spirit and one of matter — and we humans assigned ourselves a place in the invisible world of spirit. We (purposely) set ourselves apart from the rest of creation. This separation may account for the abusive way we currently relate to our own bodies, to people different from us, and to our fragile planet with its many species of life — all of which is considered inferior to ourselves because we claim to be spirit. We have preferred to think of ourselves as *aliens from another world* rather than accept the obvious: we have evolved from and are sustained by this planet and our sister species to whom we are intimately, inextricably related. Our analysis, simple as it may be, is sufficient to create the suspicion that our relationships, under the regimen of two-world Platonism, have been characterized by a destructive alienation and anthropocentrism. We have detached ourselves from the earth and seated ourselves among the gods. We tried to escape from our humanity. We thought of ourselves as eternally *alive* because we called ourselves *spirit,* and we called everything else *matter,* and treated it as if it were *dead.*

Such was the legacy of the theory of the two worlds.

IV. "Spirits" and Immortality

I believe this question of human *spirit* is the major difference between the ancient and modern view of the world. The modern world does not believe that it is necessary to posit the existence of a human "spirit" to explain any of the phenomena of human consciousness and relationships. That doesn't mean that what we've experienced in ourselves and others as "spirit" has disappeared, nor does it devalue those experiences. It only means the philosophy that required assuming that there resided in us an *unseen reality* different in kind from our body-persons, and that there was an *invisible world* where that reality belonged, has disappeared. Our scientific perception of reality is radically different from the ancient Greek scientific world-view in which our religious beliefs — and the faith based on them — were born.

Assault on Religion?

Religion in the West has traditionally identified itself with the *belief in the existence of spirits* instead of *the significance of the experience of spirit*. But what we have also not realized is that, historically, the notion of "spirits" as literal, factual entities was elaborated as a part of Plato's *cosmological theory*, just like the notion of the "One." It was accepted as the only possible explanation for the existence of "universals," i.e., abstract ideas, the shared "forms" of created things and the phenomena of human mental functions, especially conceptualization and reasoning. It was quite natural that yearnings for immortality and other "spiritual" experiences would be assimilated to this notion. These were scientific theories.

Since then, however, science changed. *Spirit is* no longer considered necessary to explain these things. Many will argue that modern "science" has not proven this case. "Spirit" exists, they say, until proven otherwise. Such a statement, of course, has nothing to justify it but tradition. But, whatever their strictly logical value, in practice, these attempts to maintain the past don't seem to have had much impact on the overall view of the world characteristic of our times. Modern science does not see the world as peopled with invisible spirits, and to an ever greater degree as time goes on, we the "people of faith" tend to agree with them. The scientific community has long since begun to carry out its experiments on the exclusive assumption that the various phenomena for which "spirit" was thought to be uniquely necessary, are now thoroughly comprehensible as functions of "matter." As that general theory guides exploration into new areas of inquiry, evidence accumulates that corroborates their hypothesis: you don't need to have "spirits" to account for the phenomena they once explained, including the "experience of spirit." This has been increasingly clear over the last three or four hundred years, and phenomena that range from the movements of the stars and natural disasters, to psychic, intellectual, moral and even mystical phenomena have been proven to be completely explainable without recourse to the existence of invisible "spirits."

A change of such magnitude constitutes a new context for faith. But there is nothing exceptional in this. Throughout history, radical change of scientific context has affected the religious project. There is no terminology, outside of the prevailing contemporary science, in which the religious person can intelligently express his/her faith, without encountering serious internal conflict. We are, inescapably, what we are — the children of our time. And it's *what we are*, that must find a way to sing.

Faith?

This is the authentic religious project — *to sing*. Ultimately, the metaphor means that faith is a relationship of *thanksgiving*. The central role of *thanksgiving* is not an elusive insight of anthropology nor an arcane religious mysticism. It's a simple human reality: *we are supremely glad we're alive, such as we are.* It's as simple to understand as it is perhaps difficult to sustain. *It is good to be here.* Faith as *trust* is an integral, essential element of the process of living, not a mental contortion designed to deny dying, much less a shibboleth-code that grants us access to another world.

Faith, by embracing *the world as it is and ourselves as we are* (which means accepting our parabolic life-line leading from birth to death), paradoxically takes away the sting of death. This parallels the Buddhist perspective which seeks a solution to our problem without imagining a world that isn't there.

This is exactly the heart of the matter. Faith is not Disneyland, a fantasy world that some say is mainstream religion's proper subject. Faith feels and expresses *gratitude* for the world that is *really there*. The point is not as obvious as it seems. We have been conditioned by our tradition to accept something else entirely. Traditional Religion insists that reality is *other* than we perceive it, and does so under the rubric of religious belief. That won't work. You can't conjure into existence a world that isn't there. Faith is not about imagining realities we can't see; it's about embracing as sacred the realities we can see.

Even while admitting that there are people who are quite content to accept the world as the ancients envisioned it, there are increasing numbers, like myself, who are just as sure that the structural features of the Platonic Universe — like the existence of "spirits" — are pure fantasy, and choose to accept wholeheartedly what the discoveries of relativity and quantum mechanics, evolution and psychoanalysis, have taught about the reality of ourselves and our world.

Subsistent Forms and Human Immortality

By insisting that in spite of all appearances, human persons are really "self-subsistent forms" (souls, spirits) that inhabit "matter" (their very own bodies) as if they were separate and alien substances, traditional Religion has tried to make obsolete science an item of belief. Why cling to such anomalies? Nostalgia for traditional formulations, to my mind, isn't sufficient motivation in itself to explain Religion's increasingly irrational insistence in this particular case, so contrary to the view of science. There is a much more important reason for it, and I believe it is our *immortality*. The supposed ability of the alleged human "spirit" to exist and function independently of the body has also been the justification for the claims of the exclusive human transcendence over dying — our *immortality* is the reason we cling to "spirit." It is a denial of death.[64]

Coping with the disaster of death is central to the Religious Project. We might all agree. But I believe there are various ways of trying to cope with death. Fantasizing a world that isn't there is just one of them; and I believe it is ultimately ineffective. We need to explore ways of coping with death and our thirst for immortality that don't involve imagining *a world that isn't there*.

---

[64] Cf the work of Ernest Becker, *The Denial of Death*, Free Press, NY,1974

After constructing its traditional imaginary world, Religion then proposes a relationship — an act of faith — with the "God" who rules that world of immortal spirits. This is a falsification of reality and therefore inimical to the act of faith. If faith is the active perception of the world embraced in a sacred relationship, projecting *a world that isn't there* turns faith into an excursion through a Mr. Roger's neighborhood, a make-believe world for children. As soon as these imagined perceptions reveal themselves as such, the show is over. There is no faith possible in a non-existent world.

Alienation — The Original Sin

Being human, just like every other form of life that we know, is a vulnerable and evanescent phenomenon. It's not just that it takes a lot of work for a human being to stay alive. But in the end, the achievements of life, however painstakingly accumulated and carefully protected, run like water through our fingers. We are perpetually assailed by anxiety about loss and inevitably, death. And well we should be, for in the end, all our worries prove true; we lose everything we ever achieved or possessed, and we die.

If we were ever inclined to console ourselves by saying *all* living things suffer the same fate as we do, we are quickly reconfirmed in our misery because, we realize, *we alone are aware of it*. We imagine — probably correctly — that the animals are happily ignorant of the inevitable doom they share with us. As far as they know, today's meal has achieved the immortality their hunger intended to conquer. This suffering of ours created by death stems from our brilliant, crystalline, magnificent consciousness. It isolates us in a world teeming with fellow creatures who seem oblivious to the dark secret that festers in our hearts, robbing us of the joy of life and our ability to sing. We envy the birds who sing with abandon. They sing, we say, *because they do not know*.

The escape from this relentless insecurity and ultimate dissolution — the search for permanent life and its assurance — has been the quintessential quest of humankind, it seems, since we first emerged into the light of self-consciousness and realized our solitary predicament. The list of the human experiments throughout the ages created for the ultimate purpose of rectifying this design flaw in our human reality — from our technologies, through our political constructions, our monuments, our literature and art, our religions — would be so extensive as to explain nothing. Or rather, it would explain *everything*; for it is all of human endeavor. The necessary labor for our "daily bread," reasonably extended to include "provision for tomorrow" is almost *unconsciously overextended* into the irrational attempt to provide "for eternity" — to find or create a permanence that is *just not there*. Each day's victory over death, the fruits of hard labor, instead of accumulating to immortality, turns out to be, like the grains of sand pouring out of the hourglass, the relentless subduction of elapsed time. Our yearning to live another day only brings us one day closer to our last.

So, I interpret our quest for permanence as a natural instinct that goes too far — an unfortunate pathological excess that is a most natural extension of the life-process itself. Nothing could be closer to the classic definition of a tragic flaw, what the Greeks called *harmatía* — Sin. For me it's the original sin.

Escape Velocity?

Then, at a second and perhaps more distressing level, there is the pain and frustration generated at the perennial *failure* of these escape vehicles of ours — our attempts to achieve permanence — to carry us beyond the gravity of our condition and into self-perpetuating orbit. Nothing as yet devised for this purpose has worked. And we've been at it, apparently, for millions of years. Besides the frustration, I believe the *attempt to escape from death means to escape from what we are*. Escape is harmful for us. It distracts us from whatever real potential may exist in our impermanent condition, such as it is. I believe many of our conflicts, both personal and political, are reducible to this obsession with the impossible — this lust for permanence that drives us to forge rings of power and immortality.

There is no such ring. It's a fairy tale. And the attempt to acquire it or the illusion that we have found it, distorts us and makes us capable of violence in its quest. Many of our most cherished projects are nothing but surrogates for permanence. The slightest reflection reveals them for the empty substitutes that they really are. *The denial of death is the escape from humanity.* The projections of Religion, in this regard, especially those that imagine a world that isn't there where our persons supposedly continue forever, run the risk of being just such a denial. Denial will hijack our lives and subject us like sleep walkers to relentless illusion.

There is no escape from death. We are what we are. And it's *what we are* that must learn how to sing.

Another Kind of Immortality

But if, as we are coming to realize, we belong to this one immense reality of matter-energy *out of which* our body-persons have congealed, and *with which* we have been fed and sustained and *into which* we return at death, we may imagine another kind of immortality, quite different from the imagined permanent existence of our ephemeral personalities. It is the immortality of the substrate, the Whole, matter-energy, of which we are made, imbued with an intrinsic vitality that is the palpable power behind our pulsing life. This enormous vitality we experience as our very selves is the energy of matter, its *vital impulse,* its *interiority*, its *primordial divinity.* It is not something we have, it is *what we are.* The functions and operations of our body-persons are an expression of it; they are not separate from it. We have no being apart from it. We are it.

As we see the temporary form and function of our individual body-persons dissolve in death and our matter-energy become available for other temporary forms and functions, we suspect that this is an endless affair. This may also suggest to us that *perhaps Our Real Self is the Whole,* the Universe of matter-energy, the Cosmos of divine living being — the dust from which we come and unto which we shall return. That this imagery and terminology is reminiscent of the great mystics of our tradition (and, we are learning, *of all traditions*), should serve to confirm our sense that such a conception as we propose is not as untraditional as it first appears.

The "Selfish" Self

Perhaps the most fascinating convergence with tradition may be seen in the universal insistence of the ascetic masters on the suppression or neutralization of the individual "ego" or "self" as an essential element of spiritual growth. Some of the greatest teachers even spoke of the "obliteration of the self," as we will see in a later chapter.

Of all of these, the Buddha was perhaps the most austere and radical because he seemed to ground his demands for transcendence over the self in its *non-existence*. Also, since he proposed no doctrine of a personal "God," this self-transcendence appeared not to contemplate an absorption in a larger "Divine Self," as do some other traditions. This is the Buddhist doctrine of *anatman*, that the "real existence" of the separate human self, or "I," is pure illusion — the source of all desire and suffering. There is no self, says the Buddha, there is nothing there. Buddhists claim theirs is *not* a metaphysical doctrine, however, and that the injunction is ascetical and the doctrine merely phenomenological. We may dispute the claims of this one philosophy, but it is harder to dispute the remarkable agreement across time and tradition in this matter of the "reduction" of the self.

This is most contradictory in the West. This ascetical imperative, the "mortification of the self," so emphatically preached by Western mystics, seems to ignore the supposed *metaphysical importance of our individual persons* which one would have considered a vital corollary of the presence in us of immortal spirit. What does such a strange inconsistency imply? There is no denying the emphatic language that all the Western ascetic masters bring to bear on this issue: the *self must be* suppressed, subjugated, conquered, transcended — some even said *obliterated, eliminated, abandoned* — if one is to permit the "new life" of which they speak to take over "in the soul." According to Meister Eckhart, a mediaeval Dominican and successor to Thomas Aquinas in the Chair of Theology at the University of Paris, the *obliteration* of the "false, finite, *selfish self*" is the absolute precondition for *its replacement with the Divine Self* which he identifies literally with the "Son," the *Logos* of God, and ultimately with Being itself. The "Birth of the Son [of God] in the soul" as he conceives it, is not just a psychological attitude but a *real metaphysical event* and resultant state: true divine Sonship for the "soul." Ultimately, in a most unexpected teaching, Eckhart even counsels transcending the Trinity itself, as we will see, in order to achieve a *totally unencumbered oneness* with Being, similar to the oneness with Being that we enjoyed "before we were born" when, he says, "I was what I wanted and I wanted what I was."[65]

If we ignore Eckhart's Neo-Platonic allusions to a pre-existent "soul," this imagery brings to mind the alternative immortality we've been suggesting.

These extraordinary people all seem to agree on the importance of an achievement of self-transcendence that evokes the notion that "our real self is the Whole."

A Spiritualist "Theology of Death"

Another remarkable concurrence between our conjectures and tradition is on display in the case of the mainline Catholic theologian, Karl Rahner. Rahner's little study, *On the Theology of Death*, offers a brief sally into a theory of the "soul's" *all-cosmic* relationship after death. Rahner by no means would agree with the non-existence of "spirit" that we are proposing here. His views are developed well within the traditional world-view, and yet in spite of that they bear a striking resemblance to what we are suggesting. The following comes from pp 26-27 of the Herder edition of 1962 translated by Henkey:

> ... For the soul, as united to the body, must also have some relationship to that "whole" of which the body is a part, that is to that wholeness which constitutes the unity of the material universe. ...
>
> If the soul also has a relationship to this radical oneness of the universe, the question must arise: does the separation of the body and soul in death also imply the end of the soul's relationship to the world, in such a manner that the soul becomes a-cosmic, "out of the world"? Or does the termination of her present relation to the body — that by which she maintains its structures and delimits it from the whole of the world — imply rather, and principally, her entrance into some deeper, all embracing openness in which her cosmic relationship to the universe is more fully realized? Or in other words: does the soul, in death, become strictly out of this world or does she rather, by virtue of the fact that she is no longer bound to an individual bodily structure, enter into a much closer, more intimate relationship to the uni-

---

[65] Eckhart, sermon: *Blessed are the Poor*

verse as a whole? We mean by this latter phrase ("universe as a whole") that basic oneness of the world, so difficult to grasp, yet so very real, by which all things in the world are related and communicate anteriorly to any mutual influence upon each other.

What seems to me most relevant for our discussion is the vision of the relationship of the human spirit after death *with the entire material universe*, what Rahner calls an *all-Cosmic* existence. Granted he has not abandoned belief in the *metaphysical* reality of the human individual existing after death, the traditional "immortal soul," but he is clear about saying that he might consider such an existence *phenomenologically* all-Cosmic — meaning experientially unlike our present consciousness of ourselves as human individuals delimited by the specifics of our particular bodies.[66]

If one were inclined to pursue this matter further, one would have to ask, "what does this do to individual judgment after death, and the reward or punishment claimed to result?"

V. Being Human

What is it to be human?

Descartes said, *"I think, therefore I am."* For him it was a formula for knowing, not for being. He wasn't saying that thinking created him, or made him human (though, based on this formula, others do say this), only that his awareness of his own thinking was a clear evidence of his existence. He needed it to make his geometrical methodology work. That it also happened to be constructed on a highly individualistic image of the human being was less of a co-incidence than the author may have suspected.

For, while Descartes' *Cogito* apparently had a methodological intent, it drew its fundamental persuasive power from ancient metaphysical roots which it assumed and exploited even as it claimed to ignore them. The individualism characteristic of modern Western culture arose from here. Using the mathematical

---

[66] In this regard, we should note the concurrence of religion writer Diarmund O'Murchu *Quantum Theology* Crossroads Books, NY 1999, p.170.

genre so beloved by the 17th century, the *Cogito* recapitulated the *mind vs matter* bifurcation of reality set in immutable stone by the ancient Greeks two millennia earlier. But, before examining the rationale and challenging the hegemony of that ancient world view, I would like to pre-empt its privileged position in our imagination, if I could, by first presenting a world-view that I think is ours, an experience we have of ourselves appropriate to the knowledge of our times.

I offer a different formula ... a formula for being, *being here,* being human:

I am related, therefore I am.

I mean this in a metaphysical sense, not as some kind of chic mysticism. It says my *presence,* my *being-here,* is nothing but the sum of the relationships that constitute and contextualize my existence, the focal point of the valences that sustain me. Saying it this way is very important. The formula says that I, literally, do not exist on my own. For to say *I am my relationships* means I am part of a Whole by which I am not only sustained, but receive my being and my way of being — *being here and being human.*

Let's consider:

I require air. My presence-in-the-world is totally dependent on a set of connections that permit me to *consume oxygen* virtually non-stop and in unlimited quantities throughout my entire life. I am sustained ceaselessly in and by the material in the gaseous envelope of our planet at every moment of my life. Sever my intimate and constant relationship to the air, and like a fetus without an umbilical cord, I am gone.

The continuous combustion with oxygen in the hidden furnaces of all of the cells of my body *is* my very life, my *self.* My life process is so identified with the uninterrupted burning of oxygen that I might be tempted to ask: how am "I" the actor in this drama? What is really going on here? I appear to be a passive instrument for the conversion of oxygen into heat and energy, over which I have little control and no independence.

I consume food which for the most part is the remains of other living things that exist on our planet whose organic particles I require many times daily in a suitable volume, or again, I die. These particles don't sustain me, they *are* me. The remnants of other living things are broken down into their elemental components and used by my body to replace *itself* continuously throughout my life. It is estimated that this cycle is completed approximately every seven years. I have an entirely *new body* every seven years built out of the plants, animals, air and water that I have taken in from the earth around me. There seems to be no independent core to this onion. However far you penetrate you will find only these components made of *matter-energy*, nothing more. If there is something *more*, it is not evident.

What am I? Am I me, or am I the air, plants and animals around me?

My body was not chosen, nor constructed by me. The form it has, came from the genetic material of my parents. I inherit everything I am, my species, my gender, my size, my health, my strength, my weaknesses, my longevity, my raw mental abilities, my disposition, my looks. I was fabricated by forces I do not understand according to patterns decided upon not by me but by the most primitive components of my parents' bodies. Everything *I am,* I have exclusively through them. My very cells are theirs.

Our particular life-form that we call human has a complex of anatomical features which were themselves the inheritance of eons upon eons of previous lives, proximately our human forebears, and then, more remotely, the life forms out of which our humanity evolved. If I have five fingers on a hand, if I have two lungs, so does every other human being on the face of the earth. But also so does every other mammalian vertebrate on the planet, including whales, horses, squirrels. All of us mammals have been shown to have similar anatomies because we are related to a common ancestor. Five fingers, two lungs. This is an inheritance, not an invention, a gift, not a possession. It's standing evidence of the role of the Universe in the formation of my *self.* I did not decide to be, nor did I decide *what* I was going to be.

I have yet to see what makes me, *me*. Where am "I" in all this?

O.K. Let's talk about "me." My very own personality, that which identifies me as the unique individual that I am, by which I am called by *my name*, is itself the result of familial relationships that have given me my language, my culture, my psychological make-up, my morality, my preferences, my tastes, my dreams, beliefs and attitudes toward the world and other people around me. I am dependent upon multiple chains of connections both vertical and horizontal, in the present and through time, that sustain and explain my individual existence. At the level of my individuality, *my person*, I am fully the product of human society; so much so that there are sciences that, with a reasonable degree of accuracy, are able to predict my personal behavior based on the group to which I belong.

My personality derives whatever psychological *balance* it may have from the familial, friendship and work relationships that sustain me. Take away any of these connections, and if they or their equivalent are not replaced I suffer serious pain, along with an emotional imbalance that can result in permanent deformity. Chronic deprivation of these relationships will change "me." I will not be the person I was; I will not be "myself."

We are the sum of our relationships. If we leave out or suppress one of these core constitutive elements, we lose, or truncate or distort our humanity. *I am related therefore I am.* "I" am part of a Whole.

Corollaries

There are some immediate corollaries to this thumbnail sketch.

The first thing is that the *independent sustaining reality is the Whole*, considered as the Universe of things. Individual human beings, and even the species itself, exist only in dependence on the Whole. The Whole is not as directly controlling of its components as that of an individual living organism, but it approximates it because it determines everything they (we) are. Saying this does not erase the undeniable reality of the individual. But, it is clearly meant to challenge the older substantialist view, inherited from the Greeks, that focused exclusively on the falsely assumed *independ-*

ent reality of the individual substance.[67] In that perspective, the only even pale reality in our shadow world was the separately identifiable *substance* — i.e., in our case, the human person. Relationship was relegated to the category of "accident." And *the Whole* as such, therefore, could not be considered the proper subject of existence. This has profound implications for our conception of the immortality available to us as matter-energy.

A second corollary that may be derived from our observations is that among the co-existent parts of the relational Whole individuals are now to be understood more in terms of their *connectedness* to one another, than in terms of their separateness and difference. This is a new angle for those of us who have been trained to define things by *genus and specific difference*. For now, how things are related to one another is *constitutive* of each, and therefore each thing enters into the very definition of the other, and the Whole into the definition of *every* thing.[68]

In our case, for example, the attempt to define *humanity* apart from its relationship to the matter-energy out of which it is constructed and by which it functions and survives, falsifies its reality. The same is true of its relationship to the other species by which we survive. A solipsist definition omits the factors which determine the depth and range of human activity, thus eliminating the bases for understanding the *significance* of *being-here and* of being human, as well as the *significance* of the Whole of which *we* are a part. This corollary grounds ecology in metaphysics, not esthetic preference or voluntaristic morality.

Third, the contingent evolutionary processes that elaborated the various species in time, are now understood to be the sole source of their "forms," i.e., "what" they are — what the scholastics used

---

[67] *The centrality of "substance" (a thing) was the result of the Aristotelian displacement of Platonism, accomplished in the 14th century, creating the "modern" world. Aristotle rejected Plato's theory that "form" was a separate reality, but he continued to rely fundamentally on the "form" of a thing to ground its reality. "Substance" was still an essentialist conception. But for Aristotle, substance was the only real thing in the world.*

[68] Whitehead, op.cit.p. 597 *"The obligations imposed on the becoming of any particular actual entity arise from the constitutions of other actual entities."*

to call the "quiddity" or essence of substances. This restates the above conclusions about intelligibility but it introduces the concept of the Whole as "Creator." It represents a radical departure from the older essentialist view which held that "creation" was inexplicable except as the insertion of a "form" into "matter" by a form-generating Creator-Mind — a "Spirit" God. In that ancient conception, the *significance* of human beings was determined by their relationship to the "*Mental Spirit*" who made them and Whom, as *mental spirits,* they recognized and imitated. This new concept of creation entails a new concept of "God" which we explore more fully in the next chapter. But here we can sketch out some of its implications.

Evolution, human nature and "God"

In the evolutionary conception the *significance* of human beings is established by our relationship to the Whole Universe whose elemental components — *matter-energy* as observed and measured by science — are the determining factors of our potential for development. We can become only what our substrate allows. But reciprocally, what we actually do become indicates what the substrate really is. It reveals the *significance* of the potential in the Universe and its components. It is only in retrospect that the original potential of the *mater-energy* of which the Universe is composed, is unveiled and identified for what it truly is. For many theorists it is *consciousness* as a truly generic phenomenon that retroactively defines the *significance* of matter-energy.[69]

Evolution has replaced the Greek World of Ideas and the "Mind of God." Evolution means that the "whatness" of things is designed and produced *by the Whole,* using a process of survival-orientated interaction among its related parts to produce unforeseen consequences.

Likewise, the notion of a static, fixed essence or form — a *human nature*, for example, that remained the same throughout time — was shattered by evolutionary theory. Evolution says things were not only shaped by the evolutionary processes, *they continue*

---

[69] Teilhard, Whitehead and Bergson all support this transcendent feature of reality.

to be modified as they pass through time. What we call "human nature" is an arbitrary abstraction, a false conceptual snap-shot taken by the human brain that artificially freezes what is really a continuous flow of evolving "form." Imperceptibly perhaps, but irrepressibly, our "human nature" is changing within us as we speak, moving beyond us just as it changed *into us* from that of our hominid forebears. Human nature is not a fixed form and it does not require a single unchanging Craftsman, whose Mind was a "World of Fixed Ideas," to account for its reality.

"God" for the ancient Greeks was a conclusion of *science.* "God" was the product of logical reasoning, a cosmological hypothesis that explained the world as they believed it was structured. Species-life, which the Greeks knew in conceptual form as *universal ideas,* is at the heart of that vision. "God" was posited to explain the existence of the phenomena of the many individuals of the same kind. Species-life in the Greek Cosmos required shared "forms," which had to be *ideas* because we humans form *generic concepts* of them. The Greeks reasoned that there had to be a "Mental Spirit" over the Cosmos, responsible for generating such mental realities, ideas, just as there had to be a "mental spirit" in us to recognize them.

"God" is no longer needed in that capacity. And since we no longer define things by their forms or essences, but rather by their interrelated survival functions, it is not necessary to claim we humans are "mental spirits" for knowing them. One does not have to know the *idea, the essence* of things to relate accurately to the way they function. Our mental operation, like the science that dominates our times, is now more appropriately considered an analytical instrument developed for survival purposes; it is a more efficient version of the consciousness evident in the higher animals. Consciousness is most properly a practical tool not a speculative one.

Some, like Teilhard de Chardin, have claimed that God is still required to explain the presence of the evolutionary capability itself which he also believes is embedded as a seminal force in all the particles of the Universe. He calls it the *interiority* of matter, as we've mentioned, and claims it is a *potential for consciousness* as revealed by the direction it has taken toward the evolution of humankind. All of this remains to be explored. We will do some of it in Chapter 3. But in all cases, even for Teilhard, it seems that the notion of "God" as a "Cerebral Craftsman," has become so reduced in function as to be virtually absent. *For Teilhard, as for all evolutionists, "God" does not design and make species.* "God" may indeed be there, and we may relate to that reality, but for Teilhard it will have to be in a way different from the traditional notions of Creator and Provident Guardian as imagined in the West. This constitutes a problem for Christianity which established its foundational credibility on that once-scientific ancient Greek concept of "God." "God" corresponded in every respect to the demands of the Hellenic Cosmos and seemed corroborated by the Yahweh found in the Bible of the ancient Hebrews.

This is an overview of the ancient theories that lie at the base of the Western cultural mindset. While they are no longer scientifically relevant, these notions continue to dominate our imagery and assumptions. Those ancient "beliefs" explained a world that, for us, is no longer there. A new Cosmos implies a new relationship and therefore a new "idea of God." How has this momentous change affected our idea of ourselves? And what is "God" really like?

VI. The Nexus ... Sexus

Always talking about sex.

It's hard to convince people that my harping on the question of the Church's attitude toward sexuality, a central issue in the first Chapter, is really not just my individual problem, or axe-to-grind. And even when I'm able to persuade them that it's due rather to the sexual fixations of early Christianity, many will conclude it must have been attributable to the personal pathological obsessions of individuals like Augustine of Hippo. But that would be a false reading of history.

What most people do not realize is that the attitudes of early Christianity toward sex emerged directly from the very core of the

Roman world's ancient Platonic beliefs of the realities of "spirit" and "matter." It was a generalized phenomenon that went well beyond the confines of the Church. It characterized all the religions that stood as alternatives and rivals to the officialist state cult of the Roman gods: Diaspora Judaism, Manichaeism, neo-Platonism, Mithraism as well as Christianity. Opinion about sexuality in that world was intimately connected to the belief in the existence and transcendent purity of "spirit" and the fatal corruption of "matter," — "flesh" as found in the human body. A disdain for the "flesh" became a fixed feature of Christianity in late Antiquity when the Western Church assumed its official status as the Religion of Imperial Rome, and the thinking of Augustine of Hippo dominated the terms of Christian discourse. It hardly needs to be said that it was accompanied by an ironic fascination

Contrary to popular belief, the ethics of the Hellenic world were ideologically antagonistic to liberal sexuality. Images of Roman "toga parties," wild sexual orgies and rampant promiscuity, both hetero- and homosexual, while not non-existent, are in large part the residue of Christian propaganda. Christianity had a "theological" axe to grind. When the Church said the gods of the myths were *false*, it did not mean that they were nonexistent, rather they were all-too-real — they were *demons disguised as gods* who falsely represented divine goodness and God's will. The Church said that anyone who consorted with these "demons" would end up in wanton, uncontrolled depravity. In order to sustain this point, Christianity was invested in claiming that the Greco-Roman world, under the aegis of these "gods" was totally and irremediably corrupt. Little wonder that the very word "pagan"[70] evokes in us today images of orgiastic frenzy and sexual licentiousness. But in fact, much to the contrary, the pre-and praeter-Christian Greco-Roman cultural mindset was traditionally moral.[71]

---

[70] *paganus* in Latin means *rural,* and refers to country people, as opposed to city people. Since Christianity was an urban phenomenon for many centuries, the country people were the last to be converted, hence *pagani* became a term for non-Christians.

[71] Brown, op.cit. *The Body* ... p.21-22. Brown says, *"The evidence ... gives little support to the widespread romantic notion that the pre-christian Roman world was a sunny 'Eden of the unrepressed.' Still less is it possible to explain ... the austerity of Christian sexual*

Spirituality and Immortality

We are all familiar with the fact that carnal austerity was preached by Christianity. We are less aware that Christianity was not alone in its promotion of sexual renunciation, in fact, it was not even the originator. Philosophers like Pythagoras, Plato and the Stoics, convinced that the human "spirit" was a prisoner trapped in a "material" body, had espoused *liberation from corrupt flesh* through a severe asceticism that often included virginity and life-long continence. The Pythagoreans even had monasteries. These men lived and wrote centuries before the appearance of Christianity.[72]

Diaspora Judaism represented by Philo of Alexandria, from which the earliest Christians inherited their moral categories as well as their theology and exegesis, displayed the unmistakable influence of this Greek value system. Philo was particularly enthusiastic about Greek moral values and spirituality which was dominated by the transcendent Greek paradigm of the holiness of the rational "spirit" and the utter corruption of "matter," the body, "flesh." This enthusiasm carried Philo far beyond the traditional Jewish respect for marriage and into an altogether unwonted blanket denigration of sexuality.[73]

The traditional Christian attitudes towards sex were thus locked into place by its parent-religions: the Hellenic and Jewish-Diaspora world-view which believed that the human body with all its desires and urges was thoroughly corrupt, a punishment for sin, and the cause of death — the *only* cause of death. Spirit was considered naturally immortal. It followed that if spirit could ever free itself from the shackles of the body, it would also free itself from all suffering and the curse of death. The renunciation of sex was seen as the vehicle of that liberation. It represented transcendence over the

---

ethics and the novelty of the Christian emphasis on total sexual renunciation, as if it were nothing more than an understandable, if excessive, reaction to the debauchery that prevailed among the cultivated classes of the Empire."

[72] Ibid., p.21

[73] Philo exhibits these attitudes throughout his works. Specifically cf *On the Cherubim II*, XIV (49) (50); *Allegorical Interpretations III*, XXIV

body. Sexual phobia in the ancient Mediterranean was not a prudish peculiarity, a pathological penchant. It lay at the very heart of the Platonic philosophical world view and became the ascetical center-piece of ancient Mediterranean culture.

Each Christian theologian from those early formative years, the men we call "Fathers," had his own take on exactly how sexuality fit into the scheme of salvation, but they all shared the same general perspective and conclusions: sex was a corrupting force of great power arising exclusively from a material, animal body that overwhelmed the purity and rationality of the spirit. In the moral squalor created by sex, the thinking went, marriage hardly played a redeeming role; rather it was more often seen as part of the problem. Some Fathers even alleged that marriage was responsible for keeping the present *evil world* going and postponed the *parousía* because *it provided for the procreation that mimicked immortality.* Transcendence over the sexual function, and that included its suppression within marriage, amounted to the triumph of the *spirit* over the forces of the flesh — *matter.* Continence seemed the very essence of what was required of a real Christian. It was salvation itself. The great St Jerome stated that even the blood of martyrdom was barely able to wipe away "the dirt of marriage" from a Christian woman.[74] Similar anti-sexual attitudes were found, quite explicitly, in the Apocalypse (14:4).

Augustine, as we saw in the first chapter, even though forced by his reading of Genesis to admit that *theoretically* the body was created "good" by God and therefore sex was natural, found a way to concur with the contemporary sexual repugnance by claiming that the sexual function had been *completely corrupted* and made unmanageable by the fall of Adam. He declared that "concupiscence" — sexual desire as we know it — was an *unnatural* scar left in our bodies by Original Sin. He believed that had Adam not fallen, the act of human *coitus* would have been carried out completely without passion, as an act of tranquil rationality.[75]

---

[74] Brown, *op.cit. The Body* ... p.397

[75] St. Augustine, op. cit. *The City of God,* XIV, Ch 26, p.318

The Doctrine of the Soul

So sex was considered corrupt, unnatural and inhuman by Greco-Roman Christians. In the practical order, that meant that Augustine promoted virginity for the unmarried, and continence for everyone else interested in Christian perfection. Marriage, in the eyes of most of the Fathers, was hardly better than fornication, tolerated only for those too weak or too uncommitted to take their Christianity seriously. Many of us will recognize these attitudes. They were still prevalent only 50 years ago and were functional in our own formation.

Some of the Fathers that preceded Augustine, including his mentor, Ambrose of Milan, held even more radical views on the body. Ambrose believed that *Mary's virginity* was the actual causative factor in Jesus being born without original sin, since the *contagion was passed on by sex*.[76] The body was the source of death. The Fathers, with the exception of Clement of Alexandria, one of the very few married men among them, saw absolute continence — the refusal to engage in sexual activity of any kind — to be an essential element in the reassertion of the dominance of *spirit over matter* and the beginning of the progressive liberation of the soul from the body which was, as we've seen, immortality.

The Church in later eras inherited these notions from ancient times, and they were cemented into a morality, practice and discipline that displayed an endemic animosity toward sex (and thence logically, toward women). The momentum of this hostility continued in future epochs even long after the original theoretical justifications had been forgotten.

The connection between these two sides of Christian creed and practice — belief in the existence of *spirit* and sexual repression — should by this time be clear; the one is the flip side of the other. Augustine took the accepted Greek wisdom that went back almost a thousand years by his time, and simply re-formulated it in Christian terms, viz., since we are *spirit*, tranquil undistracted rationality is our ultimate destiny and complete happiness. The upheavals and hungers of bodily needs, like *carnal lust* (please note the adjective), are the categorical opposite to contemplative peace. Repres-

---

[76] ibid, pp 341-365

sion of sexuality, therefore, was the most natural and obvious of ascetical programs, designed to return us to the emotional quiescence that our *spiritual* nature supposedly finds normal. That the other alternative religions in the Roman world — Diaspora Judaism, neo-Platonism and Gnostic-Manichaeism — were all in *absolute agreement* on the fundamentals of this anti-sexual perspective, served to confirm it for Christianity. But the very fact of such across-the-board concurrence should have been a tip-off that the source was the culture and not the "word of God."

There were also other motivations suggested by modern psycho-social theories of character formation and social construction that might be the proper subject for cultural anthropology. In these theories the word repression is substituted by the word "sublimation." I would like to include them briefly in this analysis.

Sublimation

In Freudian theory, the kind of self-control that converts and channels sexual energy into other forms of human activity is called sublimation. Sexual sublimation was considered by Freud an essential element in the construction of all civilization.[77] It was a requirement of Greco-Roman civilization was well, of course, where it was intimately connected with institutionalized slavery — the economic foundation of the ancient world.

I am aware that from a psychoanalytic point of view "sublimation" and "repression" are contrary notions in Freud. It would be incorrect of me to use these terms as if they were synonyms. But my perspective is societal. I'm proposing that sexual suppression, demanded by the Platonic Paradigm and promoted by the religious authorities, also served double-duty as a sublimating mechanism for the construction of the Empire and the maintenance of a system based on slave labor.

The ancient Mediterranean was the home of a tightly structured slave-driven society maintained by a militarized upper class. It could not function without a ready obedience from the slaves, and a vigilant authoritarianism sustained with an iron self-discipline by

---

[77] Sigmund Freud, *Civilization and its Discontents,* Vienna, 1930 cf Herbert Marcuse, *Eros and Civilization,* Random House, NY 1955

the warrior-overlords. If sex came to be used by the upper class males for self-transcendence and self-projection, I believe it was due to this context — which pervaded the entire ancient world, not just Rome. It also ironically insured that sexual restraint would be official policy.[78] This helps explain upper-class sexual repression in the West and thence in Christianity. We are not dealing here with some excrement-related obsession peculiar to the Church or to one or another of its influential thinkers. We are looking at the throbbing heart of Western culture, the source of its vision and its energy.

The Greco-Roman vision, which functioned to liberate the individual creativity of the privileged, reciprocated with the belief that human beings were *immortal spirit* and did not "belong" to this *material* earth with its lustful, death-laden bodies. Death was an illusion as were the bodies that bore it. And the West's triumphant vitality came from the channeling of the energies harvested from those conquered bodies for the transcendent purposes of society. The citizen (read: man of means) lived for the glory of the *polis* and thus achieved a living memory, a political immortality.[79] The civilizations built by these forces attest to their effectiveness.

There was a licentiousness that developed in the Roman upper classes where the new wealth of empire as well as Greek philosophical education had its greatest impact. As we've mentioned, this was not a characteristic feature of Roman culture, nor encouraged by its religion. Licentiousness ran counter to the austere responsibilities of traditional Roman "family values" and the authoritarian requirements of a volatile master-slave economy.

The growing decadence introduced by empire had economic and political ramifications: family responsibilities among the warrior aristocrats were being avoided to such an extent that it caused the Roman State to fear a serious depopulation of the ruling cadre. This was a threat to continued Roman control.

---

[78] Brown, *op.cit.* p.22f

[79] cf.Hannah Arendt, *The Human Condition* Garden City NY: Anchor, 1959

Caesar Augustus, at the very birth of the Empire, understood that this "un-Roman" sexual liberality engendered a "desublimation,"[80] a self-indulgence that threatened ruling class control of the slaves. "Immorality" was deeply deplored and loudly denounced by the Imperial leadership and many social commentators.[81] A society with such a forced unnatural stratification as *slavery,* ever under the threat of rebellion, required a firm hand. And indeed, during that first century of the Common Era, a massive, armed slave revolt under Spartacus, and three successive mutinies of the enslaved soldiers of the Roman Legions on the frontiers of the Empire, very nearly toppled the established order.[82]

It was for this reason that the *imperial moral codes* were enacted, initiated by Augustus himself and maintained as official public policy throughout the ensuing centuries. Those codes, conspicuously aimed at the upper-classes, punished childless aristocrats (who were purposely avoiding family responsibilities) by disinheriting their estates, exiled and in other ways castigated adulterous and other behavior deemed flagrantly immoral or corrupting, and introduced juridical measures to promote child-bearing by officially converting marriage into a *legal contract focused exclusively on the procreation of the species.* (We saw in the last chapter how this was taken over, as a "principle," by Christianity and functioned as the overriding obstacle to Post-Conciliar official Catholic reform of the prohibition against birth-control). It was in violation of the laws against immorality that Ovid, possibly the greatest Roman poet, was exiled to a remote Roman colony on the Black Sea where he died in bitter disgrace. Augustus even exiled members of the imperial family for immoral behavior.

It might be plausibly argued that Christianity was chosen by Rome to replace the discredited cult of the gods as its official Religion, precisely because it represented the return to the Spartan values and rigid disciplines, especially in the sexual area, that the Romans were convinced were the source of their original success.

---

[80] This is a term coined by Herbert Marcuse. But for the allusion see Brown, op.cit.p.6
[81] cf the Satires of Juvenal, the odes of Horace
[82] cf. Tacitus *Annals* I, 16ff, 31ff,

These were the values they saw being emasculated by the decadence of the times. The campaigns of literally centuries of Caesars to restore public morality, when periodically re-invigorated (like the persecutions of Christians), were applied with unusual severity.

Pseudo-sublimation

In a male-dominated society such as Rome, there was also another phenomenon that represented an analogous "purgation" of sexuality, a transcendence of a kind that had the *effect of sublimation.* I'm referring to the cultural transformation of *coitus* into an act of *selfish egoism* for men, involving the erection of a haughty distance between themselves and their "passive" sexual partners, women (or submissive men), along with a rejection of the tender mutuality, the emotional equality that sexual intercourse implies and engenders. Sex as a mutually deferential exchange of tenderness between equal partners was considered "feminine" and "decadent" in the Roman cultural complex. It would have placed the warrior male on equal footing with the female and that was not acceptable. The suppression of tenderness acted as a *surrogate mechanism* for the maintenance of the *warrior ethos*.[83] The sexual act in its misogynistic form became a symbol of male domination. It was also an aspect of the relegation of women (and "womanish" ways) to secondary status. The suppression of women was the foundational level of the exploitative social edifice of Imperial Rome as in other warrior dominated "male" societies. It required that sex be defined exclusively from the point of view of the performing male, his purpose (procreation), his person (paternal prerogatives), and his pleasure, rather than any dalliance with a "relationship" between man and woman that had the color of equality. It hardly needs to be said that this was a cultural imperative later inherited by the entire Western European family of people who shared the Roman-Christian heritage, and it is operative to this day.[84]

---

[83] Brown, *The Body ... op.cit p 17 ff*

[84] ibid., p.26ff

Though we may seem to have wandered far afield in this discussion, it's important to emphasize that the entire structure of sexual mores was either built on or made to synchronize with the two-world Platonic view of reality. The "male" gender, its qualities and characteristics were projected as supposedly obvious expressions of rational "spirit" while the feminine was defined as emotional, "carnal," material, "of the flesh." The domination of male over female, therefore, even at the less respected level of marriage, was interpreted to represent the conquest of "matter" by "spirit" and hence the liberation, development and ultimate triumph of humanity over animality — for the Greeks and ultimately for the Christians, *immortality*.[85]

Such is the role of sexual repression and manipulation in the Greco-Roman world. Philosophically, societally and ultimately religiously, through the association of the Church with this overall view of things, we developed our peculiarly western ways that alienated us from our humanity.

And at the root of it all was the Platonic fantasy of the two-worlds.

VII. A One-World Morality

The relevance of this excursus should be obvious. It provides an historical context for understanding the strange sexual antipathies of the Catholic Christian Church which became the cultural and moral guardian of the Roman Empire and therefore, in turn, its propagator. It points out the absolutely decisive role that the Platonic vision of dual reality — spirit and matter — played in the development of the traditional Western mindset and morality. And on a more general level it reminds us that *morality*, which is the fundamental expression of human responsibility and represents the injection of *purpose* into human life and society, is a

---

[85] ibid., p. 113-114

matter of culture and historical conditions, not revealed religious absolutes.

This is more iconoclastic than it may seem. For we in the West have always thought of our morality as revealed truth and/or rationally indisputable and therefore *absolute*, "objective" and universal, transcending culture and history. We believed our morality was derived directly from the mouth of God in scripture and confirmed by our *scientifically* determined place in the *Whole*.

As with all other aspects of "truth" in the ancient Christian worldview, scripture and science corroborated one another. And where necessary, they were made to agree by the "allegorical" interpretation of scripture. Notice, this inverts the claimed order of priority by subordinating scripture to moral choice and insight. But it demonstrates that there was only one "truth" in the ancient world and it was fundamentally Platonic philosophy. Scripture was believed to use stories and allegories to express the selfsame "truths" elaborated by the Platonic sciences. This was Philo's lifelong project. John Scotus Eriugena stated this explicitly as late as the 9th century. Christians in those days were quite certain of their view-of-the-world, including most especially the great *division of spirit and matter*. All the moral and spiritual conclusions drawn inexorably from this view, were believed to be the accurate reflection of the way Whole Cosmos was structured. Christian morality was equally the result of rational enquiry and the revelation of God.

Since we moderns arrived on the scene relatively late in the historical narrative, much of our morality is already locked in place, determined by what was considered both revealed and "rational" in the past. This may not be acceptable to us for any number of reasons. We see ourselves differently from our forebears. We find ourselves, unfortunately, obligated to sit in judgment on the moral codes we've inherited and if necessary readjust them to square with how we now perceive our place in the Whole. I say "unfortunately" because the potential rupture with the past in these areas is painful and destabilizing. Adjustment may not always be possible in the practical order. But since we are dealing here with the *significance of our humanity*, we will prescind from what may be practical or "realistic" and consider some of the theoretical questions that bear on morality. This may yield less than practical results. But I am more interested in finding guides for our reflections than new "commandments" to replace the old. The best service we can render ourselves in the recovery of humanity is to try to lay solid foundations — to determine our place in the Whole, our significance. Sound practice will follow in time.

The task that confronts us then, is to get a fix on the most basic behavioral readjustments that our newly perceived place in the Whole may call for. What, in other words, is different about the way we look at ourselves, and what does it mean for what we do? What are the moral implications of what we've been saying?

1. A World of Spirit vs. Matter or a World of Matter-Energy

The first difference is foundational and determinative: reality is *not* divided into two-worlds, *spirit and matter*. There is only one world and it is composed of *matter-energy*. There is no other. Whatever *is*, exists in and as structured by, *matter-energy*. All qualities, functions, relations, and phenomena of whatever origin and associated with whatever organism heretofore attributed to "spirit," are an expression of the potential of *matter-energy*. What was once considered necessarily a product of "spirit" is now understood to be a product of the interactions and re-combinations of *matter-energy*. In sum, *without denying in any way* the existence or the quality of experiences we have heretofore called "spiritual," or "transcendent," we are now saying that none of these requires a ground in another world, based on any other principle of existence than the properties and potential of *matter-energy* as it actually exists in this world where we live — revealed and defined in scope, depth and capability by those very same experiences. "Spirit," in other words, is now understood to be *a property of matter-energy*, not a separate genus of being or mode of existence residing in a different world.

I believe that's been said clearly enough. The implications for our morality that derive from this difference are decisive. Such a sea-change in our perception of our own reality in relationship to the other species around us will have an impact on virtually everything we used to consider "forbidden" or "commanded," that is, what placed us under moral obligation.

For example, since in our earlier view we believed that we humans were the only examples of "spirit" in the world, we alone were "persons," so we alone had prerogatives and "rights," like the right to life, which could not be violated. "Thou shalt not kill" (another human being), was considered *an absolute*, regardless of the many exceptions made for other "transcendent" cultural values, such as war, political control, protection of property, personal or societal vengeance, the rage of sexual betrayal, etc. This very same "spiritual nature" which granted such protections to us, simultaneously declared all other species of life to be *without rights*. All animals, even those like chimpanzees who are known to be our genetic cousins, could be killed at will, *with or without reason*. All the animals, domestic or wild, existed simply as our possessions, to be exploited or used for our purposes — food, clothing, work, sport, affection. If we permitted animals to live anywhere within the precincts under our control, it was simply because they served *our* purposes. There was nothing intrinsic to the animal itself that could demand that its individual life or its species be respected.

I think we have to admit that this state of affairs still obtains. Please do not misunderstand. At this point I am *not* opting for this or that practical change in our moral code. This essay is a theoretical reflection. I am analyzing the structure of our universally accepted moral imperatives in order to elucidate the ground on which they stand — which is a ground within us. That ground is the Platonic Paradigm: the theory that there are two kinds of realities, matter and spirit; and humans are the only example of spirit anywhere on the face of the earth.

This approach could be fruitfully applied in case after case to clarify the foundations of the moral demands of our culture. Let's take the "right to private property" as another example. In our culture, this "right" is also based on the transcendent value of the *individual person*, and similarly justified by appeal to our spiritual nature. Bundled in this right to property there are our "reproductive rights," which have traditionally entailed the right to control and discipline children, the rights of the male over the female in the household, the right to privacy. All are grounded on an alleged "spirituality" which is claimed to separate us not only functionally, but *metaphysically* from all other living things, making us *persons,* the denizens of another world.

Our controversies over the questions of abortion and euthanasia are profoundly connected with our erstwhile beliefs in the presence of a special "immortal soul" in the human being. Mediaeval debates on the morality of abortion centered specifically on *the precise moment* in the gestation process when the "spiritual" soul was "infused by God." Some claimed it was at six months as the "form" of the human being became discernible; others argued it was at the moment of conception. As the controversy remained in theoretical deadlock, the Church decided that *ad cautelam* (just in case), the opinion of "at conception" would have to be the standard in the practical order.

It is significant that at the root of the debate was the exclusive question of the presence of "spirit." If there were no "spirit" until six months, one party believed, then abortions prior to that time *would not be murder because the fetus was not a human being;* it had no "spiritual" *soul,* just a "material" soul like the animals and therefore could be killed with impunity. The only issue for them was the presence of the "immortal soul." There was never a prohibition against killing a "potential" human being any more than the future humanity of male semen, for example, requiring some absolute ban against the death of spermatozoa. Masturbation was considered "contrary to nature" and therefore a sin, but it was not murder.

The issue of euthanasia, similarly, turns on the fact that the human being has an eternal, immortal soul. The human person, therefore, is directly under the care and guidance of divine providence and another human being may not pre-empt the prerogatives of "God" in determining *when and how* that person will die. "Thou shalt not kill" came to be grounded on "God's" use of death and suffering as instruments of spiritual education, and moral conversion. Hence, the generalized western prohibition against terminating life, even in cases of tortuous, debilitating and interminably extenuated end-of-life suffering characteristic of many diseases and pathological conditions. Such deference to the divine prerogatives was not applied in the case of the death penalty, however, and one may question why.

But if there were a change in world-view ... if the qualities associated with "spirituality" were not considered exclusive to humankind but were accepted as an intrinsic element of *all* things each in its own way, then the question of respect and responsibility for life can be disentangled from this overpowering issue of the presence of an "immortal soul" in just one species of semi-divine being. Respect and responsibility can be applied appropriately and proportionately to all of life in its own way, to all the species of plants and animals, for the benefit of each and all — for the Whole.

Regarding both these issues of abortion and euthanasia, there is an increasing conviction among the general population that responsible behavior does not necessarily correspond to the cut and dried mandates of traditional morality. I see implied in this willingness to entertain other practical possibilities — even without having confronted the theoretical question of the spiritual soul — that there is a growing perception that the issues of abortion and euthanasia are not reducible to the presence of "spirit." There are other moral factors at play that are considered more important. This further implies that the existence of the two-worlds, whether it is believed or not, is not *necessarily determinative* of moral behavior in these cases. To my mind, this represents a significant shift in the priorities that control morality.

I believe that this shift is taking place because *we know* we have evolved from the very same life forms, the animals, whom we are so ready to kill, respectfully and responsibly, of course, without the slightest compunction or remorse. The unavoidable implications of evolution are, *minimally,* that the functions of our *consciousness* that had served as a proof of the presence of "spirit" in us have also evolved. This means that "consciousness," as Teilhard, Bergson and Whitehead have all tried to explain, is not an exclusively human characteristic but a *graduated phenomenon*, expressed in a proportionate manner by all the life forms on the planet, revealing *its primordial presence as potentiality* in the very "essence" of *matter-energy* itself. I am talking about an *interiority* that is an intrinsic property of the quarks and muons, gluons and neutrinos of our Universe. "Spirit," if we must insist on the use of the word, is now understood to pervade our universe. It is not a quality exclusive to humankind, and obviously not the denizen of another World. Far from setting us apart, therefore, "spirit" forms another brick in the foundation of our community with all creation. Whitehead believed that these primordial elements — the *quanta* of matter-energy — are themselves, collectively, *ipsissimus Deus,* "God himself."

Whatever they may be *in themselves,* we would all have to agree that the *quanta* of matter-energy are, *at least,* the collective building blocks of all Cosmic construction, from stars to star-fish, from black-holes to bacteria. They are reality; they are *our* reality. We are THAT. What does this do to our imaginary world built on the fantasy of an insurmountable division between matter and spirit? What does it do to our behavior, honed and refined, rewarded and punished, internalized and sublimated over millennia, that derive from and support that imaginary division? The implications are staggering.

At this point we should not allow ourselves to be daunted by the dawning awareness that moral obligation in our world might have to change in ways that are, practically speaking now, *impossible.* We are engaged in a speculative exercise here. We are trying to *understand.* How we may decide to manage our new awareness is a bridge we can postpone crossing until we come to it.

2. A Morality of Relationship

A second major determinant in the elaboration of an appropriate morality for our times is the revolutionary significance of *process* and therefore *relationship* in our metaphysical understanding of reality. A reality in flux, in this case, the Whole Universe, cannot be defined by its component parts — substances like us — because they (we) are no longer perceived as having a fixed and independent significance. Process necessarily concentrates metaphysical significance in the Whole, subordinating and thereby relativizing the individual components.

A relative reality implies a relative morality. A *relative* morality is *anathema* to many of us, accustomed as we are to moral absolutes. This creates another great anomaly. In a world in process, moral mandates can no longer be considered in fixed terms. "Commandments" and "prohibitions" modify themselves continuously as our place in the Whole is perceived differently through time. The key word is *relationship*. Our morality will be determined by our relationship to the Whole and our relationships within the Whole. That is our significance, our meaning, what we are.

Since we are bodies, we are in intimate and constitutive *relationship* with the entire Universe of material particles, and the other species of life made from them, from the very beginning of our existence. Our special cognitive functions, traditionally called "spiritual," by which we identify what we are as human, are themselves the efflorescence, the outer display of the inner potential of this very same *matter-energy*. We are related to these micro-entities as the components of our bodies, our brains, as well as the micro-power plants of the intense pulsing vitality that we experience as our very selves. Since we *are* our bodies, we *are* those elemental particles, and those particles, in one of their most developed combinations, are *us*.

What moral responsibilities does such a vision evoke? If we are an expression of the elements of all things, are we not therefore necessarily involved in the preservation and enhancement of the Whole? Anything else would seem irrational. To me, that sounds like the sufficient and necessary ground of an eco-centered morality and a corresponding mysticism. Our very being depends upon our relationship to this Cosmos of composing-decomposing elements. We must be intrinsically invested in the health and protection of the environment that produced and sustains us. It's not a charitable service we render as to another. It's a declaration that our own inner life *is identified* with the Whole. It is an expression of our gratitude for our very selves, our joy at being *exactly what we are*. ... It's our way of saying, It's good to be here!

VIII. The "Doctrine of the Soul"

These have been a series of related reflections on what it means to be a human being. They are part of re-thinking the accepted notions that we have used to define ourselves for the past two thousand years. It hardly needs restating that for me the crux of this question is The Theory of the Two Worlds, the Platonic Paradigm that imagines the existence of an unseen world of "spirit."

My rejection of that hypothesis, as I've said throughout, is in no way intended to deny the existence of the phenomena of human experience that the theory was designed to explain. To my mind I have simply reassigned all such data to a new ground: the homogeneous material energy — the scientifically observed and measured quanta of the Universe. But so there is no misunderstanding, I would like to repeat: I acknowledge the depth and intensity of this human dimension we have heretofore called "spiritual." This dimension defines us as human and sets us apart from all the other species of life that we know. We are identified by our morality, our aspirations, our mysticism — our sense of the Sacred. This is essential to the integrity of the human being and the basis of true human community.

There is no intention here to question the real value of "Justice," for example; but when we call Justice a "reality" we should be clear about where this reality actually resides. No one should think that Justice is a cosmo-ontological entity that exists somewhere out on its own. Justice is not a subsistent reality; and our thinking it does not put us in touch with another world or plane of existence. Justice is a human mental construct that does not exist outside of our minds except as the behavioral expression of our projections and aspirations. The "reality of justice" for us proves neither our "spirituality" nor its independent existence in the "Mind of God."

Simultaneously I claim that the *quanta* of matter-energy and their intrinsic dynamism are the source and explanation for everything: cosmic development, tellurian evolution, the vitality of life, the yearning for immortality, the quality of consciousness, the source of the moral impulse, and the ground of mysticism — the sense of the Sacred. In a later chapter the scope and reach of this universal attribution will become fully clear since I will further identify matter-energy as *being*.

It should be clear by now that I imagine my very own person in every sense to be whole cloth with the rest of the world of *matter-energy* in which we live. That Universe elaborated my way of being (being human), created it, sustained it, and will re-embrace all that I am in order to share it with others after I die. This world of matter-energy is as Mother and Father to me.

I come upon these realizations in a hostile context. My Christian Religion and its many local incarnations do not agree with my assessment. The vision I present here is contrary, if not contradictory, to theirs; and theirs has been the accepted wisdom in the Western world for two thousand years.

The ideas I espouse here, while a view I share with many others, represent my own personal grappling with the theoretical positions that our Religions have proposed as the ground their vision. This grappling led to the transitions in thought that you see represented here. My conclusions are first and foremost personal discoveries that I believe will allow me to have faith and to live with thanksgiving. And the exercise of trying to embrace in love and gratitude the world and ourselves *as we really perceive ourselves to be* is, I believe, the religious task.

Beliefs intend to embrace the reality of things, *such as they are*. And within that perception faith remains, as ever, a surrender — intimate, inexplicable, personal, unique. Surrender cannot be parsed. Like our primal energy itself of which it is the most immediate expression, faith-as-thanksgiving is not explained by anything beyond itself. We are instinctively drawn to surrender. *Surrender is our portion of the primordial energy of the Universe opting to rest in the acceptance of its own secure, inalienable, eternal vitality.* It is a self-acceptance that by-passes by light years, the clinging, possessiveness of self-involved Narcissus.

Narcissus fell in love with the face he saw in the pool. It was a tragic mistake. Surrender lets go of the person we see in the mirror, the face we love. Surrender embraces our humanity as *neces-*

sarily evanescent — how else can our matter-energy be shared with others as it was shared with us? — and so it accepts our humanity *as it really is.*

Keep the Sun on Your Face

I believe the Church is no longer guiding us to a sacred acceptance of our humanity as we now understand it. This is symptomatic of what I've called "the escape from humanity." The Church is not concerned to respond to our human condition, such as we perceive ourselves to be by the science of our times, but rather to project her own antiquated view of the world, brooking no exceptions, turning ancient Greek science into divine revelation.

We are human. We have to find a way to love ourselves, such as we are. Don't be fooled by the apparent simplicity of this formula. It's more difficult than it seems. Because we have been conditioned and even trained to our self-estrangement, we have to *apply ourselves* to self-acceptance.

Furthermore, we cannot *live* without this self-embrace which I have dared to call by the words, faith, thanksgiving, surrender. We cannot afford to wait for the Church to have its own conversion and decide to work with us on this. The Church is not God. The Church does not dispense relationship with God, the acceptance without which we die, as if it were its own. The Church is a *human construct*, an instrument for self-acceptance in a world of apparently random interactions. The Church should be our shelter in a Universe that seems to offer precious little reassurance that we are loved and our existence intended. It's an instrument in the service of humanity.

The tool that no longer functions is exchanged for another. The fig tree that bears no fruit is torn out and another put in its place.

This is not a vengeful statement. It's said out of dire necessity. The relationship of faith is not an esthetic preference, a refined hedonism, a romantic predilection. Faith is not optional. It is intrinsic to our human way of being — being conscious of death. Without faith we die as human beings, swallowed up in the randomness of an evolutionary process whose goals are too long-range for us to see and too transcendent to understand. Alienation is our relentless, ever-present enemy. We need a reliable tool that works for us, first time, every time. The task of embracing our humanity — *thanksgiving* — is always upon us.

Thanksgiving

Is this focus on *thanksgiving* another a *priori* I have inherited from the Church? I have no trouble acknowledging my debt. Her doctrines and disciplines, in the context of the "science," the world-view of the times in which many of us were raised, turned our faces toward the sun. It's not something you forget. The memory of the warmth of the sun on my face even in my groping and blindness has served as a primary irreducible datum for me. I *know* what direction to look in. I am still oriented in the same direction, and if I am to continue that way I need to embrace the humanity that my times now have illuminated for me. If the Church won't help me with that, then I'm forced to find a way to do it without the Church. Thanksgiving is not optional, because our pulsing vitality, *life* is not optional, nor is death.

Thanksgiving is our most fundamental relationship. It defines *religio,* the binding of our persons to the Source of our being in recognition and love. It corresponds to a profound self-acceptance. If traditional Christianity in fact encourages us to express gratitude to "God" for *what we know we are not,* our relationship-in-faith and gratitude becomes a myth of make-believe. Gratitude's potential implications — the joy of life, a sense of abiding peace, a loving spirit, — evaporate. Without thanksgiving Religion degrades into a forensic formality, a public mouthing of words, a statement of intent, rather than a penetrating absorption by the sheer ecstasy of the gift of being and life. True gratitude expresses our self-appropriation of the life we have, *as it is*. It allows us to say without reserve, *"It is good to be here."* It is ultimate existential security, the casting out of fear, the joy that gives reign to great-hearted generosity, the fruit of surrender, the abandonment of our "selves" in the embrace of our Source and Sustainer, our Fashioner and Friend. These are not "definitions," they are *metaphors* for the unknown darkness from which we come, to which we shall return, in which we remain always immersed — like a sponge in the sea — a darkness we can *trust*.

Unbelievable "Beliefs"

I cannot live with what the Catholic Church says I am. This is not an attack on faith. It doesn't have to do with theory but with what I consider *basic fact*: I am *not* an example of Plato's Charioteer, a disembodied spirit that runs my body like a motorboat.

I also do not believe I am the contagious carrier of Original Sin, the disinherited child of an angry Father-God who requires the sacrificial death of his first-born Son to assuage his wounded dignity. This was never part of traditional Judaism which produced the Genesis story, nor the message of Jesus, nor the teaching of the very early Church.

I do not believe there was a fall from natural (or supernatural) immortality; I believe that was a prejudice of the ancient Greeks who chose to be offended by death. Intolerable as it appears, I believe death is as *natural* for us as it is for all the other living things with which we share life on this planet. Also, I cannot accept that my bodily functions, such as they are, are a corruption that results from Original Sin. The physical similarities that I share with the higher animals demonstrate that these functions are *natural*. I do not believe I need "salvation" from this imagined "corruption and death." Nor do I believe in the sex-obsessed Platonic morality and spirituality officially promoted by the Church.

I do not believe that either Catholicism or Christianity is the "definitive plan" of God. I believe the beliefs, rituals and practices of *all people everywhere* are equally efficacious in drawing those of their cultural milieu into grateful relationship with the Source of our being. The goal is faith, *thanksgiving,* surrender to the Sacred, not Religion.

There's still more: I believe that Jesus was a human being who embodied relationship to the Sacred with such fidelity that I feel drawn to follow his example and advice. I sense that his "take" was so accurate that I am inclined not to argue with those who wish to call him "divine." To require, however, that Jesus be acknowledged as "God" in the philosophical terms of the ancient

Greco-Roman world, is a moral and intellectual travesty. Notwithstanding the claims to infallibility from those who insist he was "God," Jesus himself denied it.[86] I think I'll side with him on this.

I once lived in the world the Church said existed; but no longer. If you are honestly among those who inhabit Plato's world, more power to you; the Church will keep your face to the sun. But if you live in the same world I do, Catholic Christian doctrine will have to change radically if it is to provide the possibility of *faith* for us.

---

[86] Mk 10:18; Lk 18:19

CHAPTER III
Rethinking the Doctrine of God

INTRODUCTION

Reintegration, the recovery of faith, may not always be a slow process. In my case it was. There were no clean breaks for me and I'm inclined to say that's what qualified my particular journey. I separated from the Church and its ideological world-view over a long period of time — twenty-five years, maybe thirty. And it was only as I discovered new and what seemed to me better responses to the questions traditional religion claimed to answer that I could fully let go of the old ones. It's easy to spend time talking about the things that contributed to the disintegration. I would like to also tell the story of what was replacing them.

First, I want to say up front that I think the religious quest is natural; therefore virtually unavoidable. And I believe the source of it is to be found in the very elemental particles of which *all* things are made. This is clearly a preemptive position. You may ask, with some justification, doesn't a statement like that already stack the deck?

I concede the point. Yes, I begin with a conclusion. I won't even defend myself by saying it's what everybody does. I'll only offer this: my conclusion comes from my experience. I don't mean visions and revelations, though I can understand why people with similar experiences might feel driven to use those terms. This experience that I have had in this body of mine and in this wide world that cradles me, is as much a part of nature as the life-giving air I breathe and the miraculous light by which I see clouds and mountains and the faces of the people I love. I don't feel a need to imagine invisible sacred entities that speak to me from another world because I believe the visible world that I see and touch is Sacred.

But of course, I go further. Every world-view — everybody, every culture, every age — is capable of sustaining a relationship to the Sacred. This follows directly from my premises. I'm conscious of preparing to explore a tautology here. For, by the definition I'm giving to the term, if you empty the concept of "the Sacred" of all its "objective" theological content and historical context, if you erase and maintain under erasure all the religious imagery associated with that word, what I'm calling the "Relationship to the Sacred" *is* the very initiative that is responsible for all existence. Whatever else it may be, it's also unavoidably cosmological. The Source of the Sacred in itself might be eternally beyond our ken. But our *relationship* to it is our very existence; therefore it is real, current and necessarily palpable. And so too it is as near to any one of us as to another; it is absolutely universal. This relationship precedes any perception of it on our part. It is the ground of possibility of our being here at all. *This relationship for us, in other words, is our very presence in the world.* If we're here, it's here. And it is Sacred for us, if for no other reason. What more reason do we need to call it Sacred: *it is good to be here.*

Even without having the details of *exactly how*, we know this relationship makes possible everything we are, everything we see and everything we do. This is not something we decide, nor is it something we can define as we might prefer. We wake up to it, as it were, as an accomplished fact — an entire Universe of things, that, like us, *are here.* We cannot look at it from outside. All we can do is explore our common "*being here*" as it is. For the way it is, is what we are. All this is bundled in my experience of being Sacred in this Sacred Place.

Furthermore, I am convinced this experience of the Sacred is essentially the same as that of the Buddha, of Mohammed, of Moses, of Jesus. These people, among many others less well known, were instrumental in the creation of great religions. In the estimation of many, they were radically different from the rest of us. Some were even thought divine. They were considered at least to be in possession of very special powers and privileged with very special experiences.

I don't believe that. I think they were all just like me — smarter, better for sure — but otherwise, just like me. They were human beings. I don't believe any of them had special powers, except in a human sense perhaps — a power of persuasion stemming from self-confidence, clarity of vision, capacity for trust, compassion, love. And I say my experience is just like theirs. I know, because it corresponds to what they said about themselves. I suspect that I'm not the only one who has noticed this.

So, even before I start, I've already got myself outside the mainstream of traditional belief on a number of counts:

- I do not believe there are entities and beings, like spirits, different from us that exist in another world different from ours. We explored this in Chapter II. There is only one world.

- I believe that what we call the religious instinct is really an extension and development of the inner reality of all of us, the "*being here*" that characterizes our universe of things and of which we humans are an integral part. It is the source of our sense of the Sacred. It is *matter-energy*. It is an intrinsic property of the infinitesimally small component elements of the Whole to which we belong, and hence of everything that they compose of whatever size and complexity, including us.

- And I do not believe that the people who founded the great religions were very different nor experienced anything very different from what I and other ordinary people have experienced.

You may not agree. Let me try to convince you.

Part I
The Doctrine of God

I. Divine Providence

Where to begin. I think we should start "where the rubber meets the road," where religion touches everyone most intimately: the question of *divine providence*. It's the place where most people are likely to bump into "God." It's also the place where most of the doctrines characteristic of traditional religion are operative directly or indirectly. It's where the human being is most likely to be concerned and invested — therefore interested.

> [Note: *I write "God" in quotes throughout this chapter to emphasize that the word refers to a human concept — a construct — rather than to a known entity. This is not intended to deny the Reality in question, only to emphasize that it is, as all the great traditions assert, <u>categorically unknowable</u>. This also implies that our concepts are to be taken as "metaphor." They symbolize, evoke, and temporarily represent our current projection of what the Reality might be "in itself." As such they are most accurate as relational descriptors, not as scientific definitions.*]

I will recount two quick stories from my time as a priest, each representative of many that were similar. They both have to do with the question of divine providence, and they illustrate a dilemma that Christian ideology is unable to avoid. They will also serve to introduce the question of the doctrine of "God," which is at the heart of the religious project.

In the first, a man came to me who had cheated on his wife. He was a very committed Catholic Christian and a devoted husband and father. Let's call him Fidel, for he was basically a faithful man. He was mortified that he could ever have done such a thing and was truly sorry. But he was also disturbed at a deeper level that was more difficult to deal with. *He could not understand how "God" could have permitted him to have done what he did.* He had what he felt was a personal relationship with "God" and the lapse left him feeling betrayed.

Of course, it was clear that his complaint was an excuse for his behavior. But aside from the obvious deflection, there were a number of features to his dilemma that stemmed from Catholic doctrine (to which in this case most Christian denominations conform). He was extraordinary in that he had dedicated himself to living a morally impeccable life and to relating to "God" daily in prayer. Part of his commitment to the Church was that it offered *a guarantee*, not for miracles and "blessings," he was well beyond that, but simply to live a good and holy life. You could not fault his motivation in the least. He was a simple man, and completely imbued with the teaching he had received. He knew that "God" watched over every act and every event that occurred anywhere in the world. That was no problem, for "God" was all-knowing, and omnipotent. He also had been taught that temptation was often permitted as a trial from *"God" who would "never allow him to be tempted beyond his capacity to resist."*

Well, here was the material for an endless dialog with himself and with "God." From his perspective he had obviously been tempted beyond his capacity to resist; for he could not be accused of *wanting* to do what he did. (Note the echoes of Paul's lament in Romans.) According to Fidel, the one who failed to honor the contract was "God." But how could that be? "God" is good. So either "God" did not see what was happening, or, ... the unthinkable — "God" could not or would not do anything about it. Wasn't the very work of "God" in the world to make us holy?

At a second level, he had been taught that Catholic ritual, the sacraments, provided assistance *ex opere operato,* automatically, and with infallible efficacy. His active involvement in the Church had to do precisely with this extra guarantee that he would be the recipient of a special "grace" to lead the life he wanted. So he was faced with a dilemma about the Church. If, as I was telling him, miracles were not likely — the guarantees he thought he had been offered did not function in the practical order — then really, from his point of view, there was no difference between the Christian and any other man in similar circumstances.

Fidel felt betrayed by "God." What had been an intense and intimate relationship with "God" seemed to hang in the balance as we parted. I'm not sure that our conversation that evening was enough to stem his disillusionment.

A Sadder Story

A second story is more painful. I was asked to go to a wake for a teenager, who had drowned. It was summertime. He had been at the beach with friends and one of them got caught in the undertow, was dragged out beyond the breakers and could not make it back to shore. The teen-ager went back in after him and in an attempt at rescue, drowned. Ironically, his friend made it back safely.

A sad story. At the funeral parlor after the prayers, I went over to spend a few minutes with his mother. As we chatted, I noticed she had a little girl with her who was acting in ways that seemed more infantile than you would expect from someone her size. I asked her about it. The little girl, she told me, was her daughter and was retarded. She explained that she was a widow with four children. Her husband died while she was pregnant with this daughter. While the child was still an infant, there had been some glitch and the welfare check didn't come, an occurrence that was not all that infrequent. It was winter. The landlord's many renters were all welfare recipients. When faced with yet another non-payment of rent, he turned off the heat as way of getting the tenants to put pressure on Public Assistance to send the money. Her daughter got sick. She ran a high fever for so long that she sustained permanent brain damage.

As I returned home afterward I was thunderstruck by the overwhelming suffering that this poor woman had to sustain. It became my problem far beyond the social activism that I was involved in at the time. One could rail against the system and blame the selfish slumlords. One could demand that the welfare mechanisms currently in place be honored. But in this case, as a matter of fact, the retardation of the little girl was caused by a series of relatively minor offenses, all of which may have occurred even in a "more just" social order. The welfare case worker had screwed up, probably unintentionally, and a case overload turned into a check that didn't arrive. The landlord did what landlords are tempted to do — turn off the heat, a harsh and punitive response to be sure, but hardly life-threatening — in order to force the resolution of a legitimate grievance. And the poor mom, not expecting a fever could be so damaging, responded too late to a very dangerous situation. This time I was the one with the "problem": where was "God" in all this human frailty?

We all recognize this experience as representative of a myriad of similar cases where people have gone through protracted and accumulated sufferings — excessive and unfair by anyone's standards. Yet, based on the doctrine of "Divine Providence" we blithely ascribe to "God" the capacity to inflict tortures that would make a hangman wince. The horrors visited on people from long-term debilitating illnesses, paralysis, dementia, natural disaster, personal brutality, social rejection, economic exploitation, political oppression, old age or even sheer stupidity which, in theory, "God" *could have* prevented or at least mollified, scandalize us all.

It was this idea of "providence" that drove Augustine of Hippo to generate a theory of a "Divine Wrath for Original Sin" that condemned even newborn infants to hell. For, Augustine concluded, "... the appalling sufferings of the human race could only be permitted because [God] is angry."[87]

I did not and do not believe in such a "God." Hence, for me, the doctrines of providence that insist that everything that happens has been foreseen and permitted and therefore positively intended by "God," in my opinion, are slander and blasphemy. These theories effectively render "God" an accomplice in the perpetration of unimaginable cruelties. My question was and still is, how can any of us possibly believe that a good "God" could ever permit much less "will" such atrocities?

Of course I knew the stock answers; I had learned them in the seminary. They were never very satisfying even then. But seeing the effects in the flesh, made the ecclesiastical explanations virtually meaningless.

---

[87] Peter Brown, *Augustine of Hippo,* U.of CA Press, Berkeley, 1967, new ed. 1999. p. 397-98, with fn to *De Civ.Dei,* XXI, 24,78, "for mortals, this life is the Wrath of God."

There comes to mind the classic dilemma. *If "God" is good, then "He" is not "God,"* because "He" is powerless against negative events; and *if "God" is "God"* and is all powerful, as they claim, *then "God" is not good* because "He" permits awful things to happen to people.

Providence?

These objections are ancient and have been traditionally answered by recourse to the omniscience of God. "God" knows all things, and that includes everything in the future. If terrible things happen, they were foreseen by "God" and permitted for a reason. In this scenario, whatever happens is a priori called providential. In another view, more reminiscent of the 18th century Deists, "God" could change events, but "God" respects what "God" has created and therefore does not intervene. Omniscience does not obviate our freedom nor the processes of the natural world. This doesn't really answer the dilemma, it escapes from it. For by saying that "God" knows but does not ever act, it implies that, in fact, there is no "providence" as we had been led to believe.

There are aspects to this dilemma that have an impact on human morality. Let's say you accept the Christian argument that "God" could intervene but has reasons for permitting horrors of this type, presumably for some "greater good" foreseen by "God." Is this then a model of morality provided for us by the "God" in whose "image and likeness" we have been made, whose "perfections" we have been invited to imitate? If we are willing to accept a "God" who permits "evil" while having the power to avoid it, does that introduce *in principle* the possibility of such behavior by us? Why should we work to prevent the occurrence of events that "God" does nothing to avert?

Similarly, imagining a more complicated version of this same problem: if I myself, through *culpable negligence, fail* to prevent a foreseeable evil, let's say a life-damaging event, can I expect a provident "God" to circumvent my failure? But if subsequently "God" does nothing to stop the damage from happening, doesn't it imply that that event had been foreseen by "God" to have a place in some future benefit? Why else would "God" *not* override my negligence? If that's true, does that mitigate for me *my guilt* in not averting it? And if I had averted it, would that have thwarted "God's" plan? Would "God" have found a way around my saving intervention? Why am I called negligent and guilty for not preventing foreseeable damage from taking place, and "God" is exonerated for the very same inaction? Is "God" an accomplice in my negligence? Why are we obliged and "God" is not?

Don't scoff at these questions. They only seem ridiculous to those who don't believe "God" ever acts amid human events. They have obviously occurred to other believers in the past and have been answered in various ways — not always in accord with what we now consider morally upright. Here's an example. If "Christian" missionaries foresee a greater good, like people's "conversion to the true faith," can they, like "God," be allowed to permit great horrors — conquest, genocide, murder, torture, the social disintegration and subjugation of vast numbers of primitive people "for their own good"? What about the murder, impoverishment and starvation of "evil" people, or those in "gross error," like heretics, Jews, Muslims, *sinners*, perpetrated by ecclesiastical authority? Does any of this sound familiar? Is it possible that some of the more obscene episodes of violent repression carried out under the auspices of official Christian institutions are somehow in collusion with an inadequate vision of divine providence and the "God" that it fantasizes? We were always warned that "error is dangerous;" does the obvious damage done in these cases allow us to argue retroactively that, perhaps, it stemmed from *an error* in our concept of "God"? If the grounds for the ancient Christian apologists' argumentation against the capricious gods of Greek mythology are valid, then might they not hold true here as well: a "God" whose morality is inferior to the subjects "God" rules, no less than a morally loose Zeus or a flighty Aphrodite, is legitimately called a myth and a farce. "God" must be at least as good as I am.

So, questions about divine providence lead to other questions about morality. But what is most vulnerable in this situation is our "idea of God." Providence presumes divine omnipotence and omniscience. How could "God" be "God" without them? These are the operative factors in "God's" purposeful intervention in human affairs. "God's" existence is irrelevant if it can't reach us, touch us, affect us. Without these characteristics, it seems, "God" is no longer connected to human life as we have believed and come to rely on. We realize why Augustine had to arrive at the conclusions he did. Without providence, traditional religion disappears.

We are reminded that Augustine also elaborated the infamous doctrine of *Divine Predestination,* presaged in Paul's letter to the Romans. Since Augustine was determined to preserve "God's" omnipotence and omniscience at all costs, he *had* to say that God "predestined" some to do good and some to do evil. Paul had called Pharaoh a "vessel of God's wrath" — the analogy being that "God" is like the potter who makes out of clay whatever he wants.[88] Predestination displays the grotesque consistency of Augustine's theology. Once you grant the premises — the very same premises that underpin the doctrine of providence — the conclusions necessarily follow. "God" wills some to be evil and some to be good. And contrariwise, from our point of view, if we decide the conclusions are absurd on their face, it implies a re-examination of the premises from which they were drawn.

Our admittedly brief discussion suggests that there is no "providence" as we have been led to believe. For either "God" *knows and can act* but (inexplicably) does not, which eliminates God's benevolent connection to us, or "God" *cannot* act, which means "God" is not a cosmological force at all. In other words, as traditionally understood, "God" is not "God." In either case, if there is no "providence" as we have believed, "God" ceases to relate to humankind's daily concerns, and at best functions to reward or punish us in the afterlife.

It's claimed that Providence *always* transcends our ability to discern. That maneuver obviously cannot be challenged. But it's a solution only for the logician. In the practical order, it solves nothing; for we're left impaled on our dilemma. Given the unspeakable horrors that occur regularly under this "*providence,*" you are again forced either to impugn the goodness of "God" for not devising a

---

[88] *Romans* 9: 14ff.

more humane route to whatever end was "willed," or to say that "God" doesn't have the power. To claim there is a providence but that we cannot understand it, therefore, borders on being an empty declaration — a saving of the words alone. It amounts to a denial of Providence. Practically speaking, in the traditional world-view and imagery about "God," to deny providence is to deny our relationship to "God."

The traditional belief in Providence has led to a concept of predestination that continues to function today to demonize the poor and to justify and even canonize wealth and power. This effect, generally associated with Calvinism, is not confined to that tradition. It is in fact pervasively found throughout Christianity, especially fundamentalist versions.

For Calvin, earthly success presaged salvation, for "God" was believed to "bless" those whom he predestined. We often speak of the well-off as being "blessed" by "God." And correlatively the poor, the unfortunate, the infirm, the mentally ill, are considered in this view, somehow *punished* by "God," or at best *not* blessed, and therefore of little account. This obviously supports the arrogance of the well-off, but it also encourages judgmentalism and blaming the victims for their plight. Thus is *natural human compassion thwarted by a Christian ideology* built on the traditional belief in providence, and the "God" that providence presupposes.

Fundamentalist Christians routinely ascribe natural disasters to "God's" punishment, even daring to know what exact "sin" angered "God." The Great Plague of 1348 was routinely attributed to "God's wrath," and in many cases that was identified with the continued presence of the Jews in Christendom, leading to pogroms throughout Europe at that time. How exquisitely "christian."

"God bless America" means to the popular mind, that America should thrive and be prosperous, prevail over it's enemies. In a most revealing example of how this attitude can impact geopolitics, in the winter of 2003, the Vice President of the US, Dick Cheney, sent out a Christmas card that said "If no sparrow falls without his knowledge, can an empire rise without his consent?" From this perspective, whatever happens, must be "God's will" because everything that happens, happens with "His" permission.

The Problem of Evil, or the problem of "random"?

In contrast, there is another view. Natural events, however destructive, are random — not evil — random. They are simply following natural laws. Aristotle uses the example that when a gale wind blows, the same wind harmlessly knocks leaves off trees, but also can knock over small boats and drown the people in them. Neither effect, each the result of the same impersonal natural forces, is in itself more "evil" than the other. Good and evil are relative terms that reflect what *we* would prefer the world to be.[89]

But it seems clear in this case that to suggest that "God's" providence should be functioning to prevent the boat from having the same fate as the leaves, means that we expect "God" constantly to be performing little miracles — suspensions of the laws of nature — to accommodate us. And by the same token, we seem to be quite willing to accuse "God" of "punishing" those who drowned, for instance, because "God" did not stop the wind from blowing or the vessel from setting sail. It seems clearly *unreasonable* even in the most traditional terms to demand that "God," after having created the universe with all its forms and forces, would then accede to micromanaging each event personally and miraculously just because there were human beings involved.

If we were to state this as a principle and combine it with the observed fact that *in our experience "God" does not prevent bad things from happening whether their cause is the force of the natural world or human judgment and choice*, we realize that our expectations for that kind of providence are pure fantasy. *A "providence" that is not simply reducible to the original foundational design of the universe, does not function in any way that is discernible by us.* A providence that is not discernible is hardly "providence," as far as we are concerned. And to say that the original foundations of the material world are the only "providence" there is, is similarly to deny providence in everything but the word. This was Thomas Aquinas' exit strategy. But no one

---

[89] Cited by Moses Maimonides, *The Guide for the Perplexed*, (1175), Dover, NY reprinted 1956 (orig. translation 1904). p. 268f.

really accepted it; and the "anthropomorphisms" he warned against remained in pastoral practice the order of the day. But this problem will not disappear with the wave of a sophist's wand. What's on the block is our traditional relationship with "God."

That is why, in order to remain convinced of the existence of that relationship, believers have been deeply invested and eternally occupied with the attempt to *identify* the action of providence in their lives even to the most minute details. Presumptuous claims to know accurately "God's" providential purpose behind apparent horrors, even though they have resulted in opinions that were outrageous in the extreme, were motivated by this need to uphold the traditional notion of "God." Take the reactions to the disaster of Hurricane Katrina in 2005. They were, many of them, morally judgmental in the extreme.

In the *City of God* Augustine "justified" the rape of Christian women by Alaric's "Christian" Goths during the sack of Rome in 410 by saying "God" was *punishing* those Roman women for taking undue pride in their virginity.[90] (It would follow, then, that "God" had also *predestined* Alaric's soldiers to commit rape.) We are appalled at such outrageous impertinence on Augustine's part. But it's important to realize that it was driven by Augustine's desperate need: to maintain the traditional idea of "God." We must understand that without such interpretation, the "idea of God" created by our culture, evaporates. It is no surprise, then, that we cling to the naïve doctrine of providence in spite of its anomalies.

These are some initial reflections that suggest that our traditional "doctrine of God" (and the relationship it entails) is at the root of the difficulties we're finding with the question of providence. It means we need to do more than just review what we thought providence was. Our very understanding of who and what "God" is, needs an overhaul.

---

[90] St Augustine, *The City of God,,* Bk I, ch 28

II. The Traditional Doctrine of God

The traditional "doctrine of God" is called into question by our enquiry into divine providence. The classic Christian idea of "God" was inherited from Greek and Hebrew notions which were syncretized during the first centuries of Christian history. There are, to my mind, three major characteristics that define the image of "God" we have received from our forebears, and they all impact the question of providence. The tradition that we have received says that "God" is a *Spirit,* "God" is a *Person,* and "God" is *powerful.*

- "God" *is Spirit*; that is, invisible, immaterial, has no body and is not limited by the parameters of physical location, size, duration in time, change, etc. "God's" "spirituality" partly explains "God's" omnipresence and omniscience. This is projected on the ancient assumption that there is another *kind of being* and another world altogether, a world of "spirit." If that world is not another physical place then it is at least a plane of communication and experience completely separate from matter where "spirit" alone can function.

- "God" *is a Person.* This is fundamental to the issue of providence. We call God a "person" because we are loathe to say "God" is less than we are, like a stone, or a tree or an animal. Our experience of "person," however, is entirely limited to human beings and includes the notion of "individual substance" or entity that modulates in time through successive cognitive and volitional states. "Persons" also respond to other persons' intentions, as manifest in communications or deeds.

- And "God" *is powerful* in the cosmological sense. "God," in other words, is not limited by being "spirit" but *can and does act in the material Universe,* intervene in human affairs, create, destroy, suspend natural laws, reward and punish. We may include *omniscience* in this category of power. This attribute, like that of "person," also assumes that there is a clear and unmistakable *separation* of the entities of "God" and the world.

There are many other features to our concept of "God" in the West. But I believe these three characterize the imagery that dominates our thinking, our prayer-life, our morality, our relationships with others — and our sense of Providence.

Power, Person and Spirit

First, a few general remarks. We realize that some of this imagery is clearly *anthropomorphic*. Anthropomorphisms imagine "God" under categories that come from our human experience. They are metaphors. Frankly, if we realize that we're using them, there should be no problem. Given our limitations, it's the way we have to function. But it requires a substantial correction. Especially in traditional circumstances, where faith is more lively, the danger that a vivid anthropomorphism will not be taken as a metaphor but *literally*, is more likely. This was certainly true of the European Middle Ages, and is characteristic of all fundamentalism today.

The mediaeval theologians were quite aware of this and, in fact, did try to correct anthropomorphism. What "God" was like, they taught, could *not* be said simply and directly in any sense. They said very clearly, very often and with great emphasis: *the only thing that can be said about "God" is what "God" is not*. This way of negation worked together with the method of "supereminence."[91] This procedure, however, insured that while certain categories, *technically* speaking, could be applied to "God," the contents of the concepts were virtually *empty* of all human significance. The images that may have remained after this conceptual evacuation, in my opinion, could only be taken as a *symbol*, more or less arbitrary, that stands for something without really providing any factual information about it. "Wisdom," for example, or "intelligence," once you negate the human dimension carried by those words, you have nothing left that strictly speaking characterizes "God." It is an empty exercise.

This is true of "person" and "powerful," as applied "God." The terms were uncorrected anthropomorphisms that came from tradi-

---

[91] SCG Bk I, ch 30, [2],[4]

tional Greek and Hebrew imagery. I believe it is improper to imagine "God" using these traditional terms. Some try to get by with calling them "metaphors." Metaphors supposedly say nothing factual; but they still evoke the ancient images and tend to re-create the ancient relationships. Calling them "metaphor" will erase their scientific claims, but it may not suppress their human impact.

This is an important question. We have to be careful about the "God" we imagine, because we tend to *become like* the "God" we imagine.

Let's look at these three characteristics in more detail.

1. God as Spirit

Calling "God" "spirit," does not give rise to the same obvious anomalies we encountered in the last chapter in the case of the human soul, which has also traditionally been called "spirit." Human beings have bodies. Proponents of the theory of human "spirituality" are forced to step outside of the experience of bodies, deny the evidence of their senses, insist on the suspension of the laws of nature, and reject the obvious similarity between the human organism and the organisms of other animal life, in order to make their assertions about the human spirit.

The case of "God," however, is different. We don't see "God." There is no way to examine the claims of divine spirituality. And while there have been experiences recorded in the sacred writings of all peoples adduced as proof of "God's spirituality," they are universally ambiguous. Every one of them, whether visions or voices, could as easily be explained as the mental-emotional resonance of insights or events that occurred to their recipients. This is not to deny that the experiences were truthful or even of "divine" origin. Those are separate questions. All we are saying here is that they are *not* proof that "God" is *spirit*.

So we can't answer the question, "Is God Spirit?" But the more fundamental question is: Are there spirits at all? Is there a category of being called "spirit"? Is there a world other than this one? We tried to deal with this in Chapter II. I think it's an indication of how deeply embedded this assumption is in our culture that the assertion that "God" is Spirit is rarely challenged. To suggest that "God" may have a body, or at least a material dimension, that "God" resides in this same world as we, or that "God" might change and develop, is considered irrational and ludicrous. There is an anomaly here as well. For, in the popular imagery about providence, "God" is anthropomorphically pictured as interacting within the material universe, while the official theology claims that any such response would represent a change in God, which is impossible. Gregory of Nyssa, a sixth century Greek Christian philosopher-theologian and mystic, noted the dilemma in his treatise on "Man," and, typically, took circular recourse in the "power" of "God" to resolve it.[92]

Besides, we rarely focus on the *irrelevance* of "God's" spirituality. Consider: whether or not "God" is spirit does not matter for faith, because faith is relationship. Faith does not have to do first and foremost with *what* "God" is, only *that* "God" is and *how* we are related. So from that point of view, the statement that "God" is spirit is both gratuitous and unnecessary. I recognize that this disproves nothing.

But it doesn't mean we can ignore it. The real importance of the question of the existence of "spirit" historically derives not from an inquiry into the nature of "God" but from the implications of the existence of spirit for humans. In other words, it's a deflection. I believe the heart of the matter is that we humans are deeply invested in imagining *ourselves* as spirit and different from the rest of the Universe for we are convinced that it is only as spirit that we are *immortal*, and escape the fate of matter, which is death. Therefore we feel bound to say that "God" is spirit. We cling to the image of the two worlds: the one we live in where everything perishes — ourselves only apparently — and the other, where we have imagined "God" lives, nothing perishes and, since we are spirit, where we will live forever.

So I believe the attribution of "spirit" to "God" is essentially a *reflection of our own denial of death* and our desire to transcend it. Our traditional beliefs in this regard have less to do with what "God" may really be like and what we need to know to relate to

---

[92] Gregory of Nyssa, *Treatise on Man*, XXIII, 3 and 4.,

"God," than as support for our cherished fantasies about our own immortality.

Is Plato's vision of a Reality divided into two worlds, one of spirit and the other of matter, a fact? And if not, and I believe not, then who are we, and what is "God" really like?

2. God as Person

Our claim that "God" is a person is where our anthropomorphism rules supreme. It's because the traditional (scholastic) definition of "person" as applied to "God" is completely abstract and empty, that the *human meaning* of the word "person," in fact, if not in intention, determines the content of traditional belief. The problem is that no matter how smart or powerful, "God" is *not* another human being; and to have our image of "God" dominated by the idea of *human personality* is seriously to distort any relationship built on it. How can we relate to "God" correctly if we approach the relationship with a twisted sense of "God's" character?

The extent of this distortion is in evidence with the question of Providence. I believe the "providence paradox" has been a perennial stumbling block in the West precisely because our idea of "God" is dominated by human imagery. For it is incomprehensible to us that another human "person," with both the power and the knowledge that we attribute to "God," would refuse to intervene on our behalf, or ever permit the horrors that occur daily under the aegis of "Providence." My friend Fidel was fatally scandalized by a "God" whom he believed was a "person" in anthropomorphic terms. If the beliefs he was taught had not been *so dominated by fantasy* in this regard, he may have been disposed to face his own failure more honestly and maintain his relationship with the "God" he loved.

The Western theological doctrine of "God" cannot get beyond anthropomorphism largely because "person" is impervious to transcendentalization. In other words, as we said earlier, "person" is only really applicable to human beings, not to "God." Thomas Aquinas says the component elements of "personality," in "God" are *intellect and will*, characteristics obviously derived from our experience of humanity. To attribute intellect and will to "God" properly, according to the practitioners of our traditional theology, is a highly rarefied extrapolation that pretends to go beyond what we know of our species. To counteract anthropomorphism, as we've said, they insisted that we apply the corrective of "transcendence" or "super-eminence." That means we must say (and think) that these attributes *go beyond anything we can imagine*. But this is clearly a technical exercise that only allows for the use of the word. What the theologians didn't tell us is that this requirement in effect neutralizes whatever real "information" about "God" we thought we had gained from the use of the term "person." If we do as they say we should, the word becomes meaningless.

In tandem with this, another major theological factor influences the discussion. In scholastic theory. We are supposed to realize that all the divine attributes *are* the divine essence itself. There are no distinctions of any kind in "God." In other words "God" is such an unalloyed simple unity that what we call "God's" intellect, IS "God's" will, IS "God's" essence. Therefore, since there are no conceptual distinctions admissible among the "attributes" of God, it is useless to use the terms, intellect and will; *there is no difference between them; nor are they any different from "God's" other "attributes" or his "essence." So they are absolutely empty of meaning.* The only thing accomplished by the scholastic insistence that it is appropriate to use the word "person" of "God," is to insure that the vacuum left by its conceptual evisceration will be filled by grossly misleading anthropomorphic imagery applied literally. This absolutely defeats the purpose of the exercise. The conclusion is inevitable: We cannot think about person except in human terms. Fidel's disillusionment was a set up.

"God," is *not* another human being. Since, even in scholastic terms, we have *absolutely no idea* what it means for "God" to be a person, using the word "person" can only create catastrophically false expectations. A relationship built on an error of such magnitude is bound to be monumentally skewed. I am convinced this has been a major element in western alienation and the impoverishment of religion. We had an infantile idea of "God," and when we grew up and looked at the world around us, we stopped believing in it.

The entire projected Christian relationship to "God" is based on the belief in "God" as a person, which I contend is unavoidably and falsely *human*. All the difficulties that we encountered in those examples where we expected some evidence of the operations of divine providence are directly related to thinking that "God" is someone who responds with a recognition of the occurrences that befall us in time. We think that this recognition will result in a compassionate reaction, a discernible solidarity of some kind "as from one person to another."

The word "person" implies *all that* when applied to "God." Why else would we pray? And why else do the contradictions of the doctrine of providence perplex us and leave us feeling betrayed or punished? But, given the required scholastic corrections, there is no way the word "person" can be permitted to mean anything sequential or active or interactive when applied to "God." In reality, once corrected, it is supposed to say *nothing*. Whatever data we think it gives us is in fact supplied solely by our imagination.

The scholastics tell us when it comes to "God" we know nothing. If we were to follow the explicit advice of Thomas, it would be more accurate to say that "God" is NOT a person than that "He" is. In fact, because of the probable inaccuracy of *any* term, we are better off saying nothing at all.[93]

A "God" of Righteousness

---

[93] There is one sense of the word "person," however, that might be used validly of "God. It corresponds to the fact that according to traditional theology, "God" is not metaphysically opposed to us in any way. If "God's" being is our being, then *our personalities* which are the very expression of our being, our gathered interiority, are also a manifestation of the very being which is "God's." In this sense of "person" God is not known conceptually as "a person," which was the fallacy that entailed the inevitable anthropomorphisms we've been criticizing, but rather *subjectively experienced* as this particular named being, i.e., *oneself*. We each experience and intuit our own persons as *subjects* most intimately (without a generic or conceptual dimension), and we also experience others in a similar way, as *indefinable subjectivities* in the process of self-elaboration, not as entities conceptually defined and confined by genus and specific difference. We experience "God," in other words, as subject, not as object, and more specifically as *ourselves*. This grounds relationship but not power.

This perspective corresponds to the experiences of "God" recorded by mystics of various traditions. They have testified that they experience "God" in the "depths of their souls," and as the "Source of their own inner selves."

One reason for the Western penchant for imagining "God" as a person is that "God" has traditionally functioned in the West as the *scaffolding of morality* — and in two senses. "God" is the *lawmaker* who gives "commandments" about human behavior which are to be observed. "God" is also *the enforcer* who guarantees their compliance. "God" will *punish* those who don't obey and reward those who do.

Since the end of the middle ages "God" has been presented as the source and authority behind moral behavior in a *voluntaristic* or juridical sense. Morality is not deduced from the *nature of "God"* as Exemplar, nor does it come primarily from an analysis of human nature. It was increasingly derived from the *will of "God"* (as expressed in Scripture and/or taught by the Church) apart from any other consideration. In other words, morality in modern western Christianity has a *non*-rational dimension: it is *revelation,* not strictly a matter of rational analysis. Moral behavior is an obligation because "God" *commands* it and for no other reason.

Conceivably, in this perspective, since morality is only what "God" *wants, if "God" had a change of mind* about the moral law, "God" could permit evil to happen. This voluntarism at the root of the western image of an exclusively transcendent "God-person" allows for the outrageous conceptions of Augustinian predestination and the irrationality of his doctrine of providence. The autocratic "God" who lived in Augustine's Imperial Roman imagination was quite capable of permitting evil to happen, using Roman brutality and greed to prepare the way for Christianity, punishing women with rape. His was a "God" as arbitrary and unaccountable as the worst pampered prince imaginable. But, why are we surprised? Augustine was an upper-class Roman. These anthropomorphisms faithfully reflect the models of the exercise of power characteristic of hieratic (sacred) authority of the societies of those days, and in particular, that of the Roman Empire. This concentration on the *sheer will of the lawmaker* is a predictable aspect of the divine "personality" as conceived in the Roman world.

The Romans inherited from Mesopotamia and Egypt the doctrine of the divinity of the emperor, whose commands, whether arbitrary or not, were considered sacred because the person of the lawgiver was sacred. The buck stopped — on a dime — at the throne of the autocrat. No further justification was forthcoming. Nothing was more natural. Why would Augustine's "God" be any different?

Laesa Majestas

The notion that God is a royal "person" also gave rise to the theological use of the Roman juridical category of *laesa majestas,* an offense (a tort) whose level of gravity is solely determined by the *status* or "majesty" of the individual offended, not by the nature of the crime. This functioned decisively in the development of the doctrine of "Original Sin." In the Augustinian interpretation of the Genesis Myth of the Fall, *laesa majestas* explained how Adam's disobedience could seriously be considered to entail the condemnation of *the entire human race* to eternal perdition, including newborn infants who happened to die before the ritual of baptism could "forgive" them. The one offended in this case, of course, was "God," a "personage" of such infinite *majesty* that the crime, even though in other respects a minor infraction, took on infinite proportions. In the hands of Anselm of Canterbury in the 12th century, the further application of the Teutonic category of "equal restitution" to this situation *demanded* that the offense be "repaid" by nothing less than the sacrificial death of a "personage" of equal majesty, i.e., the very Son of God.[94] Hence the word "redemption," which originally meant "ransoming" captive humanity by "paying off" Satan with the death of Christ (itself an incomprehensible imaginary construction). came to mean "paying God back for Adam's insult." Only another "God" could do that.

This classic Western Christian theory of redemption was historically conditioned by the mindset of the ancient world. But more fundamentally it was based on the belief that "God" was a "person" just like us. The entire western conception of sin and redemption would thus be unthinkable if "God" were not considered a "person" of juridical status capable of being insulted in virtually the very same way as a human being — from which the imagery

---

[94] Anselm, *Cur Deus Homo.*

was clearly derived. Why else would it not occur to Anselm or Augustine that it is inconceivable that the immutable "God," who dwells in self-contemplating bliss, could ever be offended by our petty disobedience? It is a gross anthropomorphism, an imaginary definition of "God," one of many on which western Christian culture has been erected. The anomaly mentioned above is here as well. God's "anger," projected by Augustine, is, theologically speaking, not possible.

God as King

"God" as "king" is a key image based on the "personality" of "God" that lies at the heart of mainstream Western religious life. *Laesa majestas,* in fact, derives from the concept of nobility or royalty. This notion of "God" was concretized in the writings of the Hebrew Old Testament and given its final form probably no earlier than the 5th or 6th century BCE. Even as it represented a monotheistic advance over the polytheistic gods in the Semitic neighborhood of the ancient near east, this Jewish God, Yahweh, was himself still a primitive warrior-god who issued commands and ruled his tribal family like a powerful Sheik. It was an image that, because of the later diffusion of the Hebrew scriptures into Christianity and Islam, came ultimately to dominate the Western World from the borders of India, across Europe and into the Americas.

This image of "God" in the Old Testament, even by ancient Greek standards, was unacceptably anthropomorphic, requiring a considerable amount of "adjustment" if it was to be used by Christians. The Alexandrian development of the *allegorical method of biblical exegesis* (interpretation) used extensively by Philo and followed by Christian theologians like Origen in later centuries, allowed for what were considered essential modifications to the descriptions of "God." Without allegory, the Old Testament Yahweh was not very Christian at all.

One of the earliest and most divisive of heresies was led by an Anatolian Greek Christian named Marcion in the 2nd century CE. Marcion believed that the "God" of the Old Testament was an *evil demiurge* from whose legalistic, wrathful and punitive control Jesus liberated the world, substituting Love for Law. For Marcion, the "Father" of Jesus and the Yahweh of the Old Testament had to be *two different and contrary deities*. Marcion had a great following. This serves to indicate the serious extent to which the Old Testament Yahweh was perceived to be out of phase with the view of "God" promoted by Greek Christianity — at least in the second century of the Common Era.[95]

It hardly needs to be pointed out that all this primitive anthropomorphism, centrally based on the image of "God" as a personal, commanding and punishing Ruler-Warrior-Father, in spite of being rejected and corrected throughout Western religious history as woefully inadequate, incorrect and misleading, has continued as the central image for "God" in our culture. For the purposes of Western culture, "God" could not function in "his" traditional roles if "he" were not a "person."

But, after all this discussion, following the unambiguous advice of Thomas Aquinas we can conclude that "God" is *not* a "person."

3. God is Powerful

One of our favorite Western terms for "God" is "Almighty." Power as applied to "God" has been conceived as a cosmological, physical force. It is absolutely bound up with the Western image of "God" as moral whip, rewarder and punisher of human behavior. A "God" who could *not* "do" things — create and destroy, reward and punish, perform miracles, save and condemn — could not perform the role the West has assigned to "him."

The philosophical excuse for maintaining that "God" is powerful, is a category of judgment called "analogy." "Analogical attribution" is a scholastic device that justifies making statements about an otherwise "incomprehensible" "God." We've already seen it function in the case of divine "personality." It is based on the theory that if there is a quality possessed by creatures, then it can be said of "God" by way of "super-eminence" as we've mentioned. This was considered appropriate because the essences of created

---

[95] Jaroslav Pelikan, *The Christian Tradition,* U of Chicago Press, Chicago, 1971, vol I The Emergence of the Catholic Tradition, pp 73-75

things were believed to be copies of the divine ideas, the "image and likeness" of the Creator, a product of God's self-knowledge. Power is considered an essential creaturely quality; therefore "God" must possess it to a super-eminent degree. Thus it is said that "God" is powerful *by analogy*. It hardly needs to be said that the very basis for making such an attribution is *anthropomorphic*.

What I would offer in opposition to this gratuitous assumption, is a very simple datum and analysis: "God" *does not act in history in any way that is humanly discernible*. If "God" does act and effects change then it must occur in a way that is *totally indistinguishable from the natural forces* that are operating in any given event. That was, in fact, Aquinas' definition of providence.[96] "God" works exclusively through "secondary causes," i.e., the order of nature; "God," in other words, *does not* perform miracles. The theologians knew it quite well; and the priests were quick to point it out whenever the people complained that their prayers were not being answered. This was my penitent Fidel's dilemma. That this major correction, however, was not established as part of the ordinary teaching for the faithful was possibly a reflection of how effectively "power" functioned for the requirements of ecclesiastical interests. The notion of "God" as all-powerful kept reward, punishment and potential miracles (even refined "spiritual" miracles, as in Fidel's case) constantly before the eyes of the people. That it could also be used to justify coercive political power as well as the lucrative ecclesiastical marketing of influence with "God" by selling sacramental products, many would agree was a corollary that did not escape the notice of the Church managers.

There was no attempt in the West to build up a doctrine and an image of an immanent, *powerless* "God" that would have led to a deep mystical spirituality. The significance of an immanent "God" for our Religion is absolutely revolutionary. An immanent "God" is not "opposed" to us; such a "God" *can only be our relationship of metaphysical dependence*, which means our own intimate relationship to *our very own being* — our existence itself. The immanent "God," therefore, is available in the interior relationship we

---

[96] Thomas Aquinas, *Summa Contra Gentiles,* III, ch 76, passim.

bear to ourselves. Where in fact this preaching was done, as by Meister Eckhart in the 14th century, the Inquisition condemned it as *pantheist*. But even when not condemned, these views were marginated from the mainstream, a "minority report," an esoteric spirituality confined to the monasteries. I dare say, it still is.

Traditional Scholasticism and the Doctrine of God

The philosophers identified "being" with "God. The doctrine of "God as being," newly interpreted in the middle ages, also introduced a new understanding of the relationship between Creator and creature. It proposed a unique vision of "God's" *immanence-in-Creation* as the fundamental descriptor of "God's" presence, character, "power" and function — and every creature's divine inheritance.

The profound implications of this insight were never explored. Given its historical context, scholasticism was held hostage by traditional Christianity. The mediaeval doctrine of the immanence of "God" as "being," therefore, *remained a well-kept secret*. The Church shelved it. Ordinary laity were considered "incapable" of understanding it. That assessment continued down into our era. Normal homiletic practice still continues to present "God" as the same All Powerful Paternal Lawmaker, an image that was selectively taken from the least poetic passages in the Old Testament. There were many others, passed over, that would have supported another vision.[97] It is my opinion that the Church preferred to live with the paradoxes of providence created by authoritarian anthropomorphisms than to deepen its notion of "God" and deny itself the crude imagery that lay at the core of its control over "the faithful," its life and livelihood.

This doesn't argue against the Sacred; it argues against the way the Christian West has traditionally conceived "God" and manipulated that conception for its own political and economic purposes. It argues against our religious doctrines. And in this case, it goes to the heart of *naïve separatist theism*: the anthropomorphic notion that imagines an invisible "God" to be a "person" like we are, who

---

[97] cf for example I Kings, 19: 9-13

stands above and outside the world, who sees omnisciently, judges and acts omnipotently on it. In my view it projects an image of "God" that is a completely gratuitous human imitation and that has been rejected as misleading by traditional theologians throughout Christian history. Inverting Genesis, our western culture has made "God" in its own image and likeness.

Maybe that's not avoidable.

If we are to elaborate an alternative vision of "God," we must do it in the context of another system of thought where the prejudices and presumptions of the western cultural predilections can no longer distract and deceive us. It will be the burden of a later chapter to establish the foundations of such a system. But the broad brush strokes of how a shift from "being" to "becoming" as the basic feature of Reality, will renew our "Doctrine of God," can be sketched out here.

Part II
God and a Universe in Process

I. The Evolution of Evolution

Evolution is the *leit-motif* of a Process World.

It was the Theory of Evolution presented by Darwin and others in the latter half of the 19th century, that was the final factor that transformed our view of the world totally and irrevocably from the unchanging substances of the ancients to the modern vision of a reality in flux.

It did not happen overnight. The Theory of Evolution, while it sums up the significance of this momentous modification in Western thought, was not the only, nor the most critical factor. Since the 14th century the elements of Platonic thought which underpinned the permanence of species in the *philosophia perennis* had come under increasing attack. There has been a progressive erosion of the accepted wisdom of the fixed and static essences, in vogue when Christianity was born, and which sustained the characteristic two-world structure of matter and spirit.

The problem started with Platonism. Ancient Greco-Roman Christianity had embraced the two-world Platonic Paradigm so thoroughly that aside from the concrete events of Jesus' life, Hellenic Christian ideology was in all fundamental respects identical to Plato. And it was this platonic element still at the core of the mediaeval synthesis that was responsible for preserving the Christian theological imagery that included a Creator Spirit-God whose self-contemplating Mind was the World of Ideas which all creatures imitated. These Ideas, like the "God" whom they mirrored, were fixed and eternal, the perfect reflections of the Perfect Being. Once established as scientific fact, that "other" world became the residence of anyone's favorite fantasy: immortal disembodied human souls, heaven, hell, angels, devils, sanctifying grace, sacramental character and other invisible "realities" that were said to belong to and function on the plane of "spirit."

The schoolmen tried to integrate Aristotle into this world-view. The result was precarious and proved short-lived. Aristotle, although in principle a dualist, denied the existence of substantial forms, and a world of Ideas they inhabited. He was the nemesis of Plato. In hindsight the subsequent erosion of the platonic substratum seems inevitable. Plato's demise meant many of the fundamental beliefs of Christianity lost their rational foundation. There are many aspects to this breakdown, but the central issue was the basis for the ancient theory of the two-worlds. When it began to dawn on Western thinkers — under the influence of Aristotle — that this division had *no provable basis*, the one-world view we call modern began its long journey into the light of day.

A New Direction

Barely had Aquinas finished his life's work three-quarters of the way through the 13th century when the scholastic world-view of which he was the most prolific architect, began to crumble. The men who followed Thomas, like Duns Scotus and later William of Ockham, were Aristotelian master logicians who felt no loyalty to Plato's theory of Ideas. They said there are no independently existing *genera.* "Humanity" in other words, only existed in the individual existing human being and nowhere else. This means that there are no subsistent ideas, nor independent "World of Ideas" where they reside and therefore our concepts do not connect us with that world. The traditional Christian translation of Plato's "World of Ideas" to mean the "Mind of God" disintegrated. So any connection between human knowledge and the "other world" except through revelation and faith was eliminated.

As a consequence, this view likewise denied any direct "scientific" knowledge of the immortality of the soul, or any of the divine "attributes" which had been "deduced" from the independent reality of the concept of Being, identified as "God." Without Plato's theory of the spiritual significance of human conceptual knowing, the existence of a *genus* of being called "spirit" which had up to then been considered scientifically indisputable, was no longer provable. That didn't mean that 14th century Christians didn't believe in "spirits," but it did mean that the existence of "spirit" which was once an item of unassailable *science,* was reduced to an article of faith. This was not insignificant. The outer structure of mediaeval Christendom remained intact, but the foundations of the culture had taken a direct hit.

As more and more of the Christian edifice which was built on these theories proved incapable of maintaining itself *as* "science" against the onslaughts of rational analysis, more and more of the ancient assumptions were relegated to mere belief — assertions supported solely by Church authority (or scripture) without foundation or conviction. This did not disprove the tenets of Christianity, but it severed Christian "truth" from its once *scientific* bases and ruptured the integrity of the social construction of reality that stood like a granite Cathedral at the heart of Mediaeval Christianity.

It also encouraged *voluntarism* in religious morality, which grounded the "commandments" in the will and predilection of "God" (known through the declarations of the Church and the text of scripture), and not in the nature of things. Science and the "real world" it studied became progressively alienated from Religion. The eventual result was the emergence of the one-world, "unspiritual" view that characterizes modern scientific thought and its separation from religious "truth." Western culture became a schizoid phenomenon ... with a religious, moral and juridical view of the world based on one premise, and a physical, chemical and mathematical view of the world based on another.

If we look at the sweep of events that contributed to opinion-change as it proceeded from the initial turning point in the 14th century, there was a progressive transformation that took centuries to complete:**1350**, the Black Death which killed a third of Europe's population and profoundly eroded confidence in Providence, the benevolence of God, and the power of the Church. This coincided with the discreditation of Platonism as reliable science.

- **1500**, the discovery of the Americas which shattered the naïve mediaeval vision of a universal Christian World — a flaw which the "missions" and the *conquista,* like the Crusades before them, were designed to repair.

- **1600**, the Copernican Revolution inverted the image of the heavens, discrediting biblical reliability and undermining ecclesiastical authority,
- **1700**, Newtonian mathematics, in which the Cosmos was shown to have run *on its own* like a clock without need of divine intervention since the time of creation
- **18th century** Empiricism and Kantian Idealism that challenged the validity of the philosophical principle of causality confirming the distrust for *ideas, and any permanent or essential intelligibility*
- **The early 19th century**: the political and industrial revolutions which eliminated the divine rights of hereditary authority and completely altered the ancient view of the social and economic world.
- **Also in the 19th century**: Hegelian Idealist historicism, belief in a pre-ordained, divinely-inspired scientific and political progress.

We realize the road to evolution was prepared by five centuries of drift from the mediaeval monolith. When Darwinian evolution arrived in 1859, what it did was to provide the crowning capstone, the symbolic summation of everything that led up to it.

Evolution and the Doctrine of God

Evolution subverted the traditional Western world view because it proposed definitively to displace "God's" traditional cosmological role as the Creator and Provident Guide of the Universe. All the questions for which only Plato's fantastic World of Ideas (the Mind of God) seemed to have had answers previously, were now apparently resolved by evolution — and with elegant simplicity. The creation of the immense variety of living species that inhabit our world was now considered accomplished *inerrantly and automatically* by evolution — a process entirely contained within nature itself. "God," as the Creator of living things, therefore, ceased being a cosmological requirement. Since it was claimed that evolution functioned by random variation coupled with natural selection, it meant that the myriad of living things that cover the earth in a panoply of magnificent diversity, once considered proof of creative design and hence of a Creative Designer, were actually produced by forces indigenous to the living things themselves. ... forces that weren't even conscious, much less intelligent.

But it did not end there. The discoveries of astronomy and the physics of the atom made in the 20th century, brought to light even more incredible operations occurring in the formation of the Universe itself that seemed to be an extension back in time of the evolutionary principle of random variation and natural selection. These discoveries unveiled a self-constructed Cosmos where aggregates of matter composed and decomposed in the swirl of subatomic *quanta* packets, the residue of an initial explosive distribution of matter-energy. These were the same elements out of which our earth-sun system ultimately congealed and from which all species of living things are made. It suggested that throughout the virtually infinite reaches of space there is a homogeneous substratum. The real creator of the variety of entities that populate our world was a dynamism, an energy, we know well — because we see it everywhere, even in ourselves — but do not understand.

Newton's clockmaker "God," the 17th century upgrade of Genesis, after a short reign of only 300 years seemed suddenly superfluous. The interactions and recombinations of the same infinitesimally small sub-atomic energy packets, the *quanta* building blocks of matter, muons, quarks, "dark matter" and anti-matter (now all thought to be simply the different vibrations of mysterious homogeneous "strings"), were responsible for the construction of the stars and galaxies of the Universe as well as the genetic material of all living things. At the base of a universe of huge structures, infinite variety and minute mind-boggling complexity lay a single simple homogeneity — *matter-energy*. Everything was constructed of it — and it was all self-elaborated.

Randomness

Evolution seemed to confirm an already skeptical Western Europe in the perception that reality was riddled with a randomness so contrary to the human sense of purpose as to be psychologically intolerable. It was ironic that even as evolution showed that humanity was organically one with the rest of creation, by incorporating *randomness* as an intrinsic factor of structural design, it also drove in the final wedge separating humankind from the Universe of things. In the older view, the human capacity and penchant for *orderly choice* was seen to be whole cloth with a Universe whose intricate orderliness was purposely chosen by an Infinitely Intelligent Parent who designed the order we see. Creation based on random variation, on the other hand, suddenly made our human sense of purpose seem utterly alien, unnatural and inexplicable. Orphaned by our lonely intelligence, we became a thing of fear and loathing to ourselves, a freak mutation in a world built by other forces, strangers in a Universe that had once been our home, where we had been the first-born, the apple of "God's" eye. Random variation as the corner-stone of evolution made *alienation* the principal descriptor of the human condition.

If we're honest, we'd have to admit we always had our suspicions. Aristotle was not the first to realize that a gale was a random force. Life was full of randomness, chance, luck. The pre-Christian Romans believed that *Fortuna* was a goddess, as all-powerful as she was whimsical and implacable. Karl Orff's acclamation of *Fortuna* in *Carmina Burana* evokes a bitter disillusionment with Providence that borders on the demonic. "Lord, I believe, help my unbelief," was the desperate prayer of those who struggled with "Providence." The evidence for the rule of randomness has been there all along. Is it possible that we had been so spoiled by our imaginary projections of a benign hovering Parent that we by-passed an adult adjustment to the way things really are?

II. Going Somewhere?   Evolutionary Finality

There is a possible variation on evolution that some believe may save us from plunging into the abyss of the random hypothesis — namely, that there is a *finality,* a purpose at the heart of becoming. Is it possible that the process of Evolution is going somewhere? Wouldn't that also imply a Conscious Designer?

Is Evolution going somewhere? The question for us today is not entirely dissimilar from what it was for the scholastics: Does *becoming* (which for us means evolution) have a goal and not just a termination? In other words, is there a purpose to it all? Is evolution being directed by a Final Cause? Is there an Omega point?

For traditional neo-Platonic philosophy, the Final Cause of all created being corresponded to the desire of all things to return to their Origin in the "World of Ideas." So *Omega* for the Greeks was really *Alpha*. It was used to explain *becoming*. That Ideal World was the very Being of "God," the One, the Alpha, the Beginning from Whom all things arose, Who from another point of view was also the Omega, the desire and the destiny of all things. Existence exhibited a symphonic symmetry, a cosmic harmony: reality was resolved in the very chord that gave it rise.

This vision was embraced by ancient Mediterranean Christianity. The Greek-inspired Christians enthusiastically identified "God" with the platonic "One," the "Mind," which was the origin and the model which all things imitate. We have to keep in mind, this was a *cosmological* vision. It had to do with the entire physical universe in all its parts and particles, not just a few disembodied spirits. The neo-platonic doctrine of the "return to the One" came to be identified with Christianity's belief in the Second Coming — that Jesus was expected to return in triumph at the end of time, transforming the entire Universe into an immortal, divinized *pleroma*.

There were key differences between the "pagan" Greek and the Christian conceptions, however, and they were not insignificant. For the Greeks *matter* was the big problem. A triumphant finality meant the individual human spirit's self-liberation from death-bearing *matter*. For the earliest Christians who were more influenced by Jesus' Jewish roots, contrariwise the goal was a *physical immortality*, "the resurrection of the body," a sheer gift from "God" transforming the Whole of Creation. The "soul," according to early Christians, may have been spiritual, but it was definitely not immortal.[98] And *immortality* was what they were after.

Triumph over *death* was the goal both views shared. The association of death with "matter" and life with "spirit" lay at the heart of the Greek understanding of reality. The Greek interpretation eventually predominated; it penetrated Christianity to such an extent that belief in bodily resurrection became less important than the practical business of achieving immortality through individual liberation from the flesh — by sexual and other forms of renunciation — as the focus of Christian energies.

Evolutionary Omega and Christian Omega

In the aftermath of Darwin, the possible concurrence between an Omega point of cosmological evolution and the projections of the Church, was not lost on alert Christians. Interest in this line of approach was alive well before Darwin. From early in the 19th century, many were persuaded by Hegel's transcendent vision to see the progress of their times — evidenced in the political, scientific and economic transformations taking place before their eyes — as the elaboration of the purposes of the "Spirit," which Hegel presented precisely as a dialectic of the Christian Trinity played out in human history. If human history was the progressive expression of a *divine reality*, as Hegel proposed, biological evolution fit neatly as a *prequel* into that scheme of things. The Spirit, in other words, was working even before history. For these Christians, when Evolution finally came along, far from denying, it was believed to vindicate the Christian vision.

The mainstream partisans of Darwin's theory, however, disagree. They say the evolutionary process is not going anywhere in particular. Gavin de Beer, for example, writing on evolution for the *Encyclopedia Britannica* in 1979, says that with the emergence of tool-making humans in Paleolithic times, "for the first time on earth teleological purpose made its appearance."[99] He believes the process of evolutionary development is driven exclusively by ran-

---

[98] See Chapter II
[99] Encyclopedia Britannica, 1979, "Evolution" (Gavin de Beer), Macropedia, vol 7, p 21

dom variations selected naturally and *automatically* by their ability to survive. There is no pre-formed plan, no purpose, no Final Cause. The purpose is survival.

Theistic evolutionists like Pierre Teilhard de Chardin and Alfred North Whitehead are at the other end of the spectrum. Fully committed to embracing evolution as a divine project, they envision an Omega Point toward which they claim the entire process is directed.

What's at stake for us in this discussion, is the character of "God."

De Chardin and Whitehead

De Chardin, a Jesuit priest who was also a paleontologist, accumulates arguments to the effect that there is an identifiable upward and intensifying trend that defines species as they have evolved through time. Progressively, species develop larger and more intricate brains; they become more intensely conscious and more thoroughly socialized as they emerge the one from the other. He says all matter possesses an *interiority* which he expressly identifies as the root of "consciousness." The potential embedded in this interiority, functioning through organic instinct, is activated in the evolutionary process of complexification. Humankind is the exclusive apex of that development.

For de Chardin, evolution does not degrade. It does not move backwards into less complex and less conscious forms even though they may even be more "viable." This for him indicates an unmistakable linear *growth upward* implying purpose, intention, finality. It allows him to elaborate a modern vision of reality with a Christian significance, explaining human consciousness and culminating in the "Second Coming" which he calls the "Omega Point" of evolution. It is *the human species* that is evolution's "point of the lance" for Teilhard, and he imagines that humanity will develop into a divinized form he identifies with the *parousía*. He calls the process "Christogenesis".

Teilhard sees "humanity" as special. As the bearer of consciousness, the human species was the necessary goal of all previous evolution. It can never "go extinct" until it lives out its evolutionary destiny as the vehicle for the emergence of Omega.

For Alfred North Whitehead, however, a mathematician turned philosopher, the developing organism is *the Universe* itself considered as if it were the "body" of "God." He has no problem declaring "God" the immanent principle of energy and direction of the physical universe, and the ultimate subject of all becoming. For Whitehead, the "purpose" of evolution is the elaboration of the "*Consequent* Nature of God," the *conscious* end-point of universal development. He declares the "*Primordial* Nature of God" the *unconscious* energy embedded in things bearing direction and purpose through *inchoate desire* focused on "eternal objects" he expressly associates with Plato's ideas.

Both de Chardin and Whitehead appear to be generating an entirely new model of the Universe built exclusively on *forces immanent to matter*. Both men ground these forces in "God" strictly as a cosmological factor. Whitehead's "God" is one with the universe; Teilhard's "God" only accomplishes that at point Omega, *but not before*. Teilhard has no problem acknowledging the "final pantheism" this conception entails.[100] Whitehead's pantheism, on the other hand, reigns throughout. Whitehead seems to make a "God" of blind desire the immanent principle of the evolving Cosmos, a kind of semi-dormant "Soul of the World," a Schopenhaurean "Will."

Purpose or Randomness?

In each of these theories, the overriding impact of *conscious purpose*, emanating from an unseen "God," dominates. To my mind those who insist that only this type of *conscious finality* can save us from a nihilistic randomness themselves present an equally fundamental anomaly: they imagine a purposeful "God" directing an inexplicably random process. It's most revealing that Whitehead proposes "God's" primordial appetition to be focused by what he calls "eternal objects" which he expressly equates with Plato's

---

[100] Pierre Teilhard de Chardin, *The Phenomenon of Man,* Harper and Row, NY 1975 (1955), p.294, where he calls Omega a "superior form of pantheism".

World of Ideas. While claiming to exclude "consciousness" from this primitive appetition, he nevertheless admits that to describe this feature of reality, he would prefer a word like "envisagement," which to me clearly implies consciousness. It seems Whitehead's claim of "unconsciousness" for the Primordial "God" is ambivalent.[101]

This serves to illustrate the dilemma that haunts theories of evolutionary finality. If evolution is *going somewhere*, then, it is claimed, something conscious and purposeful — like Plato's ideas, the Mind of God — had to point it in that direction. That means that cosmic development is consciously directed and the randomness we see is *only apparent*. In a universe directed by a conscious, purposeful Being, this deceiving randomness in turn needs to be explained. Why would a consciously purposeful "God" deceive us about the significance of being and try to make us believe the material universe was the product of a random process?

As in most creationist conceptions of *cosmogenesis*, the *process of becoming* is left more unintelligible than ever. "Becoming" made sense to the neo-Platonists because they imagined that becoming was "being" (form, idea, spirit) trying to overcome and eliminate non-being — *matter*. But we no longer give any credence to the theory of matter and form. What then is the "purpose" of all this evolutionary groping? Impermanent evolution is a strange way "to create" if "God" is using it only *to get past it* to something "permanent." 99% of all evolved species, plants and animals, have gone extinct in an infinitely prolonged, halting process that has covered more than 3,000 *millions of years*. This cosmic trip with its attendant suffering and bitter failures would seem to be some kind of demonic game — a sadistic child's idea of fun, like pulling the legs off ants and watching them try to run. A "God" who actually intends permanence *should create permanence*

---

[101] Alfred North Whitehead, *Process and Reality,* Macmillan, NY, 1968 (1929), pp 58 & 60: "... eternal objects, as in God's primordial nature, constitute the Platonic world of ideas." He also says that to describe the "appetitive" process by which God utilizes "eternal objects" as the source out of which the "concrescence" of "actual entities" takes place, he would like to use a word like "envisagement." (p.39) How all this remains "unconscious" is hard to imagine.

once and for all. Our sense of the goodness of "God" is offended by such a conception.

So, we find ourselves again at the familiar dilemma. A "God" who would do this — who would consciously preside over eons and eons of mass extinctions and incalculable numbers of discarded genotypes — is a strange "God" at least, and perhaps even not a very *good* "God" at all.

The "good" is a very important category for us. It guides what we strive for; and we have used it since time immemorial to determine what "God" is really like.

III. The Good "God" — Our Final Cause

Another meaning of the words "Final Cause," comes from our religious traditions. From this perspective "God" has been the Model of human behavior and "spiritual" growth. There is a sense of direction exclusive to human beings, that is bound up with our *discernment of moral goodness*. Does this kind of "finality" have any influence on evolutionary development, or on our understanding of the "character" of God? What follows are some reflections on this question.

The doctrine of Providence confronted us with a dilemma: the goodness of "God," or the power of "God" — given the evidence, it seemed you couldn't have both. If we had bet on *goodness* (implying God has no power), we would also have to say that blind evolutionary groping is not "unnecessary" at all. For if "God" is *truly powerless* as the dilemma insists, then "God" not only does not intervene providentially, but we are led to conclude that "God" *does not create* as our ancient tradition imagined, either. The two questions are really the same. The ability to create and the ability to intervene providentially in the flow of events involve the same cosmological capacities and relationship. The existence of a powerless "God" is consistent with the absence of conscious purpose in the evolutionary process that forms cosmic structures and the species of living things.

The fact that *it seems to be exactly the way we find the Universe* should reassure us that our thinking is on the right track. But, that is little consolation. A powerless "God?" What good is that? It leaves us feeling abandoned. If there is *no* evolutionary finality, if no one is guiding the process, then just like admitting there is no "providence," it eviscerates our traditional images of "God."

A good but powerless God? Our culture would seem to prefer it the other way around: let "God" be *powerful* — we can *always* redefine goodness, and so we did. Much of the ambivalence about violence in our traditional morality, in my opinion, is directly due to our inclusion of infinite "power" among the unchallenged characteristics of "God." It seems we are so locked into our traditional image of "*Almighty* God," that when that description proves impossible to sustain, we would rather say *there is no "God,"* than open ourselves to any suggestion that the Sacred might be radically different from the way we have traditionally conceived it. We cannot imagine "God" without power. But that is *our* problem; not "God's." "God" has a right to be whatever "he" is; and perhaps "he" is powerless.

But if we dared to continue down this unknown and unlit pathway — *a powerless "God"* — where would it lead us?

1. The "God" We Project — Our Father or Our Child?

Looking at western Christian theology throughout history, belief in the goodness of "God" is *not* as untraditional a criterion for discerning the face of "God" as some might think. We find ourselves once again having recourse to that simple, but compelling, common-sense principle: *"God" must be at least as good as I am.* This standard, however unsophisticated it appears, has functioned repeatedly and decisively in religious history. Time after time we have transcended obsolete images of "God" and created new ones *based solely on our own developing awareness of moral goodness.* As with the ancient Greek mythological gods, whose blatant adolescent immorality was an endless source of Jewish and Christian ridicule, we will *not* accept a "God" who is immoral — by *our* standards. We are unapologetic about it. We use *our humanity as the criterion for the doctrine of "God."*. The "God" that we choose to follow is the "God" that we elaborate in our hearts.

That means we are the creators of "God," in the sense that "God" is the bearer of the perfections we project and wish to imitate — the Sacred Goal, the *Omega*, of human development. But that also means we ourselves are somehow *Alpha*, the origin and source of this energy, this drive to express and elaborate the Sacred. This Alpha directedness is at least not separate from us. We are the gateway where "God," as our Final Cause, the principle of direction and purpose in our human lives, enters the world.

Are we sure we want to continue down this road?

We are certain to encounter *objections* to this apparently irreligious kind of thinking. For to say that *we* are the source of the Sacred means, for many people, that there is *nothing* Sacred. Personally, I don't understand that reasoning. What I'm trying to say is quite the opposite: *everything is Sacred,* including us. Projecting the Sacred in conscious terms and then intentionally sustaining it, I believe, is our specific role and evolutionary destiny. We project "God" as a legitimate and authentic human activity.

To say that "God" *as Final Cause of human striving* is one of the emergent features of the evolutionary process does not make "God" any the less the goal of human striving. A "God" who is our Child is no less Sacred and cherished and the object of our obedient service than a "God" who is our Parent. Parents know exactly what I mean.

It's understandable that we feel we need a Parent. Even Whitehead wanted a "God" who could "redeem" the Cosmic Process, someone to guarantee that evolutionary missteps would be integrated into future successes.[102] In the traditional view, "God," once imagined as our provident Father, served as the ultimate metaphor for Sacred Reality. The image provided relief from fear and the burden of responsibility. It was a "God" that supported a fatalism that is really nothing more than the order of nature justified as "providence," and in social terms, submission to the *status*

---

[102] ibid., p.408

quo also justified by "providence." For many people, this entirely exhausts the function of religion.

Augustine's "Child"

It's no wonder that a "God" conceived in those terms, as Augustine did, had to be a "God" who destroyed and discarded, provided and predestined. Ascribing such intentions to "God" didn't bother Augustine's conscience. His arrogance is explained to my satisfaction by the fact that he was an upper-class Roman. He had internalized the Empire. It was an absolute *sacred* horizon for him as it was for all Romans of whatever religion. As a Christian, he translated that to mean that "God" utilized Rome's bloody history to produce a divine instrument for the diffusion and universal acceptance of Christianity. Once "evil" Rome was transformed by his fertile imagination into "good" Christian Rome, Augustine renamed it the "City of God,"[103] and declared that its legions were now legitimately employed in the suppression of schism and heresy. He was the loyal subject of a Sacred Empire, providently elected by "God" for the salvation of the world. For him "God" was in *no way* at odds with the authoritarian society he knew and cherished. It was "God's" Empire, "God's" Agent for the transformation of the World. Why wouldn't "God" be just like the Emperor? And why shouldn't the emperor (and later, the Pope) act like "God"?

Augustine was a ruling-class Roman, not a Jewish rebel. He, like all of us, generated his idea of "God" based on the level of moral, political and "spiritual" development he had achieved as a human being. Like all of us, the "God" he imagined was his Child, not his Father.

With this current discussion we have introduced a controversial "subjective" factor into the equation about "God." It seems heterodox to many of us because we have been conditioned to take the traditional doctrine of "God" as revelation from on high and therefore "objective." We have not allowed the very process by which

---

[103] By Augustine's use of the word "city" in this Title he means "God's Rome." There was only one "city" for the Romans, not unlike the way Manhattan and only Manhattan is "the City" for New Yorkers.

the notion of "God" is generated and refined by us to enter into our definition of *the significance of "God" for us*, which is, after all, the "doctrine of God." If, indeed, "God" is discerned and described in terms that were forged by *our own internal criteria for goodness*, then *our* sense of goodness is creative and constitutive; it is integral to the Sacred.

This kind of thinking, however untraditional it may appear, has long been recognized as an authentic theological method and justified on ancient philosophical grounds. According to the classic view, we are made in the "image and likeness" of "God." This seminal insight served to explain and ground our religious project. In examining our own hearts and minds, it said, we are exploring the traces of Divine Goodness left there by the act of creation. The "God" we elaborate in our hearts can be trusted to approximate the Divine Reality itself because each is the mirror-image of the other. Everything about our human nature, especially its *sense of purpose* — goodness, morality — speaks accurately of "God." Thus the scholastics had no qualms about resolving thorny theological questions, repeatedly, by having recourse to *convenientia,* i.e., "what seems appropriate," as a basis of judgment.

2. The Good — Morality and Human Purpose.

The human moral impulse, the inner drive to "do good and avoid evil," is a trait that we generally accept as functioning under the overall category of "purpose." It is precisely this teleological orientation, this sense of direction of human consciousness that imposes itself on everything to which we apply ourselves. Morality is one of these; it is a manifestation of our sense of purpose. At least that is our traditional definition.

Our morality has carried the imprint of structured *purpose* under the rubric of the insistence on existence, i.e., the vital impulse, *matter-energy*. It proposes to establish an *effective connection* between means and ends. These moral ends, often expressed in terms of abstract absolute values, only appear to be devoid of practical import. But morality has essentially been conceived as connected to purpose, and the purpose is existence: being and wellbeing. It is the same human phenomenon as survival. Many of our moral injunctions are concretely related to the "well being" of the human community: do not kill; do not steal; do not lie; respect sexual contracts.

"Well being" and "being" are intimately related. As we have inherited it, *morality is the application of finality, purpose, i.e., the purpose of survival, to the existential problem for the human species.* Morality in our times is still focused on survival and existence, but has now expanded beyond a narrow focus on humanity to include the Whole. In our segregated spiritualist past, moral imperatives functioned for the protection of the human species alone, considered the sole bearer of divine "spirit." Now that we understand "spirit" to be a property of matter itself, it seems entirely appropriate that we seek to apply these protections and their associated feelings of guilt and responsibility to all the species and systems that humankind is capable of managing ... and damaging.

Purpose and Evolution

Human consciousness operates in the midst of the immense and varied community of things on which its own survival depends. Human presence on the earth has naturally had an impact on evolution itself. Human *conscious purpose* brings a new influence that goes beyond earlier factors for phylogenesis that were random or unconscious. Evolutionary transformation has always included the participation of evolved species themselves in the advancement of the process. All the atmospheric oxygen, for example, that cycles with CO_2 making life possible for terrestrial animals, was a global modification to earth's environment created by the plant life of our planet hundreds of millions of years ago. Before plants, there was not enough oxygen to support animal life. In a similar way, human consciousness has now entered the process; and like the plants that brought oxygen to the earth, people bring *purpose*. This represents the ultimate step, so far, in evolutionary participation. The introduction of *purpose* by humankind *varies* the development of species, both its own and others', and simultaneously *selects* the variations that will survive. Human purpose thus tends to take over the evolutionary process in the domains under its control.

So, "random variation and natural selection" becomes, with humankind, *"intentional variation and purposeful selection."* A clear example of it is human evolution itself. If we accept the conclusions of paleo-anthropologists interpreting the hominid fossil record, we have undeniable evidence of an *upward growth* in humankind's intelligence supported by a corresponding development in our bodies. These in turn are shown to coincide with greater social organization, sophistication of tool use and theoretical speculation.

Such correlation in evolutionary modifications have been traditionally interpreted as "top down." That is, they were considered the functions of a *consciousness* evolving directly under the pressure of an outside source (like "God" or evolutionary instinct), eliciting, in a second instance, anatomical changes, which then finally lead to more complex social behavior and technical control. But it seems more likely that the process was *the inverse*. It began with *human social patterns* which were intentionally chosen and maintained by people. These social habits then created an environment apt for subsequent adjustments in the structure of the human body like the cranium, and the brain, which, in turn, then allowed an increase in the range and intensity of conscious activity.

Along these lines, for example, it appears that some of the gender-specific anatomical differences within humankind — human male and female *secondary* sex characteristics — along with the accompanying psychological variants (the focus of so much relational energy and frustration among us), are the result of eons upon eons of sex-based social assignments. In other words, much of what is currently characteristic of the body and mind of the human male and the human female, was *the product of human society and choice*, not vice-versa.

Vive la difference is, apparently, not just a French acclamation; it seems to have been a perennial human project.

Besides the well-documented destructive impact of humankind's modern consumption habits on earth's life support systems, the human application of *purpose* has directly modified other species as well. The traditional age-old selective breeding of plants and animals to suit our purposes has now been dramatically upgraded to include *genetic engineering*. The limits of such unprecedented control over life have yet to be determined. If this ability continues and even expands, as it shows every sign of doing, it will offer a scope for human creative intervention in speciation so vast as to boggle the mind. We cannot imagine where such control may end — if anywhere.

Eco-morality

Our appreciation of this *awesome power* to affect the course of Universal development impels us to submit it to the criteria of existential finality — morality. Morality insists that purposeful human intervention bring existential benefit — being and well-being — to the Whole. That such benefit redounds necessarily to humanity's own well-being makes rejection of this principle utterly irrational, though not impossible as we are well aware.

So, morality re-applies *conscious purpose* at a higher plane, the plane of "being." We live within the one inescapable circle, the widest of all: being, *existence*, "being-here," survival. Our engagement in the Cosmic Process under the necessary rubric of *conscious purpose* demands that we subordinate our technological prowess to the concern for the "being-here" and the "well-being" of all the species and systems we manage.

It is good to be-here

We have identified three concentric applications of *human purpose*: The pyramidal grafting of *conscious moral purpose* onto an earlier pre-conscious *evolutionary purpose* which derived from an even more primitive *survival purpose* creates an all-encompassing human hegemony which now stands poised to guide "The Process" to an end — an end chosen by us.

The Process, increasingly under human guidance, as deep into the human past as we can burrow, and as far into the human future as we can peer, recapitulates the intentionality of all life to "be here," to survive.

Morality is all about "being-here." Is this formula too simple to ground a moral system? "Survival." It's what we do. It's what we *all* do. And it's what we're *supposed* to do.

Who can argue with it? *It is good for us to be here!*

But let's not get lost. We're trying to fathom what "God" might be like. We are groping our way down the "unlit pathway" of a *good but powerless "God,"* one of the two horns of our dilemma. We are trying to discern what it means "to be good" and therefore what it might mean to be a powerless "God."

IV. Human Purpose and Pre-Human Finality

In the last section we said that the human appreciation of moral goodness is a legitimate and even traditional tool for the discernment of the character of "God." We began to explore what that might mean for our quest.

Morality involves *purpose,* and purpose is generally associated in our minds with an act or an *action*. So we think of it as a function of physical power. Morality is an activist project. "Doing good" is a stock phrase that describes moral behavior. This is also true of our images of divine "goodness." Before the theory of evolution entered the picture we always considered the creation of the universe an act of goodness precisely because we thought we could discern in it the benevolent purpose embedded in the powerful *action* of a generous Designer and Giver of gifts. We called creatures good because of "God's" purposeful generous action in creating them. They were "God's" gifts. So all this made "God" the one who did it all, "good."

Evolution changed all that for us. It asserted that that the various species of living things are real, unanticipated, *unprogrammed discoveries,* carved out of chaos not by the act of a purposeful "God," but by the blind groping of the survival drive indigenous to the material entity or living individual. Evolution took design, *purpose* and the generous, powerful *action* of the Designer out of creation. By our traditional standards, that meant that goodness, was no longer an apt descriptor of the material universe, because "God" and "God's" purposes were no longer involved in making them, neither *what* they were nor *that* they were. If "God" does not act intentionally and with benevolent purpose in the world, how can the world be good and how can we call "God" good?

Clearly appalled at this implication, believers like Whitehead and de Chardin advanced theories that seemed to trump the claims of a "God"-less evolutionary universe. It was simple enough they said: *evolution itself was designed by God.* Evolution is a good "God's" generous plan and action. How else do we explain the pre-human linear, apparently upward, allegedly purposeful evolutionary developments leading to humanity's appearance? "Macro-evolution," they said, offers compelling evidence that the entire process is under Divine guidance. It is still the gift of the "Good God."

The observations of science (and ordinary experience), however, say that such evidence as there is points rather to an uncaring randomness on display in fatal dead ends and massive discarding of failed genotypes throughout geologic time. The phenomenon is too extensive to be ignored or denied. How could such a brutal process be a generous Designer's tool for the creation of species …the gift of a "Good God?" To claim that "God" is actively directing this merciless competition for purposes *that are its polar opposite* is ludicrous. Such a theory would turn the struggle for survival into a camouflage, a senseless and wasteful game set up intentionally to deceive us into thinking that there is *no Designer* — an entertainment in sleuthing prepared by the Grand Riddler. "God's" traditionally defined "goodness," as the work of an active provider, is not evident in the speciation produced by the evolutionary process, just as it is not evident in the daily occurrences supposedly under the control of "providence."

I'm referring to the naïve notion of "providence" that we examined at the beginning of this Chapter. Recall the woman who had lost her son to drowning. That's only the tip of the iceberg. Tortuous debilitating suffering is not a game nor an optional existential pedagogy used by "God" for "spiritual" instruction. There is an anguish in existence, not because "God" directs it and wants it there, but because there's no way around it. "God" can do nothing about it. It is the nature of the process of "being-here." Evolutionary speciation by random variation and the competitiveness of natural selection is faithful to our experience of reality as it really is. It is why a naïve, anthropomorphic "providence" does not work as an explanation. These facts are consistent with the notion of a powerless God.

If "God" is powerless and does not "act," how can "He" be "good"? If "God" cannot *do* good, how can "He" *be* good?

I answer by saying there is another way of being good and, I believe, it is a clue to what "'God' is like."

Maternal Self-Donation

"Goodness," the disposition to give and share cannot be defined exclusively by *activity*; because *action* is not the only instrument of donation. The Mother who allows her infants to take of her very substance — the cells of her body, first, for their very existence and then after birth, her milk for their sustenance is no less "good" for her passive generosity than the Father who actively and aggressively gathers things for the provision of his family. A simple example, but it shows goodness can also be an agenda-less, inactive self-disposition, a benevolent passivity, permitting benefits to be taken from oneself by others. And it is the others who are the active ones pursuing purposes determined by themselves alone. Each kind of donation is generous, a giving and therefore "good. Thus is a powerless "God" still "good".

This suggestion of a "maternal core" to "Gods" character may be perhaps the most apt metaphor for the creator-creature relationship — descriptive of "participation in being" — as we will see.

A. The Finality of "being-here"

There is no conscious, planned purpose operating in evolution. But that doesn't mean there is no linearity of any kind. If events were simply random and without focus, they would be unintelligible. There is indeed a directedness provided by the actors in the drama themselves that accumulates to an austere existential finality which characterizes our material universe. It is the energy of matter utilized by material things that is the *insistence-on-existence*, what we and all living things experience as our *drive to survive*. It makes us what we are and determines what we do. It is the dynamism responsible for speciation. And ultimately, I believe, it tells us what "God" is really like.

"Being-here," the survival drive, is the unconscious energy of matter. This energy is responsible for the astonishing display of directed vitality observed in all the life forms on our planet including ourselves. The tasks of survival that this vitality confronts with such verve and intensity, have produced all speciation. This energy guarantees that the elaboration of new genotypes will be an unending phenomenon — so long as conditions favoring life continue to exist on earth. The key descriptive term for this drive is *survival*.

Existence, in this conception, is not a state or a quality; it is not some "thing," *it is a self-directed dynamism.* It is a process. "Being-here" and its energy, the survival drive, the *vital impulse,* are one and the same thing. Being doesn't *have* energy. It *is* energy — an energy to survive. In classic terms, it is *becoming.*

This is more significant than it sounds. When discussing finality the assumed dominant category has traditionally been *consciousness,* thought, intention, *purpose,* not blind, groping survival. Why? Because finality means *purpose* and purpose implies vision, choice, consciousness, the ability *to see* an imagined end-point. This power to imagine what does not yet exist is a crystalline mental operation of *consciousness.* So, whether we propose a conscious Designer-God who stands outside the process and guides it, or a source of conscious design intrinsic to the process (like Whitehead's "envisagement" of "eternal objects"), so long as we insist on positing *conscious design* as the source of pre-human development we vitiate the primacy of "being-here" and render the process unintelligible, as we've said repeatedly. *You cannot explain randomness as a function of rational purpose.*

I can understand the temptation. It was Lamarck's trap. Jean-Baptiste Lamarck was an evolutionary theorist who preceded Darwin by a generation. He proposed an evolution that functioned through the conscious choice of the evolving individuals themselves. His theory has been proven completely erroneous. De Chardin is similar. He imagines an "interiority" in matter semiconsciously guiding development infallibly to human *consciousness*. The temptation also explains why Whitehead risks contradiction, trying to define his Primordial "God" as *unconscious* and simultaneously claiming it "envisages" "eternal objects," precisely in order to maintain "purpose," i.e., finality, in an otherwise random and groping process.

The issue is compounded because the finality displayed in macro-evolution appears to be directed toward humankind, as if, besides being the director, consciousness were also the endpoint, the *purpose* (understood as "goal") explaining all earlier development. In Teilhard's vision, this drive-to-consciousness is explained because matter was supposedly infused by "God" with the "seeds of consciousness" which will grow inevitably into humanity. This recapitulates the ancient Greek anthropocentric vision. The Greeks were mesmerized by the transcendence of human intelligence over all other forms of life and so they projected "thought" into the heavens. "Mind" and its ideas became the dominant metaphysical and cosmological category for them. They saw all of reality as "mind" struggling to "spiritualize" and make mind out of everything. Becoming was the attempt to convert matter into spirit. The purpose of thought was to turn the material of the universe into itself. Teilhard, in the very first lines of his forward to *The Phenomenon of Man,* announces that same ancient vision with the metaphor of sight:

> "*Seeing.* ... the whole of life lies in that verb ... the history of the living world can be summarized as the elaboration of ever more perfect eyes ..."[104]

It is the wellspring and ground of the Theory of the Two Worlds, the fantasy of spirit and matter — the Platonic Paradigm.

In opposition to all this I consider the physical properties of matter-energy a survival power. And contrary to accepted western wisdom, consciousness is not its dominant characteristic. Existence is a material energy that includes within itself as a subcategory the potential for consciousness. Consciousness is a survival strategy of existence, the process of "being-here," not a

---

[104] De Chardin, *op.cit.* p.31.

power of vision. It is ancillary to survival; it does not direct it. Matter-energy itself, existence-as-insistence, *becoming*, is the dominant and directing category. It is fully responsible for all pre-human development leading to the emergence of consciousness in humankind. Consciousness is only one of the potential expressions of *matter-energy*, the vital impulse.

The pre-emptive Platonic Paradigm

I anticipate an objection to this proposal. The objection states that we are leaving ourselves open to attack by the partisans of "intelligent design." For, as the classic argument goes, if this potential for consciousness exists in matter, *something conscious had to put it there* (the implication being "God"), because *ex nihilo, nihil fit*. We will be accused of simply allowing the re-installation of the creationist position despite all claims to the contrary. This, in my opinion, is precisely what Teilhard did. He insisted that a conscious "God," intentionally put the "seeds of consciousness" into the material substrate of the universe so that species would evolve a conscious being.

Teilhard's insistence is based on an unwarranted assumption. It assumes there is a real difference (one that is not reducible to appearance alone) between "matter-energy" and "consciousness," requiring that we think of them as two separate realities or two types of reality. The very use of the words "put there" imply the claim that we cannot legitimately conceive of matter-energy as having the intrinsic property of potential for consciousness in the same way that we legitimately say that matter-energy has other uncontested properties like electro-magnetism (potential for motion, attraction, heat, light), atomic weight and structure (potential for molecular formation and chemical combination), etc. We don't use the words "put there" when speaking of these potentialities, for we all agree they are of the "nature" of matter. None of these "material" properties were discovered before the modern age, therefore they do not suffer from the prestigious prejudices of antiquity. Not so for potential for consciousness. It is a property that has for millennia been given a transcendent assignment by the ancients — and it has come down to us saddled with those prejudices: *Our tradi-*

tion assumes that consciousness is a feature of "spirit" not matter ... that consciousness is immaterial.

I submit that potential for consciousness, to the contrary, is of the very "nature" of matter. That it has not been traditionally recognized as such stemmed from a tragically flawed interpretation put forward by the ancient science of the "Two Worlds." This property, potential for consciousness, is as intrinsic to matter as any other recognized characteristic. But since it is only one survival strategy among many, it bears no necessary pre-eminence, except among us, who are defined by it. We naturally exalt it because of the competitive advantage for survival that it gives us.

The objection, and Teilhard's insistence, is deceptive in that it is not based on principle, as it claims, it is based on *prejudice,* the western assumption. In fact it is based on the *very* same prejudice we have been confronting throughout these pages: the inveterate fantasy of the "two-worlds." It is a continuation of the unchallenged assumptions of the "Platonic Paradigm" like so many other features of our way of thinking. We presumed and, on the basis of that presumption, posited that there was a real, unbridgeable separation, a metaphysical distinction between "spirit" and "matter." Consciousness, we said, belonged to the realm of spirit and nothing "spiritual" can be inherently true of matter. Therefore, if matter displays a disposition toward consciousness, it had to be because of the invisible presence of "spirit." Consciousness has to be immaterial.

This is the classic position. It is at the core of the Western view of the Two Worlds. It has determined what we think about "God." It has defined humanity, formed our morality and focused our aspirations. It is pure projection. Its proofs are all circular. There is nothing to support it.

Now, if we simply *accept the evidence of our experience* and its extension in our instruments of measurement, we would have to say that there is nothing to prevent the *foundational energy* that constitutes the inner reality of matter from being understood to account for *all* the manifestations of energy in the Universe, vital energy, evolutionary energy, and of course conscious energy. In other words, there is nothing that obliges us to think that any given manifestation of energy, like consciousness, is not *derived from* the primordial energy at the core of matter. Consciousness, I contend, is a sub-routine of *survival,* not vice-versa.

> We should pause momentarily and appreciate the philosophical *sea-change* that such apparently obvious statements represent. Finality, we realize, has traditionally been associated in the West with *consciousness* and therefore also with *essences,* forms, which are the elements of design, the *ideas* of a Designer. And reciprocally, the distinguishing description of any given "form," in the ancient world-view, was given in terms of its finality — i.e., the *purpose* or *end* for which that *substance* was "consciously designed." Now, once you say that there are no more "forms," and as a corollary, there is no design or designer, then you are left without the traditional explanation for why things exist and why they do what they do. They have no *purpose* because no one put any there.
>
> *"Why are there flies?"* for example, would have been a typical question. It would have been answered in terms of *purpose.* *"Flies exist in order to assist in the breakdown of decaying matter for use by new living individuals,"* would have been a standard answer.
>
> But if there are no forms or essences, there is no "purpose." Then what explains why flies exist and do what they do? The evolutionary emergence of flies is now understood to be *a function of the "drive to survive"* impacting flies' ancestor species in the context of their "niche" or available food source, permitting the new species to survive, thrive and achieve stasis. In traditional philosophical terms, creation by *the drive to survive* means the "why" of things is not explained any longer by *essence,* but rather by *existence-as-becoming.*
>
> *Existence-as-becoming* provides an austere, universal finality. *For existence has no purpose beyond itself.* It is a self-embrace. It creates "forms" blindly (disinterestedly, as it were) as a by-product of its true existential obsession. It is a non-rational appetite determined not by an imagined end point (a form, which would include Whitehead's "eternal objects"), but rather by the naked insistence of existence to go on. It is an in-

> finite and indeterminate potential; it is not defined by any essence (idea, design) whatsoever. It is not specific, therefore *it is the same phenomenon in all species, as generic as existence itself.* The survival drive manifests itself equally in all forms of life, regardless of complexity or status on the evolutionary ladder. It can potentially become *anything*, given time and the proper conditions. *The goal of existence, in other words, is to exist*, not to think or to see or become something pre-determined. It is the "self-embrace of being." It is not only self-explanatory, it explains *everything*.

If there is an assumption to be made, then, it is this: *all energy is fundamentally homogeneous.* Just as the scholastics assumed there was only one "being" and all existents shared it analogously,[105] we assume there is only one "energy," vital energy, the energy of survival — the self-embrace of existence — and *all becoming* is a manifestation of it, including consciousness.

Once we eliminate the prejudices of the "Platonic Paradigm," we may be able to perceive the presence of this *immanent power* (in the sense of a non-directed unspecified unconscious potentiality) embedded in matter itself, capable of taking advantage of random variations that *may* ultimately develop into consciousness, but are chosen only because they guarantee survival.

Consciousness, however, is not a *necessary* development, despite Teilhard's insistence. There are survival solutions *other* than

---

[105] Mediaeval theologians differed about their "definition" of being. Some like Duns Scotus called it "univocal," some like the mediaeval Jewish philosopher Moses Maimonides, in order to preserve the absolute otherness of God, called it "equivocal," and still others like Aquinas called it "analogous." So much diversity of opinion was itself an indication of the confusions created by having to include both "The Infinite Being" and finite being within the one concept of being. If we attempt to define energy, however, we must do it in *cosmological*, not metaphysical terms — that is in terms of the experimental evidence, not the word or concept "energy"; and we are not obliged to include "absolute, infinite energy" within it, since we have no experience or evidence for it. That all energy is connected is a cosmological theory, not originally a metaphysical fact, because it is proven only by establishing its scientific etiology, i.e., antecedent and consequent events, not dependent causality. However, the accumulation of scientific evidence suggests metaphysical conclusions, as in this case. If all manifestations of energy can be ultimately defined as the branches of a single tree with one trunk, we have being — all of it, residing under one concept. I believe this is a perfectly legitimate common-sense application of knowledge across the disciplines in the quest for truth.

what the anthropocentric model projects. Why must survival energy be directed solely and exclusively toward human consciousness as opposed to other pathways of survival? The basic energy in the building blocks of the Universe may also be capable of generating other forms of effective survivability that we, as conscious beings, may not anticipate. Highly complex insect *instinct*, for example, may be one of these.[106] Instinct in general may be a parallel, i.e., a *praeter*-human, not necessarily a *pre*-human, phenomenon. So, if instinct is a faculty as evolved as consciousness, then the presence of potential for consciousness is an *after-the-fact* observation, not a *before-the-fact* principle, as the objection assumes, and as Teilhard declares, following the canons that make "thought" the ultimate reality. So, the *finality* that we encounter in existence cannot be used either to prove *Conscious Design* in pre-human development, or to accuse us of allowing the reintroduction of such essentialist teleology surreptitiously.

The Drive to Survive

It's important to emphasize that a "drive to survive" need not move in the direction of angelic benevolence and contemplative ecstasy — *consciousness* as Teilhard seems to imagine it, following the predilections of Christian neo-Platonism. In reality, the thirst for life, as we well know from experience, may take *any form that works,* even forms that are selfish, violent and predatory. The dinosaurs reigned on earth for *160 million* years, a breathtaking success story we ourselves may never come close to matching.[107] Such an accomplishment was the result of the balanced use of predatory behavior. And similarly, if humankind now dominates the planet, it seems to be as much because of our capacity for unbridled selfish exploitation as for any responsible stewardship, social altruism or mystical insight.

A "drive to survive," moreover, need not have moved toward humanity, and human development need not progress inevitably toward Teilhard's *parousia*. I believe these goals are not evolutionary inevitabilities. De Chardin's naïve romanticism in this re-

---

[106] Bergson, *Creative Evolution,* Dover, NY, 1998 (1911, 1907), p. 165ff
[107] The genus *homo* has been around for about 2 million years.

gard is reminiscent of Augustine's confident assurance that "God" was using Rome's bloody rapacity as an instrument for the Christianization of the world. Ultimately, the naïve Christian theism that both these men espouse accepts *whatever actually exists* and *whatever actually happens* as the purposeful choice and action of "God." It is consistent with a simplistic belief in "providence." [108]

---

[108] Henri Bergson, a process philosopher who wrote at the beginning of the 20th century, centered his speculations about evolution on what he called the *Vital Impulse* which he took as a primordial property of "being itself" and is on display everywhere. His theory bears clear similarities to Teilhard's *interiority* and Whitehead's *divine unconscious appetition*.

For Bergson the *Vital Impulse* is clearly "spirit" and is prior to matter, not in a chronological sense but in a metaphysical sense. This "spirit" emanates or evolves matter as the expression of its creative energy and ultimate focus. All evolution, then, is the continuation of that process driven by the *Vital Impulse*. It is the work of "spirit." Bergson is an Idealist in the tradition of Hegel and Schopenhauer. He believes that if *the potential for life is an intrinsic property of reality* operating at all levels of existence, it can only be so because it is an immaterial force. "Spirit" is the only reality. He thus appears to overcome dualism by declaring matter to be a derivative of spirit. The matter-spirit dualism is braided together but it is still there. Bergson, like Plato, makes this world a world of shadows.

De Chardin seems to be proposing a similar vision. He identifies *an interiority* in matter itself which functions for evolution as a "potential for consciousness." Variations that occur randomly are chosen, he says, not by natural selection, as Darwin believed, but by the *instinct* to ever greater consciousness, which is a function of the interiority of matter. He claims a theist "God" created matter with this pro-conscious interiority in order to set the process of evolution in motion towards an emerged divinized humanity.

Whitehead then takes all this a step further and says, it's not because "God" *made it* but rather because *the matter-energy of the Universe is "God Himself" in the process of developing*. Within such a thoroughly pantheistic view, all dualisms supposedly evaporate. Whitehead labels unevolved matter "the Primordial Nature of God," changing under the influence of an *appetition* focused on "eternal objects" which he unapologetically declares is Plato's "World of Ideas."

While these views all assert, in one way or another, that matter is *alive* they all recapitulate in a "process" format the fundamental flaw of western thought since the beginning: that matter is inert. All vitality is due to Spirit (implied: conscious and purposeful) as a metaphysical entity separate from matter.

But in contrast I would say the secret of the mystery of matter is not that it is "spirit" but that it is *energy,* material energy. There is nothing "spiritual" about it. This explains evolutionary direction by *potentiality* not by *act*, by being open to unknown and unchosen possibility not by a determined response closed by *conscious pre-planned design*. Randomness functions with a raw, naked finality, the finality of the desire to exist, the *lust to be-here,* the *"self-embrace of being."*

"God" as Consequent: Conscious Purpose and Eco-Morality

There is no primordial "purpose" nor Divine Conscious Director necessary to account for and explain the features of the cosmos including all the life forms on earth. In this *cosmological, essentialist sense*, "God's" role is neither creative nor providential. Evolutionary groping (with all its failed pathways) is not a divine pastime of smoke and mirrors; it is *absolutely necessary* for the creation of all the structures in the Universe. Without it there would be no "creation" of species and *a fortiori* no development. It is the work of existence, the energy which is matter itself.

But to say there is no primordial, pre-ordained, conscious design, does not mean that purpose cannot come into existence, as we well know it has. Conscious purpose evolved in the human species. Its very emergence is a proof that matter possesses the capacity to produce it and sustain its functions.

Once emerged, then, *conscious management* tends increasingly to take over the direction of The Universal Process. We humans have directed our own development for more than a million years, and with the expansion of our technological reach, human direction has come to embrace the entire planet. In time, it may go even further.

So, if we turn our attention to Whitehead's idea of *"God's Consequent Nature,"* which he conceives as the goal of evolution, I would translate it to mean a human construct which symbolizes the "conscious purpose" to which the human species decides to guide the process, which of course, includes its own destiny. We have no way of knowing whether there are others like ourselves in the Universe; if there are, we share this task with them. But assuming that we are alone, it is we who "emanate" the notion of "God" as *Omega*, and decide how we will elaborate it. We project "God" as the *pleroma*, the Final Cause to which we want the now purposefully selected Universal Process to go. We define and refine the "God" who grounds our principles of human behavior. These include the moral imperatives that are the peculiar insights of our times, *our* perspective on human responsibility.

Natural Selection and eco-morality

Morality is important. In stark contrast to de Chardin's naïve belief in an infallible process terminating in a divinized humanity, natural selection quite obviously continues to function, and now sits in judgment on the goals chosen by human purpose. Survival cannot be taken for granted. Just because we humans can exercise extensive purposeful control doesn't guarantee that our choices will be the right ones. If conscious purpose is to rule, it must learn to rule wisely, i.e., morally. It cannot simply *dominate;* it must also *submit to* the intricate and in many cases fragile valences which have taken thousands of millions of years to set in place. These delicate interrelationships form the network in which we are embedded and by which we survive.

Our aggressive methods of extracting and consuming the resources of the planet are already responsible for the widespread destruction of habitats causing extinctions of species other than ours on a mass scale. It's clear that in the offing we are also negatively impacting our own habitat, and the macro-systems — like water, atmosphere, temperature — that sustain it. Like any other species of animal, if our habitat disappears, we disappear. And, as we enter the age of genetic engineering, humankind stands on the brink of designing and re-designing life-forms — including ourselves — for whatever purposes we may decide. "Conscious purpose," as managed by the human species, is increasingly capable of driving the Process, but does it know where it's going?

The survival of humanity, and now the planet that we manage, is clearly not guaranteed in spite of what de Chardin's religious fantasies project.[109] We may be so successful at changing our environment as to generate conditions that go beyond our ability to adapt. This catastrophic miscalculation of the limitations of our planet home and our own bodies — a miscalculation that might be ultimately attributable to the false "spiritual" assumptions of two-world Platonism — may destroy the ecosystems by which we survive.[110]

---

[109] De Chardin, op.cit. p.275, states clearly that the human experiment cannot fail.
[110] Cf Jared Diamond, *Collapse*, Viking, NY 2005

Thus does "natural selection" rule "Christogenesis." Survival holds our feet to the fire. Choosing the proper purpose is serious business, and we have to learn how to do it or we will not survive.

B. Participation in "Becoming"

If we maintain respect for the indigenous authenticity of blind evolution as evident to our observations, does it leave "God" out altogether? Not if we were to focus on "God's" traditional role in Creation — *that* things are, not *what* things are. "God," in this ancient vision, is the "being" of existing things, which we experience as *being-here*. This is the "being" in which we participate, along *panen-theist* lines, as we will explain shortly. But we differ from the ancients. For us "being" is *matter-energy*, which we experience as a process, a dynamic presence, the "insistence-on-existence," the drive to survive.

"God" is *existence itself*. Nothing could be more traditional than that statement. What is untraditional in what I am saying is that *existence is the energy of matter*. *It is a process not a thing*, a duration, a vital impulse, an energy. It is survival, the process of holding on to existence. It is struggle. It is becoming.

Thus are the delusions of naïve providence overcome. For the effect of "God's" presence is the groping, clinging, fighting presence of the universe. It is the energy which is matter. "God's" presence and action in the universe is intimately and exclusively identified with the dynamic substrate itself. This mutually compenetrated presence *does nothing* more than what matter-energy is able to do at any point in its evolution. "God's" *power* is entirely absorbed *and exhausted* in this, "Her" presence-made-available-to-others. "God's" presence is phenomenologically identical with the natural order. "God's" presence is *entirely* manifest in its effects. There is nothing more of "God" that can ever be seen or experienced.[111]

---

[111] This statement is entirely compatible with tradition. The scholastic thinking on the beatific vision never claimed that the visionary would see "God" as a different *object*, but only in a different *way*. This means that even for mediaeval scholastics the *way* we see "God" now, in "his" effects, embraces the only "God" that is.

If we accept being as *becoming,* then we can define "God" not as Pure Act, but rather something like *Pure Potency* — *infinite potential,* which we have already identified with "being-here" and which we experience as *becoming,* the struggle to survive. Since "God's" passively shared *existential self-embrace* is the very *inner reality* of all things, *what things can do and actually do is all that "God" can do and does in our world* — nothing more, not figuratively but literally. There is no identifiable difference. The effect of "God's" presence remains, as ever, a thirst for presence. What "God" *does* is to be-here ... continuously and insistently ... and we in "God." That is all. We *are-here* in "Her" *being-here.* This is existence for us. It is a matrix.

The metaphor for "God" is Mother, not Father.

This means we will no longer be scandalized by an imaginary "God" who supposedly "permits" disasters to happen. Providence will literally mean *what "God" provides,* namely, the passively shared *infinite potential of "God's" energized existence* — "God's" process of being-here, "God's" self-embrace — which is the *material energy* of the Universe and which we each experience interiorly as our "being-here," *our becoming,* our personal drive to survive, our own lust for life, our personal continuity.

With this kind of "providence," then, when horrible things happen to people (and to air, and to water), what "God" sees is what we see, and with us "God" stands mute, helpless and appalled.

V. Being as Becoming

Some will condemn this position as "pantheist." There are similarities, I admit, but I intend it in a sense that should rather be recognized as *pan-en-theist*, that is, that all things exist in "God," as I hope to explain. This is more traditional than we might suspect.

Process, first of all, dominates the issue. I reinterpret "God's" being as identified with process and development, exactly like all the being we see around us, including us. There is an unconscious phase, "God's" primordial presence on display in the material energy of the Universe. It is an *Alpha* energy always actively in process and with an infinite potential for transformation, but without Whitehead's Platonic elements, like the divine "envisagement" of "eternal objects." Such features make evolution a game. All change, I maintain, is unforeseen and self-directed, a result of the self-embrace of "God's" shared existence.

Then, there is an emergent phase, stemming from the development of consciousness, both pre-human and human. "God" is a creative symbol: Omega, a conscious human product, that is posterior, derivative, a consequent development and ultimately the goal of our human self-directed evolution. There is no predicting what *Omega* will ultimately turn out to be, if indeed it is ever something fixed and finished, but in any case it is *we* who determine it, naturally, working within the potentialities of the Alpha matrix that spawned and sustains us.

Pan-en-theism. This is a relatively new term that refers to an old doctrine. The Encyclopedia Britannica says *pan-en-theism* stresses "the inclusion of the world within God, while viewing God as more than the world."[112] I use it to mean that *what we are is "God" by participation* — a concept that I understand in a way that is not entirely untraditional. I want to alert the reader, however, that I intend to avoid the dualism that was historically associated with this neo-platonic conception because such "being" as I identify is *only* the actual reality we all see, hear, smell and touch, in us and around us everyday, observed and measured by our senses and their extensions — *matter-energy* in all its forms, the energy and process of *being-here*, becoming. This is quite *un*traditional. Matter does not stand in opposition to "God," as the neo-Platonists projected. To the contrary, *matter-energy is the exclusive locus of divine immanence and creativity.* Matter-energy is divine participation made manifest. It is the "outward" display of the inner reality of "God." Hence it possesses the essential properties of that par-

---

[112] EB, 1979, Micropedia. The main article on "Pantheism and Panentheism" is in the Macropedia vol 13 p.948; cf Matthew Fox, *Passion for Creation, the Spirituality of Meister Eckhart,* Inner Traditions, Rochester VT, 1980. There are over 50 multiple-page references to "pan-entheism" in the index.

ticipation: the energy which is the "insistence-on-existence" and its necessary extension, Life. It is "God's" shared being.

As an expression of the vitality that accompanies "God's" immanent suffusive presence, the matter-energy of the Universe has an infinite potential for development. We humans are one of its emergent forms; and in that capacity we authentically project "God" as a symbol of what we think we, and the process we increasingly manage, are and are becoming, *Alpha* and *Omega*. ("Authentic" doesn't imply "authoritative," for our projections can be faulty.) So in this sense of a chosen end, the idea of "God" functions for human life similar to traditional theism. In each case our idea of "God" is the *alpha*-Model and *omega*-Goal whose projected perfections we try to imitate. In each case the object of our striving is transformation into the "God" who is our Final Cause.

The *pan-en-theist* perspective involves what may seem a confusing identification of "God" and creation, and an indistinguishable collaboration. But this is nothing new. Scholasticism, because of this neo-platonic notion of participatory existence, was itself borderline pantheism. Let me explain.

The Classic Scholastic Ontology

According to classic philosophical theology, "God's" essence is existence itself, therefore being, existence, is one because it is God's alone. There is no other being. Creatures do not *have* being on their own separate from God, not even as a gift. Since there is no being apart from "God," creatures' existence is an *active participation in "God's" being*. Aquinas said we can distinguish our being from "God's" being only *formally*,[113] i.e., in the way each

---

[113] cf. *SCG I,26* "God is not the formal being of all things." Since the essence of "God" is to exist, there is in fact, for the scholastics, no *formal distinction* possible between "God" and creatures in the strict sense. God does not have a "form" comprised of genus and specific difference as do creatures, and therefore "God" cannot be distinguished from them *by form*. When Thomas says (in SCG I, 26) "God" is not the "formal" being of creatures, he is using the word in a slightly different sense. He's referring to that aspect of the being of things which comes through their "form." It means that the being that creatures "exercise" is not "formally" as God does, i.e., necessarily. Creatures exercise being dependently; God exercises it necessarily. In other words, they actually do exist after the manner of their own forms which is not that of *Esse in Se Subsistens*. Thomas is actually asserting a tautology. He is saying creatures do not exist the way "God" exists;

exercises the same being. In other words, "God" and creation are *materially* indistinguishable. "God" is present and "active" in "God's" effects. If that's true, then Aquinas was saying that, *understood as participated being,* we are "God's" being; and so we are, in that derived sense, "God." We are "God" who, in us, is made visible, conscious, purposeful, active and suffering.

How did this avoid literal pantheism? By only one route: in typical fashion, the schoolmen made a "distinction" — they said there were *different ontological perspectives in play here.* The "being" is the same, but "God's" relationship to it is different from ours, for it belong to "God" not to us. "God" IS Being totally and completely; we exist only IN "God's" Being. There is nothing of us that is not "God," but "God" is not limited to us. "God's" being is co-extensive with our being and with every species and entity; but our being is not in any way co-extensive with "God's" being. Our being is only "God's"; but "God's" being is not only ours. We have no being that is our *own,* not even on loan. For "God," however, all being is exclusively "God's" own, *even ours.* Nothing else "has" any being. God alone "has" being; we "use" God's being. We are totally dependent on "God," "God" is not in any way dependent on us.

In the words of a Christian mystic, the 14th century English author of the *Cloud of Unknowing:*

> "... he [God] is your being, and not you his. ... He is his own existence and everything else's ... he is the being of himself and everything. He is one in all things and all are one in him, for all have their being in him who is the being of all ... he is his own blessed being — and yours too. ... in him your being has existed from all eternity ..." [114]

Now in this classic neo-platonic conception of creation as *existence by participation,* elaborated in terms of the static concept of

---

they exist in different *ways.* Creatures, in other words, do not activate *being* the way "God" activates being. But the *being* in all cases is the same: it's "God's" shared being. They share one and the same "existence" which is God's. God exercises it independently and creatures, dependently; but each exercises the same being and each does it authentically.

[114] Anonymous, *The Epistle of Privy Counsel,* c 1385 England in *The Cloud of Unknowing,* Penguin tr. Wolters, 1961 & 1978 pp 162 & 170

being, there is only one shared "existence" — "God's." Logically, the activities that proceed from that one existence should be considered primarily "God's" actions. And, in fact, classic theist theology since at least the ancient days of Philo of Alexandria (pre-Christian, Jewish, 1st century CE) has always gone beyond the mere claim of *moral collaboration* between God and the human being and rather asserted unequivocally that all our (non-sinful) works are to be *attributed to God* — literally and metaphysically and not just as a devotional practice.[115] "God" is the "primary cause" of everything. Of course, the reciprocal was true as well: everything happens on the authentic initiative of the "secondary causes," i.e., creatures.

Their emphasis on rational consistency obliged mediaeval theologians to accept these "pantheistic" moral implications. But that didn't prevent the Church in its ordinary preaching from selectively *disregarding* this classic theology, and maintaining instead the primitive Old Testament imagery of "God" as a Warrior-King who stood *above and apart from* the world. But as an image for the traditional theological position, it is quite inaccurate. The officially sanctioned theological notion of "God" throughout the millennia of Christian history has always included *immanence* as one of its essential elements. It means that because the being we share is entirely "God's," all things exist *within* "God" and "God" exists *in* creatures.[116] The extraordinary premises of defining "God" as "Being" required that the scholastics say that *human actions are truly divine actions*. And for me that means that my mediaeval Catholic forebears would agree with me that the notion of "God" projected as our chosen *Omega*, most properly, without usurpation or blasphemy, is a *divine-human elaboration*.

---

[115] Philo interpreted Cain's primary sin not to be the murder of his brother Abel, but rather idolatry. Cain claimed his actions and possessions for himself, said Philo, denying *God's ownership of being* and effectively making himself God — that was his sin. Philo Judaeus, *Allegorical Interpretations III, 46 (136)* Yonge, p.65; *Cherubim Pt II 22 (71)*. Yonge, p.87

[116] Rahner and Vorgrimler, *Theological Dictionary*, Herder and Herder, NY 1965, p.223, the authors define immanence as "an attribute that does not connote an effect external to the agent, but a self-realization; ... immanence and transcendence need not be mutually exclusive."

But I would like to repeat once again that for *the abstract "being" of the scholastics* I am substituting *the "matter-energy" of the physical universe* as currently understood by science and observed by us. It is *becoming, the process* of being-here. I am inclined to say, it is all that we can ever discern or experience of "God." And, since it *is-here*, it is "God."

Why do we pray? Are we talking to ourselves? Perhaps we have forgotten Aquinas' discussion of prayer in the *Summa Contra Gentiles* where, while admitting miracles are possible, he says our prayers have no effect whatsoever on the plans of an immutable "God," but it is good for us to pray in order for our conscious desires *to align with the order of the universe*.[117] Prayer, then, for Thomas is *our adjustment to our Final Cause*. I would suggest in addition that our calling on divine power and resources means calling upon the capacities of *our own being* which in scholastic terms, is *"God's" being*.

The scholastics thought "God" was so *immanent* throughout creation and so transcendent over any principle of limitation that they also said *you cannot speak of "God" as a separate substance or entity*.[118] That means "God" is not a "thing" distinct from anything else. Some philosophers say that paradox means that *as far as we humans are concerned,* God is "No-Thing," and as far beyond our experience as "nothingness" itself.[119] It is an expression of "God's" utter incomprehensibility.

Becoming — being is a process not a "thing"

In contrast, naïve theism has pre-conceived "God" as static substance — *a thing, an entity, a person* — rather than, as we are proposing, a *living dynamism, a field of energy*, an infinite potential, a pervasive immanent *presence* in which all existing things participate. If we reject all static terms like "substance" and "entity" as a description of the fundamental unit of reality and substitute dy-

---

[117] SCG Bk III, Pt 2, Ch 96, [8,14]

[118] SCG Bk I, Ch 25, [7] ff.

[119] Many see this as the ultimate explanation for Heidegger's use of *"das nichts"* nothingness, as the creative "horizon" of his philosophy, that which evokes human authenticity. Cf especially Caputo, who identifies Eckhart as the inspiration for Heidegger's notions.

namic images of energy, process and becoming (which is exactly what characterizes all the things we see around us), then it's not only "God" that we cease to think of as a "thing." Even our own "human nature" and our individual personalities cease to be taken as fixed realities and become a temporary "concrescence" (Whitehead's term) within a larger *Whole*, an eddy in a flux, a stage in a continuous process, a wave in the Ocean. If we consider "becoming" to be the only reality, then "becoming" or *energy-in-process* is "Being," and the arch-characteristics we have traditionally assigned to the "concept of being" can be applied to this material "becoming," including creative divinity. Individual species and substances will be identified more as *modalities of matter-energy* than as independent realities in their own right. If "becoming" is "being," then the "being" we observe and measure, matter-energy, taken as a homogeneous Whole, is essentially and intrinsically *creative* — and displays a *divine transcendence*. It is universally functional and *non-specific*; it sustains the reality of everything there is. Indeed, it *is* the reality of everything there is, and that reality is, *in its very essence,* a thirst for continued existence.

This requires an unaccustomed shift in our imagery about being. Instead of imagining reality to be *things* that then "become" or change (with the implication, "under the influence of an extrinsic force," and, "in order to achieve something fixed"), we have to imagine "emergent energy," or "creative energy" or "living potential" or "thirst for continued existence" as the *only something* there is, transcendent enough to sustain all participatory existence. This, I say, is "God's" existence. This living being "concresces" and is on display for us *as the Universe* of things — visible and *measurable* (or hypo-measurable) always and everywhere composed only of sub-atomic *quanta* or their generating "strings," changing under the influence of its own energy, its own thirst to continue. This is what I claim is "God's" being, the matter-energy by which all things *are-here* and become what they may, the process that is existence.[120]

---

[120] Possibly connected with the string theories of matter, other recent cosmological hypotheses have suggested a kind of continuing spontaneous emergence of matter, in what scientists call "quantum fluctuations," throughout the vast reaches of interstellar space.

Materially infinite? Becoming?

"God's Being" may have an infinite *material* character, just like the star-filled space that awes us on clear moonless nights. The image suggests that "God" *is maternally creative* — passively allowing "Her" very reality to be taken and used by all things. Once "matter" and "spirit" are understood to be one and the same thing, how can "being" and "God" be anything other than material energy.

As Bergson never tires of repeating, we experience "being" as *naturally emergent*, that is to say, *alive* — creative, exploratory, evolutionary, becoming. There is no more primary datum available to us. Why must we insist that "God," who is "being" itself, be different from all the actual being in which we live and move? Why must "God" be conceived as already fully emerged, completely fulfilled, "Pure Act," static, finished and impassive — separate, as "spirit," from the rest of material being? Why couldn't "God" be the energy of an infinite potential for creative unfolding, and the Universe, "God's shared being," drunk and reeling from the touch of "God's" self-embrace in the process of actually unfolding? *Why, in other words, can't "Being" be exactly the way we find it.*

An immanent "God," even in traditional terms, thoroughly suffuses finite reality which is in the process of becoming. "God," therefore, according to the scholastics, sustains and is immanent in *change*. In this conception, if the Universe changes and evolves it

---

This continuous "creation out of nothing," first proposed and discarded fifty years ago to explain a then hypothetical "steady state" universe, has undergone a renaissance in our time, to account for the recently confirmed and otherwise inexplicable *accelerating* rate of expansion of the Universe which seems to be caused by a constantly increasing amount of interstellar mass. (cf. Pasachoff & Filippenko, *The Cosmos,* Harcourt College Publishers, 2001 p 353). Physicists don't mean the phrase "out of nothing" metaphysically. They are referring to the conversion of invisible energy, below the threshold of observation or measurement, into the quarks and muons of measurable, observable *quanta.* Invisible energy may be totally imperceptible, even by sensitive instruments, but it's not "nothing." At any rate, it's a further extension on the increasing awareness that *energy* is at the core of it all. This is often referred to as "dark matter," produced by "dark energy" because for the astronomers neither is visible, and their existence is an hypothesis. Some theorists suggest other factors account for the phenomenon that dark matter was conjectured to explain. Cf *Scientific American Special Report,* (undated) Mordehai Milgrom, "Does Dark Matter Really Exist?"

can be presumed to reflect the reality of "God." Our projection therefore suggests the possibility that "God" is somehow also "becoming,"

Evolution is not a game, neither for "God" nor for us. Evolution is the process of continuing to be-here. Evolution is what "existential self-embrace" looks like.

Is it so outrageous to say that "God" is *becoming*? The reasons classically given against that notion have to do with the immutability of "God" — characteristics that were prejudicially imposed by the static "concept of being" and the Platonic fantasies about matter and spirit. We will examine the etiology of that concept of "being" in the next chapter and challenge both its assumptions and conclusions. Why should we say that the *static, supra-temporal* character of our traditional concept of being alone accurately defines the possibilities of an ultimate reality which our daily observations reveal to be temporal, changing *and powerless?*

Matter and Spirit

As we've been saying throughout these reflections, there is an inveterate prejudice against "matter" inherited from the ancient Greeks. Against the background of "spirit," once considered the unique font of life, matter was conceived as *dead, inert, virtually non-being*, unable to exist without form, hence the source of all decomposition, corruption, and death. In human beings, matter was manifest as bodies, *flesh*, therefore the origin of needs, impulses, emotions, desires, lusts, revulsions, coercions. Matter represented everything we believed we should avoid, suppress and eliminate from our lives.

I contend that we have interiorized this prejudice against matter to such an extent that it has become an unquestioned horizon in our culture. But if, as we are saying, *there is no division between matter and spirit,* that means they are not distinct modes of being, and the opprobrium heaped upon matter in our tradition, vanishes. There is no longer any reason to insist that matter cannot bear all the burdens traditionally assigned to "being." For matter as unveiled by modern science is not *non-being, but rather, energy.* And as energy, matter enjoys all the qualities we have traditionally identified with "spirit": the energy of life, the impulse toward development, the capacity for transcendence, consciousness, purpose. There is no longer any impediment to imagining "God" as having a material dimension, analogously, a body — just as we do.

Would such a "God" be just a little too much like the perishing world we live in and *have come to mistrust, disdain and exploit*? Is that why we balk? The immanent "God" of our tradition already dwells in every creature, and dies with every death, with every sparrow that falls from the sky, with every innocent human being executed by his own kind. We would do well to remind ourselves that our Christian metaphors project precisely such a "God."[121]

If "God's" energy is the core of all things, it is our core as well. The "God" we ourselves encounter in our own depths, our *selves*, becomes the Guiding Ideal of cosmic development; it is what *we, and everything else with us,* are (currently) becoming. Perhaps, as Whitehead suggests, what we are becoming is what "God" is becoming. De Chardin calls it "Christogenesis." Our intrinsic development project is, in Whitehead's terms, the "Consequent Nature of God".

---

[121] This statement refers, of course, to the "Incarnation" considered Christianity's defining doctrine. Whatever else it may be, the Incarnation will always *metaphorically* evoke the transcendentalization of matter. The exaltation of the "flesh" to divine status accomplished in the Incarnation was faithfully mirrored in the corollary "doctrine" of the resurrection. Henceforth "flesh" was no longer dead, it was Sacred and would live forever. Logically it could not be the real source of death. From this we realize original Christianity was built on Jewish theological categories in which death did not come from the flesh as with the Greeks, but rather "sin." Augustine, following Paul's lead, effectuated a synthesis between the Jewish categories and the Greek, showing how "sin" had corrupted the "flesh," and the "flesh" then became death-dealing. In this way the central Greek theological categories for death (flesh) and redemption (spirit) absorbed and dominated the Jewish. Paul's re-interpretation of Christianity for the Greek mind required exactly this kind of dualist adjustment.

Anticipating another synthesis in the future, could the Incarnation be taken as a *metaphor*, giving poetic insight into the real nature of our reality, i.e., matter as theophany? In this case the Incarnation would be salvific not because it changed reality, but rather because it allows reality *to be perceived as Sacred*, thus *making it function as Sacred for us*. Could Rahner's notion of the "supernatural existential" be used to maintain the validity of tradition without denying the metaphor?

VI. Where Is The Sacred?

Conscious purpose, to think and to choose, is one of the characteristic capabilities of our species. We are as dependent on the continued use of purpose for survival as we are on the air we breathe. Randomness, purposelessness, unconsciousness, is alien to us, and given our lack of other survival mechanisms like instinct, dangerous as well. It seems incredible to us that *randomness* may have ruled speciation before our appearance.

The randomness in the Darwinian view of evolution runs counter to our human feelings and spontaneous assumptions. Hence, the creationist argument proposing a pre-human *Conscious Designer* directing evolutionary development remains a working hypothesis for many people. It's important to note that "creationism" represents the same philosophical significance whether it's asserted of static or dynamic models — that is, a seven day finished product *a la* Genesis, or a 15 billion year evolutionary development. "God" is still running the show. But in the case of evolution for naïve theists the randomness is only apparent. Evolution can only be some form of cosmic theater.

Naïve theism, and with it the traditional sense of the Sacred, has always bound itself to some version of the creationist position. In a sense, there is no way ever to disprove this hypothesis because one can always claim that "God" installed *whatever* system science finally discovers is functioning. This hardly qualifies as science, however, and many religious people have conceded as much. They are content to surrender the quest for a rational explanation and remain with their belief. Others born into the same cultural mindset that now they do not share, have no such haven to retreat to. They cannot posit the *kind of* "God" that they say is not in evidence. They feel isolated and abandoned in a world no longer Sacred because "God" no longer functions in it as traditional Creator and Provider. Given the prejudicial theistic conditions our culture has set, if it's true that a random world implies an impersonal "God" that cannot love people, it's even more true that a world entirely without the traditional Creator and Provider leaves people without a sense of the Sacred.

For all of us who have inherited European culture, with its mechanistic science and anthropomorphic religion, the world is either run by chance or by an absurd, irrational "God." Our reflections here are saying it need not be so.

Jean Paul Sartre, Nausea at Randomness

We in the West have, by our history, proven our ability to accept an irrational "God." I believe, it's not a "Providence" permitting horrors, but rather *randomness,* that offends our cultural presets. We can't tolerate it. Randomness translates to a feeling of isolation and despair. This reaction, in my opinion, is born of the residue of the ancient philosophical assumptions that we inherited with our Christianity. Jean Paul Sartre's description of the phenomenon in *Nausea* is expressive:

> I was not surprised, I knew it was the World, the naked World suddenly revealing itself, and I choked with rage at this gross, absurd being. You couldn't even wonder where all that sprang from, or how it was that a world came into existence, rather than nothingness. It didn't make sense, the World was everywhere, in front, behind. There had been nothing *before* it. Nothing. There had never been a moment in which it could not have existed. That was what worried me: of course there was no *reason* for this flowing larva to exist.[122]

This is desperate language. Sartre seems to be displaying a bitter disillusionment. I believe his sense of despair comes from the fact that he cannot get beyond the axioms of traditional metaphysics, in which he, like the rest of us, was formed. For crypto-traditionalists like Sartre, the *absence of purpose* has the effect of conjuring up the *absurd,* which in this context feels like *non-being*. But, there is no *non-being*. Existence was here before us, it produced us, and it is not being taken away from us. There is nothing but being. The continued universal presence of being even in the *absence of discernible finality* should serve to clarify once and for all that being is not tied to these conceptual structures.

---

[122] Jean-Paul Sartre, *Nausea,* tr. Alexander, New York: New Directions, 1969, p.67

Sartre strikes a responsive chord in us because we naturally recoil from randomness. It makes us, as he astutely observed, *nauseous*. It suggests that we ourselves were spawned in like manner, without purpose. In *Nausea* he says dryly: "Every existing thing is born without reason, prolongs itself out of weakness and dies by chance." He concludes in another place, "Man is a useless passion."[123] That sentiment would empty human life of any real significance. It seems we have imagined "God" *as a person just like us precisely in order to transcend randomness*, precisely to generate this sense of familial belonging, intelligent purpose and personal love that the Universe, seen through the eyes of modern science, seems not able to provide.

Sartre himself, it should be noted, could not stand it:

Not long before Sartre's death the <u>Nouvel Observateur</u> recorded a dialogue with Sartre and a Marxist in which Sartre reportedly said, "I do not feel that I am the product of chance, a speck of dust in the universe, but someone who was expected, prepared, prefigured. In short, a being whom only a Creator could put here; and this idea of a creating hand refers to God." Sartre's former companion, Simone de Beauvoir, was shocked. She said, "all my friends, all the Sartreans, and the editorial team . . . supported me in my consternation." ... Apparently even Sartre who had early admitted that "atheism is a cruel and long range affair" could not himself live it to the end.[124]

I believe that this confirms what I have been suggesting: that "Sartrean nihilism" and despair are in reality the flip-side of naïve theist imagery and its associated "metaphysics." It reveals only the poverty of traditional thinking, and does not in any way diminish the fertile depths revealed in the process of "being-here," which we hope to explore.

The Sacred

The word "Sacred" identifies for us what evokes our awestruck gratitude for the *parental tenderness,* protection and care that we have been accustomed to assign to the Source of our being-here. Our existential vulnerability resides at the very core of this notion.

---

[123] Jean Paul Sartre *Being and Nothingness,* Philosophical Library, NY, 1956, p. 615

[124] Quoted of Norman L. Geisler, reproduced in *The Intellectuals Speak Out About God* Edited by Varghese, Regnery, 1984 p.139

The idea of the Sacred is a derivative of our metaphysical dependency. If we are *not* the result of purpose, it seems to imply we are *not loved*, and therefore not protected. We seek assurance in this apparently random universe that *our* precarious existence is *not* random, it is special, it is *Sacred*. Being *sacred* means that we are chosen by "God," and therefore *safe*; we want to know that *we will live*. We want to *be-here*. Does that sound familiar? The Sacred, therefore, is identified with our existential safety. And for that, we need to know "God" *loves* us.

We humans express our personal love through intentional benevolence, and we expect the same from our "personal" God. What we see operating in Sartre's remarks are the classic assumptions about being and "purpose" which, at the naïve religious level, have been traditionally borne by the image of a "God" conceived with the dimension of human consciousness. But please notice: it's only in the context of primitive naïve theist imagery that such assurances are even required. For if, as naïve theism assumes, "God" and created being are metaphysically distinct and distant entities then there is no ground of union between us. There is a "gap" that must be bridged. *Making a connection with "God" then becomes a moral event (an achievement) and is no longer an innate metaphysical fact.* Union must be "achieved" by purposeful choice, on the part of "God" and/or on our part — and that begins with creation itself. "God" must *go out of his way,* as it were, to love us, because we are not "lovable," i.e., of "God's" very flesh, blood and bones. These expectations of a personal intervention on the part of "God," I believe, also explain why an evolution orchestrated by a Designer "God" does not strike these people as a strange and inappropriate manipulation. It stems from the same alienation.

In a *pan-en-theist* universe, on the other hand, union with the immanent "God" is a cosmological reality — a given, inalienable, primordial fact — the basis, ground and possibility of all other facts of whatever kind. And the immanent "God" is totally suffuse in the creatures who are spawned of and *within* "God's" very being. This "God's" range of conscious, purposeful influence in the world is exactly the level of conscious, purposeful ability that matter-energy at any given point in time has acquired. It is limited to the capacities that have been accumulated through the creatures' evolutionary / moral / mystical development. "God" does not sit "above" and "outside" the world. "God" is its inner reality. What we creatures can do is what "God" can do, no more, no less.

Sartre is unreconciled to the possibility that "purpose" is a characteristic of human existence *alone,* even as he heralds it. Like him, many of us may have already decided that purpose must have been present *before us* or its presence *in us* is meaningless.

I contend that all this is a result of the collapse of naïve separatist theism which imagined an anthropomorphic "God," Father, Warrior, Sheik of our tradition Who related to us *from outside our world*. This is what evolution demolished — a conception that was all along an inadequate cosmo-ontology. Even though it is hardly ever mentioned from the pulpit, we should remember that traditional theology has always asserted *immanence*, along with transcendence, as an essential element of the creature-Creator relationship. Immanence means "God" is not *other* than us, and therefore an extraordinary intervention is not required to bridge an imagined gap between us and the Source of our Being and life. Our immanent existential union with "God" is a given. No more intimate and inalienable relationship can be imagined. We are as naturally "one" with "God," the source of life and being, as "God" is with "God's"-self. This is the primordial fact. In itself it does not require the divine "bridge-building" initiatives heralded by Christianity, and in fact may deny its very premise: an imagined chasm created by "Original Sin."[125]

---

[125] All of what was just said contrasts sharply with the world-view promoted by Christianity since Roman times. That Christian vision contends that "redemption" is precisely the initiative of God designed to bridge an otherwise insurmountable ontological estrangement between Creator and creatures ... produced by Original Sin. I am convinced that this faulty "cosmic" interpretation of the significance of the death of Jesus was born of a colossal error, suggested at first by "Paul's" thinking as represented in *Romans,* and then projected into metaphysical solidity by Augustine of Hippo. The error consisted in this: a psychological "gap," a sense of alienation created by Roman political oppression, a universalized religious doubt and a resulting moral *anomie* — characteristic of the Mediterranean world ruled by Rome at the birth of the Empire — was wrongly interpreted in ontological terms. And the death of Jesus, which coun-

The Sacred is Us

Our "sense of the Sacred" includes our familial sense that we "belong." I would suggest that the "functional Pantheism" which lies at the heart of all mysticism might effectively replace our anthropomorphic projections of "God" taken literally as a "Provident Father" that used to offer us an assurance of loving union and therefore safety, originating in another world. Even so, there is no need to avoid using those parental images *metaphorically* — they are evocative of the sense of "belonging" that our situation implies. Similar to what Aquinas said about prayer, they help us to adjust to the order of the universe. But our poetic use of such a metaphor doesn't mean "God" literally is what *we* project. It does us no good to insist on taking our metaphors as literal fact. They will be contradicted in short order by both our experience and our science, leaving us as perplexed as before and more bitter than ever. But if there is no other world, if our body-persons, in other words, really belong only to life in this one world, then we can re-define ourselves as an example of "God's" *matter-energy* — "God's" being — at a certain stage in the process of exploratory recombination. If matter-energy can be neither created nor destroyed, then we already have an Eternal Life *with and within* the "God" Who is "not far from each one of us for in 'him' we live and move and have our being."[126] We are, as some Buddhists say, like a "wave" in the Ocean[127] of Being-Becoming. Like "God," we share ourselves endlessly with others, as "God" and others from time immemorial have shared themselves with us.

---

teracted the alienation with fidelity and trust, was transformed into a "cosmic" event. It was a massive confusion between the psychological and metaphysical realms that, with Augustine in the 5th century, became set in philosophical granite. It took a psychological phenomenon and interpreted it in metaphysical terms. It was a displacement of enormous consequences that the West has lived with for millennia, and that was the basis for the character of "Western Man" — pusillanimous, grasping, distant, cerebral, cold and afraid. The Christian theological vision ontologizes alienation.

[126] Acts 17: 27-28

[127] This is a favorite image used by Thich Nat Han

The Hindus called this recurrent wave formation and deformation "Re-incarnation." Like Sartre, they originally thought of it as a *big* problem. For it implied that the material of our bodies, the source of our individual identities, was recycled to others and our self-identity disappeared along with it. The fear of death made us cling to the self we had built on that particular individual conjunction of matter-energy. But the Buddha came along and said there was no problem; there was nothing to lose *because there was no independent "self" to begin with.* The endless process of composition and decomposition created intense suffering only for those who failed to understand their self-identity with and within the Sacred Whole, which is the Immortal Universe of Creative Energy, which is what we are, and what "God" is. Conversely, those who came to understand their self-identity with the Sacred Universe, without there being any physical change whatsoever — in life, death or the things that happened to them — achieved, according to the Buddha, the transcendence over the false sense of the separate, perishing, clinging, illusory *"self"* that he said is the source of all suffering. Once they knew their real self was the Whole, the *All* of which their apparent *"selves"* were only a pale and potentially distracting reflection, they stopped "clinging." They let go. It ended their suffering.

The Buddha called it *Nirvana*.

From this perspective, that every last aspect of reality as we know it is explained as the random groping forces of the material universe, does not derogate in the least from the Sacredness of the Whole and its Creative Process, which is "God's" being, which is us. If the Sacred is what offers us eternal Life, then reality is Sacred just as it is. We are "safe" because we are "God's" very flesh and bones. The "material" Universe does not need an outside "purposeful, spiritual" source to make it Sacred.

What this means is that we and the Sacred are closer, more identical than we would ever have dared to imagine. It means that the immanent "God" of the scholastics is more immanent, more inseparably one with us than we thought. And, when you come down to it, how immanent is "immanent"? In scholastic terms, who is to say that immanence must allow for some identifiable line of demarcation between the immanent "God" and the entity "God" "immanates."[128] By definition, immanence totally suffuses the entity it sustains; any part of it that exists, exists in "God's" being. This holds equally true if we identify being as matter-energy. Can we say this matter-energy is ours? Whose, then, is it? How do we differentiate what is of "God" and what is of us? We can't. To say that we and "God" are one, is more literally true than our legalistic tradition — focused as it was on controlling behavior with reward and punishment — has prepared us to accept.

Isn't this Pantheism?

Functional Pantheism

We have been pursuing a speculative quest for the "face of God." But in the final analysis, the most this quest can hope to accomplish is to make reasonable a practical choice that overrides speculative doubt and theoretical hesitation: If we want further assurance, practice, that is, *experience* will have to provide it. That is what the mystics do. In two later chapters we examine the testimony of the mystics.

We should not be distracted by imagining that we *once* were Sacred and now we are *not* (due to a "fall" based on ancient Greek myths that matter is evil, or fantasies about an "Original Sin"). It is simply a pernicious prejudice that says the Sacred *must* be something *different from* us, that comes from *somewhere else*, another world that conditions our sacredness on a code of behavior or a "justification" imposed from outside. If we cannot distinguish what is of us and what is of "God" then maybe there is no distinction, or at least no distinction that matters.

Such a *choice* means the end of the Platonic Paradigm. Accepting the intrinsic Sacredness of our Universe of matter-energy means there is no need for a second world, that one out there, pure and eternal, necessary to redeem and "save" this one here, corrupt and perishing. There is only one Universe and we are not only *in*

---

[128] Raimundo Panikkar, in his book *The Trinity in the Religious Experience of Man*, Orbis, 1973, p.32f, ridicules a naïve notion of indwelling that imagines "God" residing like a tenant in some little corner of the "soul" when the correct image is complete suffusion and commensurability.

it, we *are* it. It's because it is *Sacred* that there must be only one. There is no need for another. This is not an admission of defeat, a cry of Sartrean despair. It means the holiness we seek is ours by birth; it resides in the *quanta* of energy of which we are built. These *quanta* are "God's" creative energy turning itself inside out for us in time. It's not "bestowed" on us; we do not acquire it, nor can we ever lose it, though we can, unfortunately, lose the sense of it, and we can betray it. It's what *"God" is*. It is the energy of evolution, the thirst and capacity for Life.

Our moral behavior, then, is a *response* to this awareness of the Sacred matrix in which we live. Moral behavior does not make us holy, it is rather, like prayer, our adjustment to the natural order, to what we really are. It's our acknowledgement of the holiness, the oneness with God and therefore all things, that we enjoy from birth and can never lose.

How should we identify it? Is material energy itself the ultimate Sacred Fact? Or is it, as the ancient mystics of our spiritualist tradition say, only the "mask" of an even more deeply hidden, incomprehensible "Fact" that pervades it all, beyond the reach of our knowing? Or are they simply indistinguishable, making the question irrelevant? In any case, the mystics of every time and tradition testify that for them "heaven" has begun here. This explains the spinning inebriation of the Sufi mystic, Rumi, the ecstatic abandon of Francis, the Nirvana of the Buddha, and Jesus' unshakable sense that, like him, we are the sons and daughters of a loving "Father."

At a recent gathering a young student photographer was displaying some of her work. One picture was illustrative of this point for me. She had taken a close-up of a tattoo on the upper arm of a friend. The tattoo — no graphics, just a simple sentence in small caps, read:

TREAT EVERYTHING AS IF DIVINE

Please note: the "as if" makes the theoretical question of "pantheism" or "pan-en-theism" academic. Academics may be inclined to pursue the question further; for my purposes, however, we have come as far as we need to. For, in practice, the all-embracing Sense of the Sacred *is the same*.

Perhaps what *we are* — directly or by participation — is precisely what our tradition has *not* prepared us to accept. Insecure as we feel, prone as we are to selfishness and oblivious to the needs of the Whole, we are easily persuaded that we cannot shoulder this "divine" responsibility to manage and direct *The Universal Process*. We are not sufficiently practiced in the secure self-acceptance and deep centered stillness — Meister Eckhart called it a sense of "spiritual aristocracy" — that such an adjustment in our assessment of ourselves requires. And so we imagine that "God" is *other* than us, distant and forbidding, someone we fear and obey, rather than the core of our very selves, allowing us to create an Omega goal of care, compassion and intelligent direction to an otherwise random and groping Universe.

Is there a "divine primordiality" here that energizes our efforts? Yes, there is. And *it is indistinguishable from us*. That gentle force that pushes our small self into the light of day, every day, like a hand puppeteer, is the "God" Whose being is *our very being*. *We experience "God" most directly as our very own selves* — and so does each thing in its own way.

Have I confused these realities? Pardon me if I don't apologize. What's the point of emphasizing what *might be* technically distinct (and the extent of the distinction, unknowable), if in any case, it's metaphysically interpenetrated and phenomenologically identical? This perception is not exclusive to the marginated mystics of our tradition. The mystics of *every tradition* confirm this. *The "God" they experience is indistinguishable from their own selves.*

Are we still looking for an outside "justification" we're not quite sure we're going to get? Or worse, have we become convinced we're just mutational freaks in a world where we don't belong?

Our projection of a Final Cause is the symbol of our appropriation of the once groping process that produced us. It is our declaration that we are Sacred; we recognize that we share, and therefore are, "God's" being in this evolving Universe. By establishing such a Sacred Project for ourselves over so many countless millennia reaching back to Paleolithic times, we have fixed our identity.

We have made ourselves the stewards of the Sacred — creatures of care and compassion, obsessed with the process of *being-here,* which is "God's" shared being, locked on course toward an *Omega* chosen by us.

That this is *totally our doing,* does not make it any the less "God's." These realities are not separable. Yes, no doubt, the Inquisitors will call it "pantheism."

The "God" whose face we discern and project "as through a glass, darkly," is the future of the Universe. We are the *theotokoi, the* "God bearers," bringing "God" into the World.

Appendix to Chapter III
(An academic discussion)

Traditional Scholastic Causality and the Power of God

Let's approach this question of power from another angle. There is a traditional scholastic (Aristotelian) category of causality, applied to "God" as creator, called *efficient causality*. What generally characterizes efficient causality, as opposed to other kinds of causality, is that it is said to produce its effects *ad extram*. In other words, an agent achieves its effects by acting *beyond and outside itself,* which could be also considered a working definition of "power." An individual has power that can act *on another*, projecting its will or influence *outside* of its own physical-ontological orbit and into that of another being.

Please note: the connotation of *ad extram* is *physical and spatial*. As an image it is obviously derived from the fact that in our material world substances appear in a given location "in space" fixed by the material mass that they are. If they project their influence onto something *beyond* their enclosed substantial localized reality, the effect will have to take place spatially *outside* of and beyond themselves, hence, *ad extram*.

But, "God" is traditionally understood to be *immanent* in all creation, and by the classical definitions, "God" does not act *ad extram*.[129] In fact the term *ad extram* does not apply in any of the relations between Creator and creature, even to the supposed initial act of creation, *since the very being of the creatures is that of the Creator* and there are no "separate" ontological orbits in play here. *Creation, for God, is an entirely interior event.* There is no *ad extram* and so there is no "power" in the sense we understand it. The power that is exercised *is immanent*[130] and works indistinguishably from the natural forces intrinsic to created being. This is traditional scholasticism.

In order to say that all natural events are authentically generated by the creatures themselves and are not the supernatural miracles of God, we have to say that "God" *does not* control them, even as, in scholastic terms, "God's" sustained *relation* to them IS their very existence. Now what kind of Creator is that? *That we, in the West, are so culturally locked into the authoritarian mindset that we cannot possibly imagine a "God" who "owns" existence but is not "in control" of it, may tell us what we are, but it does not tell us who such a "God" is.* We tend to reject any

---
[129] SCG II, 31, [5]
[130] SCG II, 23, [5]

such notion — in spite of being confronted with the evidence of it everyday. Just look around. "God" does not intervene. This is where our quest for a spirituality should begin ... and end.

But if we allow ourselves to say, as Thomas did, that creation is not an event of motion and change *ad extram*, but simply a *relation of dependency*,[131] then we might be able to imagine, even in traditional scholastic terms, a "God" who is not only "No-Thing" (not an entity accessible to human experience apart from the effects of creative immanence), but also *does nothing*. "Efficient causality," even in scholastic terms. is simply another anthropomorphic image — a metaphor for the Ontological Relationship, *the Embrace of Being*, in which all things exist within "God's" being

Final Causality

Thomas, following Aristotle, says the primary causality exercised by "God" is *Final Causality* from which he says formal and efficient causality are derived.[132]

In Aquinas' scholastic vision, the Final Cause of creation is only *logically different* from the efficient, formal or exemplary cause. It is simply another way of looking at "causality" — this time from the point of view of "becoming," or as we might say, "process." The Final Cause implies a Formal or Exemplary Cause because a finality, as the projected end point, must have been pre-programmed — "hard wired," we might say — somehow included in the organism responding to the attraction; for how else could it respond? Such a "programmed" creature necessarily has an embedded specific "form," which, from the creature's point of view, is *anterior* to the finality toward which it tends. This form directs the process of becoming and so is *also* a "cause." The schoolmen called it the formal or exemplary cause. For our purposes here, because of its anteriority to the Final Cause, we'll call it the "primordial" cause. (The allusion to Whitehead's terminology, is intentional.)

The scholastics would say that this primordiality and the primacy it seems to imply are only *apparent*. For, the Final Cause, "God," is so ontologically *fertile* that by merely "being there" "God's" simple existence alone, *without act or action of any kind, evokes* the existence of the Universe. The "hard wiring," the formal cause, the apparent primordiality embedded in the creatures, is in reality consequent — *an effect* of the

---

[131] ST I, 45,[3]; 46,2 SCG II, 17, 18
[132] ST I, 5, [4] cf Aristotle, *Metaphysics*, XII, 1072.

Final Cause. It is simply the echo in the creature of the Voice that called it forth. I believe this is what Thomas means when he speaks of the primacy of Final Causality in creation.[133]

So the three (or four) classic "causalities" are only aspects of the same *sustaining relationship of dependency, the Embrace of Being,* by which all things exist in "God." Thus the scholastics enunciated principles that are quite capable of conceiving a "God" Who is, unlike the imagery of the almighty potentates of the ancient empires that forged our culture, more like *One-Who-Is-Not-There,* doing nothing, *powerless as we define power*, "acting" only as an irresistible attraction — the object of love — drawing all things into the Eternal Embrace of Existence which is nothing less and nothing other than a share in "God's" very own being-here.

In this conception, "God" is not only powerless — "does" nothing — but this very powerlessness was also the "cause" (and therefore the explanation) of *becoming* in the sense that since "God" is "immovable" the creature must do the "moving" toward the desired end point, Perfect Being, the Final Cause.

If this is the *process of creation* itself, we may consider the "fulfillment" heretofore attributed to the "end-time" as in reality only the completion of the process of creation. Creation, in other words, now includes evolution; it will only be finished at the end, not at the beginning of "time." This may be considered the theme of this chapter.

Creation and Time

An interesting sidebar to this "borderline pantheism" of the scholastics is Thomas' treatment of "creation and time." In the *Summa Theologiae* this comes up under the question of the eternity of the Uni-

---

[133] Finality is always accompanied by some kind of directing factor existing in the creature which in a temporal flux *appears* as primordial. From a perspective *within* the process, this primordiality functions like a search engine with a pre-conceived goal. An example of this can be seen in the growth processes of living organisms, where the infallible metamorphosis (ontogeny) from infancy into adulthood is directed by a pre-existent genetic coding (DNA) embedded in the organism of the developing individual. In the *logical order*, the final cause and the primordial cause each imply the other, there is no primacy. In the *practical order* (the real world), however, an end presumes a prior beginning. All process follows a sequence that goes from beginning to end; the primordial factors are seen to direct the process and so have a temporal priority. But in the *metaphysical order*, the nature of the relationship between necessary and contingent being suggests that being is "constructed" in the opposite direction: it goes from end to beginning. There is no temporal sequence here, however — the reversal is purely *structural* in nature (the scholastics would say "causative"). Chronologically both "poles" arise at the same time.

verse.[134] Aquinas is caught between Aristotle, who says the Cosmos is eternal, and the Church which says it had a beginning and will have an end. Thomas admits there is no way of *proving philosophically* that the world is not eternal as "the Philosopher" says, but he is careful to stay orthodox by acknowledging that the word of the Church must be accepted on faith. Nevertheless, in his discussion he makes his own opinions quite clear. Before the beginning of time there was no time — hence there was no "before." Creation is an instantaneous presence before which there was *nothing at all*. There was no time before time.

Now, when we couple this observation with the doctrine of the "simplicity" of the divine essence, we must say that the Act of Creation, like all characteristics attributable to "God," is indistinguishable from the divine essence itself.[135] In other words, the Act of Creation is an *inner occurrence* to "God," identical to God's very Being. "God's" act of creation IS his essence, and since there is no "before and after" in God, Creation is co-temporaneous with "God's" existence — and the "emanation" of creation from "God" "occurs" *in* and *with* the procession of the Divine Word from the Father. Classic Thomism sees creation as *interior to* the Trinitarian processions. Creation proceeds as dependent relation, while the Divine Word, the *Logos,* proceeds as subsistent relation.[136] The difference is not "physical" or temporal or phenomenological, it is *metaphysical,* that is to say it resides in the fact of ontological *contingency*. It corresponds to the question: Who is *Esse in se subsistens*, and who exists only by dependent participation.

The Universe has no horizon beyond itself. It is co-terminous, temporally and phenomenally with "God." The only distinction, in this abstract conception of mediaeval philosophy, between "God" and the Universe is *ontological* (causative), not phenomenological. "God" is different from the Universe only insofar as "God" is its Principle, Cause, Source of Being. *In all other respects they are entirely indistinguishable.*

---

[134] SCG II, 36
[135] SCG II,35
[136] ST I,Q34,a3; I,Q37,a2; I,Q45,a6

CHAPTER IV
Towards A Metaphysics of Process

I. Becoming, Being and non-Being

If the material substrate of the Cosmos is *energy*, we realize that becoming, change, is the keynote of reality. Energy necessarily implies movement, duration and process. An interpretation based on process offers "creative becoming" or change as the fundamental characterization of Reality. This is in contrast to traditional cosmology and metaphysics which defined reality as "created being" borne by form and substance.

In a process world, *substance*, as the category of individual entities, is re-interpreted as product and appearance; it is not primary, but secondary. Substance, in a dynamic system, is not illusion; but it is derivative, and most revealing of all, it is *temporary*.

Relations within matter-energy constitute the substances which appear at any given moment in the flow. The constant assembly and reassembly of these relations — change, *becoming* — characterize the process occurring everywhere in the universe. The changing substrate is much more fundamental than the substances formed from it. Substances do not endure. Transcendence over the temporariness of substance, by which I mean continuance beyond the limited time-span of the individual, is exclusive to life and is achieved by the genetic reproduction of new individuals leading to the perduring existence of *species*, which, in turn, even though on a much larger temporal scale, also disappear.

Substance and its species, while they appear to be the "purpose" or "goal" of the relationships that occur within matter-energy, do not endure. Substances, as the Buddha astutely observed, "compose and decompose." What seems to endure is *the substrate*: undefined matter-energy, the vibrating "strings" that may constitute it, the changing relationships within it, and its potential — we may even say, penchant — for future recombination.

Matter and Form

The West lived within the parameters of ancient Greek cosmology for millennia. Its main features were completely integral with the rest of their philosophical world-view. Reality for the Greeks was composed of "matter" and "form." While in the later Aristotelian view these were considered simply abstract "principles" of being, with the earlier Platonists "form" assumed independent ontological status and came to be treated almost as if it were an entity in itself.

The form or essence, for the Greeks, was the heart and source of substances, entities. Form was considered the reproduction in the individual existent of the idea by which that entity was what it was. In Plato's vision, the idea itself was the eternal archetype of the form that created substance. The idea existed in the Mind of God from eternity, a product of God's self-contemplation, a reflection of "his" perfections. From these ideas, they said, God made all things, creating being out of nothing by inserting form into formless matter.

The idea got its "being" from "Being Itself," as an image, a reflection of God; it both "looked like" God and subsisted in God's own Act of Being. The idea in God's Mind, which in the creature became the "form," alone bore "being." Matter was considered pure potentiality, a "not-yet" anything and therefore "nothing." Matter was "non-being." When matter as potency and form as act came together they became an entity, a *substance.* To be, for the Greeks, was to have form; it was to be *something*.

For the Greeks, loss of "form" literally meant that the substance or entity dissolved; it lost "being." For once the form disappeared, matter alone proved incapable of defending itself against the regressive return to "nothingness:" the pure potentiality that matter was thought to be. This was death. Death was exclusively due to the inability of *formless matter* to support being by itself. Formless matter's fatal descent into the utter "nothingness" of pure potentiality was halted only if another form intervened, assumed the decomposing matter in question, and produced "something" else that could resist further deterioration. Hence "nothingness," chaos, was chronologically primordial, and ontologically fundamental, and "being" was cosmos, organized existence, borne exclusively by *intelligible forms* — God's ideas. "Being came through the form," was a favorite reminder of the scholastics. In the Greek conception, therefore, since form came and went, the cycle of life represented a real *coming to be* and a real *ceasing to be*. Life was the passage from non-being to being and back again.

Reality was being. *Becoming,* or change, on the other hand, was recognized as an intrinsic feature of reality, but in light of the primacy of being (and nothingness), becoming was considered ancillary. Becoming was seen as an instrumentality of being utilized to effect a transition from chaos to cosmos, from unorganized to organized, from potential to actual, from inert "matter" to life, from non-being to being. Becoming was a tool of being for the construction of *substances and their species,* and so was always subordinate to being. Substances were "real" (because they had "form"), whereas unformed matter, as we've seen, was quite literally considered nothing.

A Different View

This view of the world has long since disappeared. Beginning as early as Aristotle, the independent reality of Plato's forms and the "World of Ideas" where they resided were emphatically denied. Ultimately, in our times, as evolution came to be accepted as the "cause" of the variety of living species, even form as a "principle of being" disappeared. Today we believe there are no "forms." And if there are no forms, then substances are not the metaphysically independent realities, beings, that the presence of form signified. What we believe we see today is only *matter-energy* — an energy focused exclusively on existing — and the temporary structures that it elaborates in time, creating "forms" (meaning species) by the hunger to survive.

We are inclined to believe that *substances,* living individuals, organisms, while "really there" are not what their name implies. They are not very substantial at all. They are real but only in the sense that they are the *real modalities* of the substrate (the whole complex of *matter's-energy*) out of which all things are made. There are no substances as we used to think of them, because there are no "essences," no Plato's World of Ideas, no eternal "forms" that give meaning and independent reality to an empty potentiality called "matter." What there *is,* is the substrate, *matter's-energy* in motion — *becoming* — evolving life-forms from an inner creative dynamic, *a vital impulse,* — the self-embrace of existence — from which we humans emerged and on which we remain dependent, that we experience within our own selves. It is a dynamic whose significance we do not understand even as we live on its energy and insist on controlling it.

In general, then, we will say that "becoming" *is what is.* Becoming is *all* there is. Becoming, therefore, is "being." The "Doctrine of God" which has always been a by-product of cosmology and metaphysics, will be correspondingly affected.

Panta rei. In terms of the most ancient philosophical debates in the Western tradition, this system will represent a shift from Parmenides to Heraclitus.

We are reminded that Heraclitus was a pantheist.

Being and non-Being

It is one of the traditional axioms in western thought that "if being is, being *must* be." This is a way of answering the fundamental question, "why is there something rather than nothing?" The ultimate grounding of the principle of ontological causality is to be found in the insight that lies at the root of these statements. It appears to have become an acceptable starting point and ultimate justification for traditional metaphysics.

In classical western philosophy, as we observed in our short review, impermanent *"becoming"* has always been considered secondary to permanent "being" as the ultimate characterization of "reality" and the definitive source of its significance.

In the world as we see it, however, *"becoming,"* by which I mean "change-in-time," is the phenomenon we actually experience. It's the only thing that *appears to be,* so by our definition it seems reasonable to say, initially, it means "everything." "Being" is also a word we can use to refer to everything. If that's what we mean, then each word — being and becoming — is a synonym for the other. But if by "being" we mean more than that, like *an abstract concept elaborated from a comparison with "nothingness,"* then, it's a projection. We don't *know* "being" *as such.* If taken in this way, then the term and notion "being" is a conceptual projection created out of our imagination in order to inject into experience a meaning and a permanence that corresponds to our metaphysical (and cultural) predilections. *It's a concept that is not formed from our experience.* The fact is, all the "being" that we know, changes, and the *unchanging permanence* we claim to find — traditional "being" — was put there by us. "Being as such" is an abstraction that doesn't correspond to something that exists. The traditional western "concept of being" does not come from a primitive insight, a "knowing" of axiomatic originality, but from analysis and projection.

Metaphysical systems that begin with the "intuition of being" as their point of departure can be simplistic and deceptive. They often assume that we are immediately in touch with and know "being" in contrast to "non-being," which has been taken to mean that we somehow intuitively "know" *what existence is.* But I believe what has been labeled the "intuition of being" and the concept it generates, "being," are *not* a primitive perception at all; rather they represent the result of an elaborate unstated analysis whose biases they continue to bear.

Genus and specific difference

We understand by recognizing the *difference* between one thing and another. I know *what* a chair is and so I can distinguish it from charcoal or a chimpanzee. To know *what* something is, in traditional terms, is to know its "quiddity," its "what-ness," its essence. Since our mental process and our concepts have this formation, it seems entirely unsurprising that our perception of "being" would be couched in these very same terms. In the case of *being*, however, our concept doesn't correspond to reality, because, since *everything exists,* we can't distinguish being from anything else — there's *nothing* to distinguish it from. And so we really can't know *what* being is; all we know is *that* things are present to us. And yet our conceptual apparatus has led us to assume that what we have apprehended is a "quiddity," a difference, a meaning. But what difference could there be?

"Being," we've always answered, is at least different from "non-being."

I believe "being" is a word that's been given an ersatz significance — a false meaning — by setting it in opposition to the notion of "non-being" or "nothing", for, from what else is "being" distinguished? Without this distinction, "being" is a simple declaration of presence, "being here"; it means what "appears," what's "present," what's "there." *Without contrast to "non-being," being has no significance* — it has no *meaning* because it's not different from anything. But if it is claimed, as the traditionalists do, that "non-being" as horizon is thus *integral to the meaning of "being,"* we should next ask where the notion of *non-being* comes from? We obviously don't know "non-being" either; for what is there to know? To say that "non-being" is, in turn, known by its opposition to "being" puts us into a vicious circle. You can't do that. So we say, you can't know "non-being." "Non-being," we say with Henri Bergson, "is a pseudo-idea."[137]

What then is the source of our *idea* of "nothing"? Various pathways are suggested. Working from the assumption that what we *know* is what we experience, what makes sense to me is that the idea of "non-being" is extrapolated from the *experience of death and birth,* the generation and dissolution characteristic of all living substances that we know, including ourselves. We cannot imagine

---

[137] Henri Bergson calls "the nought" a pseudo-idea. In his 1907 volume, *Creative Evolution* (Dover reprint 1998, pp.272-298) he goes through an elaborate analysis of the mental processes that he believes account for the ersatz concept of "nothing." He agrees that this is a derivation twice removed. He attributes the fallacy to the fact that human consciousness and its conceptual structures are ordered to practical acts, not to abstract speculation. Abstractions like "non-being" are extrapolations made by an intellect designed to move from practical "lack" to practical "fullness" — the recognition of a "void" that needs to be filled. So, for example, thirst is understood abstractly at one remove to be the "need" for water, and then at a second remove "need" is understood to be an instance of the "absence" of a reality which is then interpreted as identifying a mental ability to recognize "negation," "absence of being," or "nothing." He considers such a derivation completely unwarranted and the concept devoid of information.

after-death or before-birth, because we cannot imagine *non-experience*. So we call it "non-being." But non-experience is not necessarily non-being. *Non-being, I submit, is an imaginary construct, a projection created to stand for a quasi "state" that we surmise must "be there"* because we are confronted with the reality of death which appears as a ceasing-to-be, as well as the coming-to-be which is the way birth is usually interpreted. But, in fact *there may not be any ceasing or coming to be.* The phenomena of birth and death are entirely explainable as *change*. Things are constructed out of pre-existing things and when they dissolve they are reused by other things that follow them in time. There is a universal recycling going on here. *Non-being* does not enter into the process at all. There is no "state" of non-being. There are only "things changing," i.e., *becoming.*

Central to this analysis is the "scientific" recognition of "composition and decomposition." Substance is constructed from substrate and perdures only for a time. When it loses its "form," it is no longer recognizable and so dis-appears. It is this dis-appearance that has been *interpreted as* the cessation of being, or the "introduction of the state of non-being."

But there is no "state" of non-being. It's a contradiction. Non-being does not exist in any form. There is no such thing as "nothing." This statement may seem too obvious to merit saying. Repeated *caveats* are required, however, because our concept of "non-being" as a matter of fact in this case wears the disguise of a quasi-state — of *something* — and therefore, paradoxically, what could only be literally considered "being." This contradiction is evidence that *"non-being" is a product of our imagination* and bears the features of the only knowing we can do which is of experienced phenomena. So, I am inclined to define the concept of "non-being" as *the inappropriate conceptualization of certain imagined aspects of our experience of becoming. Non-being is the unknown but imagined "end-point" extrapolated from the experienced sequences involved in generation and dissolution, composition and decomposition.* But I want to emphasize: to call this "end point" "non-being" or "nothing," is an unjustified gratuitous assumption. *There is, is fact, no evidence that anything actually* ever *"ceases to be."* What the West has claimed to be a cessation of being, is simply change. The same can be said for birth which serves as the model for creation *ex nihilo*. In our experience, substances do not come to be out of "nothing." They are made from pre-existing substrate. "Being" then, I suggest, was conceived against this naïvely assumed background, and therefore itself can only be an aspect of becoming. *It is a derivative of a derivative of becoming.* So, we are reduced to the common denominator: reality is "a substrate-that-exists-in-time-and-changes" — *becoming*.

On that once assumed foundation of "being" and "non-being," then, the whole edifice of western science and religion has been constructed. This is perfectly acceptable if we have no "scientific" pretensions about them. By that I mean, if we consider our science and religion not absolute but relative, a *cultural project,* a *poem,* if you will, not physical, factual "truth." As a poem, we should consider our intellectual edifice to be not unlike an architectural style which suits our taste and our times. All styles produce buildings that are a protection against the elements, but there is nothing *universal and necessary* about them; one style can serve as well as another. All buildings shelter us from the night. Being and non-being are characters of myth and legend, not "truths" of science and philosophy.

Presence, Appearance and dis-Appearance

So we might prefer to avoid the prejudices endemic to the use of the term "being" and rather say, as some modern philosophers do, that things are *present* — they are *phenomena;* they appear — or perhaps the term we have been using, they *"are-here-now,"* which emphasizes their concreteness in time and availability to experience. *Presence, being-here now,* does not carry any of the heavy significance of the word *being.* There is a *univocity* to this "presence": for insofar as things are *present* (*"are here"*) they all seem to be doing exactly the same thing. They are all equally available to experience. It is this "sameness" of "presence" that seduced westerners into thinking they had found a feature of the "quiddity" of being, what they called its *unicity,* the source of transcendent permanence and universal metaphysical dependence. But all they had discovered, in my opinion, was the *univocity* of the mental construct — the concept of being — utilized to refer to the homogeneous *experience of presence*. Our concepts are necessarily univocal. Presence ("being here"), tells us only one thing about reality: that *it is here*. It does not inform us, for example, that in fact things are *not* the same at all, nor does it tell us about their *congenital impermanence*, i.e., that they become something else in time. All our knowledge of being tells us is that we are immersed in a world of experience, and "being" is the word we have chosen to identify it.[138]

"Presence" ("being here") and "being" refer to the same phenomenon, but they do not have the same import, the same significance. "Being" goes well beyond the mere attribution of "presence" and has been identified as a transcendent feature of reality. The concept of being is considered *significant* because being is believed to represent a triumph over "nothingness," an achievement so exceptional that it proves the *necessity of being*. In terms of finite "unnecessary" being, that triumph is displayed in "substances," things that come and go, are born and die, *passing from non-being to being or vice-versa*. But substance, taken as modality, as we have suggested, does not necessarily "come into being and go back

---

[138] Duns Scotus among the mediaeval philosopher-theologians identified the "concept of being" as univocal. This was in contrast to the Thomist claim that it was analogical.

Aquinas said that "being" is predicable *analogously* of realities that occupy vastly different niches of existence. So being is said to be predicated of God and creatures, just as it is of humans and animals or animals and plants. All these entities are said to differ in major ways, embraced under the umbrella of analogy. In scholastic terms, beings may be said to differ ontologically, but I claim the concept of being by which we identify them as "existents" is the same for all. It is not analogical; it is univocal. Analogy is called an "attribute of predication" which suggests that it might apply to many concepts. But in fact it is used for only one — the concept of being. "Analogy" is, in my opinion, a scholastic sleight-of-hand specifically designed to resolve the difficulties that arise from the use of "Being" as the definition of the traditional theist God. Analogy supposedly reconciles finite and infinite being under the same concept which otherwise could not support both. But in fact "existence" means only one thing for us, because we mean exactly the same thing in everything that we apply it to, from protons to primates. Hence, it is univocal. Insofar as they exist, everything is doing the very same thing. I claim we experience it as their "presence," but, against the artificial horizon of "non-being" we have traditionally interpreted that "presence" to have existential significance — which we have called "being."

to nothingness;" it is, therefore, not necessarily metaphysically significant, and so neither was the idea of "being" which is derived from that imagery.

"I" am an individual substance. The fact that when "I" die, "I" am no longer having experience, is not necessarily "metaphysically significant" because it does not imply that there had been any "cessation" of being. It is only on the assumption that "I" am, from an *ontological* point of view, *substantially* more than the sum of my parts (i.e., that "I" am understood to be a being, an "entity beyond" rather than a "modality of" my parts), that I could thus claim that after "I" die, even for that short period when my parts are still apparently intact, there is a *cessation of being*, rather than simply a change in modality. There is only a cessation of *being* if I am a *subsistent soul*, able to exist without the body, and "I" *mysteriously disappear*. Otherwise, my apparent disappearance is entirely explainable as a "change" in the substrate from one modality to another.

> NOTE: This is ironic and paradoxical in traditional western terms. For, on the basis of the theory of the human spiritual "subsistent form" (the immortal soul), Western (Greek) tradition has always claimed that for people there was no possibility of a cessation of being at death. In fact, for the Greeks who developed this theory, there was no creation of being at birth either, because the human "soul" was thought to have pre-existed its union with the body. They ascribed all death exclusively to matter, and a substance that was pure "spirit" (like the soul) was ipso facto as immortal as the gods. So, the assumption of the substantial self — which Buddhism claims is an illusion and the unique source of the human "problem" — implies either, that when "I" die, I return to "non-being" (a position that has always been rejected in the West, and indeed there would be no reason to posit the soul as subsistent form if it dies with the body), or, that "I" cannot die and what appears as death is an illusion. In this latter case (the traditional scenario), human death becomes a completely unique and inexplicable phenomenon, metaphysically and biologically different from the death of every other earthly living thing from which it is otherwise indistinguishable. It would require a special explanation as to how human death can occur at all, given the presence of a subsistent spiritual form, a "soul," that is immortal. What could possibly be the principle of dissolution for an immortal "form," the will of God? As a rational explanation, all of this is unsatisfying.
>
> Even in traditional Western terms, we have none of this difficulty when it comes to the animals, because we assume they are *only* their bodies, and

therefore their individual "selves," as experienced both by us and by them, are not separate substances, they are mere *modalities of the material substrate*. That such a position similarly applied to the human phenomenon would have squared perfectly with our own philosophical categories, had never been deemed sufficient reason in the West to warrant any deviation from our insistence on the substantiality of the self which has always meant the immortal soul. The Platonic vision was invested in "spirit" as its only source of human immortality; therefore it would not even recognize the material substrate as "being." Since "being" was identified in some way with "God," and God with "Spirit," such a recognition would have amounted to a primordial, cosmic contradiction. Matter had to be considered "nothing," hence death was the introduction of "non-being" — by way of matter — into the world of immortal being which was all and only spirit.

This is the heart of the cosmological question: what is matter? If matter and spirit are not two separate metaphysical realities, there is no reason why we cannot ascribe the capacity to act, which we have heretofore associated exclusively with "spirit," to the one single substrate of "matter's-energy" or "field of energy" or vibrating strings, or whatever the scientists ultimately determine the substrate to be. This seemingly minor shift from two distinct realities to one with the qualities of both, would mean a sea-change in the philosophical panorama. It would support a cosmic vision willing to invest matter's-energy with all the sacredness and creative power that defined Cosmic Being — "God." And it would open us to another kind of immortality altogether.

In the West, the eternal existence of the individual disembodied human spirit remained for millennia the one and only conceivable theory of human immortality. It is no wonder then, that a Christian-European culture — *intensely individualistic* in economics, politics, morality, esthetic expression, religion, even mysticism — came to be built around it. The structures of "being" that are derived from "being-here" as we are discovering in this reflection, however, allow us to contemplate another kind of immortality, possibly more satisfying to the modern mind. "*Esse in se subsistens*," conceived of as the entire Universal Energy System in the process of exploration and self-elaboration, which expresses itself in its modalities — substances, entities and persons — guarantees us an immortality that is cosmic, collective and eternally creative. It is the immortality of the one Divine "Self" of which ours is a microcosm, an indestructible "Self" within which we eternally live and move and have our being.

If we allow ourselves to assume this perspective, we will quickly discover that it supports a morality of collective responsibility which corresponds faithfully to the political and ecological imperatives of our modern conscience. It encourages us to embrace a cosmic mysticism which transcends individualism and finally makes intelligible the perplexing constraints of genetics, biology and species-life on our individual existences. We will

> also find explained that mysterious, insistent natural urge to lose ourselves in a "sacred cause," a larger "self," which has so often been exploited, manipulated and turned against our best interests by clan, nation, party, church. All the above are derived from the original self-identity of the one single substrate out of which we are all made — matter's-energy. We are modalities of "one thing." Can we call it, in some way, "God," or should we try to preserve the immense sacred mystery of it all by refusing to call it ... anything?

The "Primordiality" of Non-Being

The key element in the traditional false "significance" of being is the assumed *primordiality of non-being.* This parallel phenomenon is already discernible in the question that initiates the core metaphysical "argument" for the existence of God: *"Why is there being rather than nothing?"* What makes this question seem "natural" is the assumption that non-being comes first — i.e., that *only non-being has a right to exist* (note the contradiction) without a reason. *Being,* in other words, is considered improbable, and must be explained, while *nothing* is "normal," the natural state of things, and needs no explanation. This assumption of the "primordiality of non-being" is another aspect of the assertion that "being" or existence is a *positive quality*, metaphysically significant, rather than the *ordinary and insignificant universal condition,* the foundation of everything, the only thing there is. Again, *it is the comparison with an imagined "non-being" that gives "being" its metaphysical significance.* Once we say, however, that there is nothing but being, — that being is all there is, that there is no such thing as nothing, — "being" recedes into the background and becomes simply the presence of everything. Being, I say, is normal and primordial, not non-being. There is no such thing as non-being! We cannot think "nothing" because "nothing" doesn't exist. The question, "why is there something rather than nothing," is absurd. Bergson agrees: "... the question, 'Why does something exist?' is consequently without meaning, a pseudo-problem raised about a pseudo-idea."[139]

---

[139] Bergson, op.cit, p. 296.

If we agree with Thomas' contemporary Duns Scotus that the concept of being is not analogical but *univocal* like all our other concepts, we enter a new world of possibilities. Analogy intends to resolve the dilemma of the simultaneous inclusion of *necessary and unnecessary* being within the same concept — and ultimately presupposes a metaphysical relationship of dependency between them. "Being" projected as univocal, however, refers to only one thing, "existence-as-presence," "being here," the same for God as for a house cat. God may *also* be the "ground of being" or even the "totality of being," though the concept of existence-as-presence does not *necessarily* entail either of those possibilities.

This conceptualization could be used as a virtual re-statement of the ontological axiom, "if being is, being must be," but the axiom in this case would lose its "necessary" status. For, an "existence" that does not presuppose a conquest over non-being is not "necessary," it just is — and may always have been, as far as we know. If we were to erase the "necessary" part of it, the statement bears reference only to insignificant "presence" and the axiom would be reduced to an empty redundancy: "if being is, being is." The existence of "presence" in and of itself, unlike "being" which claims to imply "necessity," gives us no new information at all.

But that's entirely appropriate, for in fact it's *all we know*. It leaves open the possibility of the evolutionary elaboration of "finite essences" without the dilemma created by having to explain their provenance from an infinite, immutable, fully complete "One" in "Pure Act." We can say that "essences" evolve from a *potentiality* within being that does not contradict being's character because we have not pre-defined being as "Pure Act," a feature which was necessary to overcome the inertial primordiality of an imagined "non-being." Without a primordial "non-being," "being" can be *finite*, which is, again, exactly the way we find it. If being only "is" rather than "must be" then we can say "being" without saying the traditional "God," or we can say "God" without saying "Pure Act." "Being" in this case, however immensely extended in both time and space, would be *open to development*, which we have traditionally called *finite* — and rejected for that reason. This concept of being taken as *presence,* in my opinion, synchronizes perfectly with the universe-in-process as we currently know it.

Being as beings

A usual accompaniment to the classic "proof" for God just referred to is the unstated assumption that the individual "things" we experience are *truly substantial* with their own definable and delimited metaphysical reality. But this commonly accepted premise is also an assumption. As suggested by our modern instruments of measurement and observation, the "common sense" belief that what we experience are "entities" rather than "modalities" of a single entity, is not beyond doubt, and may in fact be utterly false.

Traditional theists rarely mention the fact that their concept of "God" would, without any compromise to divine transcendence, theoretically support the existence of *one universal created being* (the Universe of matter-energy), a single dependent substrate with metaphysical import, all other apparent "substances" being modalities of it. I believe traditional theists do not like to speculate on such a possibility because it would call into question the existence of individual human "souls," disembodied spirits, *metaphysically distinct human entities* whose immortality (the basis for reward and punishment in the afterlife) has been traditionally grounded in their independent metaphysical reality as *substances.*

Now I suggest all these notions are bound together. Our perception of death has given rise to the pseudo-idea of non-being as well as the idea of independent metaphysical substances, beings. Because of the traditional interpretation given to the importance of our individual selves, we are locked into the assumption of the "significance" of our own persons *as being*, and by extension to other individual substances, like the animals The phenomenon of our *death,* which is the apparent dissolution of personal identity, is naturally viewed as the most catastrophic of events — for each of us personally *the end of the world* — and could hardly be considered to be *without* metaphysical significance. Given the fact that before birth we *experienced nothing* and so believe "we were not here," we naturally ascribe an overwhelming primacy to what for us has always been called *non-being* but which may only be non-experience. For *"being-here"* (the experience of presence) and *"being,"* have traditionally been assumed by us to be the same thing. Life in this modality is short, and we tend to see our "being-here" (experience) as an improbable and transcendent triumph of *being* over not-being. The experience of our personal identity, therefore, makes it difficult to assume a metaphysically higher ground. And yet everything we examine suggests that our difficulties might be due precisely to a severe metaphysical shortsightedness in this regard. What we are, metaphysically, may have already existed for 14 billion years (the current estimated age of the Universe), and may indeed have existed forever according to new theories that our current Universe is simply a new "bud" on an even more ancient tree. Accustomed and attached as we are to "life" in our modality as persons, we may not be particularly enthusiastic about this cosmic identity and immortality. But we may have no choice in the matter just as we had no choice about "being here" or about the kind of "life" that evolved for us to enjoy made out of the same cosmic energy substrate that is responsible for all evolution. Seen in this light, our imperishable identity with the Whole which conceived and molded us *such as we are,* might be appreciated by some as a much more secure guarantee of comparable future delights within the same cosmos of matter-energy (*which we are*) than any imagined separate world of "spirit" where my individual experiencing spirit-person would reside apart from the world as we find it. We must trust something, at any rate, so *why not trust the process that "put us here" and made us what we are.* The "God" responsible for all this, at any rate, seems to want it this way ... and we have little choice.

I want to re-emphasize that the metaphysical problems we have identified in this reflection are ultimately derived from an imaginary projection: the reality and primordiality of non-being. But I repeat: there is no non-being, and there's no indication that there ever was. As far as the eye can see, there is nothing but wall-to-wall being. We do not know what there can be other than being, and therefore we do not know what being is. All we know is that it's here, we are here part of it all, and it all changes.

Becoming is being

That the elements of the things we experience might possess an interior power to transform themselves radically from one substance to another, has, in our culture, been an unacceptable interpretation of the incredible phenomenon of complex and creative change within being. So, traditionally, we have tried to explain away our undeniable experience of these continuous modulations with theories of the hidden permanence of forms and substances implying the coming and going of entities, that is, *being going to and coming from non-being*. But the necessary corollary of these theories is the hypothesis of the constant injection of "non-being" into time and space (again, the contradiction should be duly noted). It implies the constant "creation" and "cessation" of *being* as it emerges from and falls back into "nothing" — as if being were "something" that could be given and taken away, and as if "nothing" were a "state" from which things emerge and to which they return. These images are obviously pure fantasy. There is, in fact, no justification for any of it. Such evidence as we have seems to indicate quite the opposite: *being is neither created nor destroyed.*

So, If we take *"presence"* in its concrete form as encountered in the real individuals of our world, it is entirely without special significance, for it is common to all things which appear as the *impermanent modalities* of a substrate that is undefined, universal and homogeneous in time and space, subject to continuous change and capable of permutation into an infinite number of modalities that were traditionally called "substances." The only justification for assigning the status of independent "entity" or "substance" to these modalities would be on the basis of a metaphysical principle — like form — that is present but not apparent. Such an attribution was in fact made in ancient times when the appearance itself was considered sufficient justification for declaring the presence of "form." Given the discoveries of science, however, this naïve assertion is no longer possible. Therefore there is no identifiable basis for the claim of metaphysical independence to "substances."

Reality, in other words, as experienced, "being-here," *is becoming*. Existence is the process of *becoming*. The time-related sequence of *substrate-substance-substrate* appears to be constitutive of all reality everywhere *and for all time*. This, I believe, coincides with the observation about the "composition and decomposition" of reality that lies at the roots of the Buddhist vision, and is the source of the Buddhist doctrine of *anatman,* i.e., that my very person (and by extension, every "thing") is the expression of a modality; it has no "substantial" existence in and of itself. That this imagery also corresponds to the models developed by physical science with regard to what the West now calls "matter-energy," suggests there is nothing about this point of view that is startlingly new.

But given our contrary traditions in the West, its implications for us are.

II. God as "Being"

The notion of "God," so central to our perennial Western philosophy, has been wedded to the *concept of being* and traditionally served in the double role as the foundation of science as well as the ground of Religion. The classic "God" of western philosophical theology is Infinite Being, Pure Act, *esse in se subsistens*, the existence of all existents and the model of all essences. God was the source and ground of both existence and thought. And what God thought was also the blueprint on which all things are patterned. This identification between Thought and Being was established with the ancient Greeks and in traditional theist circles has fundamentally not been questioned since.

The Greeks were overawed by human thought. More than any other datum, human knowledge and reasoning power was the focus and driving force behind their philosophical explorations. They were so convinced that what they saw was an insuperable discontinuity between human thought and the cognitive operations of other animals that they felt constrained to assign human nature to another world entirely — a world of "spirit," of "being" devoid of matter where the defining characteristic was thought and its products, ideas. It was a world inhabited by the gods.

God was Spirit and so God was a Mind that thought. But God was also "Being." Since "Being" comprised everything there was and everything there could ever be, God must somehow *be* all things. Being was all there was. All other things could only be reflections of God, copies of the divine Being. Being, thought and the divine ideas, therefore, all had to be the same thing — God, the One. There was nothing more to think, so God must think nothing but Him/Herself, and there was nothing else other things could be patterned on. God was all there was.

In the world of spirit, there was no "matter." That meant that in that world there was no factor of individuation, or separation (or death), for spirit was entirely beyond the limitations of space and time, the dimensions in which matter was held bound. Human thought as a "spiritual" activity, therefore, functioned beyond these limitations and was in communication with the spirit world directly, the world of ideas, which was the Mind of God. Hence human thought was characteristically focused on *universals,* the *generic ideas* that lay beyond the spatial and temporal restrictions of individualized matter. These generic ideas were the essences of created things, the forms that provided them with "being." "Socrates is human," was their classic example. In this sentence, human thought connected most importantly not to Socrates, this or that "man," but to "humanity" itself, the universal which was believed to be the original "idea" in the mind of God and the source of Socrates' being human. In discovering the idea of "humanity," human thought found its origin in the mind of God — what was *most real, most human* in every human being.

Now, the ancients considered the "concepts" of human knowledge to be the infallible reflections of the universal ideas they "captured"; our knowledge *exactly* matched the eternal idea and thus *infallibly* reached truth. This held true for the "concept of Being" as well. So it was natural that the features of the concept of Being would be minutely analyzed and serve as the source of the "knowledge" of Being Itself, God, the scientific "Cause" of all existing things. The features of Being revealed by the concept were attributed to God. In this step, since the analysis of the implications of "ideas" *was* the "scientific method" used by the ancients to further their knowledge, the identification of "God" with the *concept of being* yielded *extraordinary* data that was to rule science and theology in the West for more than a millennium. What they believed the concept of Being unveiled to them was nothing less than the inner anatomy of God.

Applying the Concept of Being to God

Whether the ancients developed their notion of the existence of "God" from its idea (Anselm's classic argument) or from another process of reasoning (e.g., the "five proofs"), "God" was always, like "being," a *derived concept.* For no one directly *knows* God.[140] The "concept" of God, like the concept of being, did not arise in the act of knowing but from a chain of reasoning. The Mediaeval focus on "being" provided not only a "proof" for "God's" existence, but a concept that would supply analytical detail about "him."

In the transition from the ancient to the mediaeval version of classical philosophy, the western notion of "God" went through a minor metamorphosis. First considered necessary to explain the existence of *species* (by positing the Mind of God as a World of creative Ideas), "God" subsequently came to be identified as the *ground of being* itself, though without loss of the earlier role.[141]

---

[140] Except, of course, the mystics ... which is another whole line of approach.

[141] The scholastics identified the being of all things as a participation in God's Being. This imagery was particularly supportive of the apophatic mystical perspective articulated by Pseudo-Dionysius, given almost scriptural status by the theologians of the middle ages. This is what lay at the root of Eckhart's mysticism. It emphasized the ontological rather than the cosmological nature of the creature-Creator relationship. God and creation were related, not only as model and image, Craftsman and artifact, but also as *existential symbionts* because creatures existed by participating in God's own existence.

Once the theoretical ground was established, the way was cleared for the pursuit of *mystical knowledge of God,* which means direct experience. But mystical experience never directly formed the basis of the Doctrine of God in the great Religions of the West. The major western traditions — Jewish, Muslim, Christian — all justify themselves with alleged revelations opposed to "common" mystical experience which latter, they insist, might be merely "subjective." Revelation is claimed to be "objective" information and therefore of universal significance. Even though such revelation is claimed to have occurred in what could only be called mystical experience, the gratuitous classification of that experience as revelation transfers it from subjective to objective status for those believers.

Paradoxically, these two "functions" of "God" — as ground of essences and ground of existence — appeared incompatible with one another because the super essentiality of infinite "being" was *logically contrary* to finite essence. (Categorically speaking, all finite essences "nest" inclusively within "being," but the concept of infinite being *as a concept,* is *formally opposed* to the concept of finite essence — they are logical contraries. In a system whose methodology was logical analysis, this was not insignificant.) Being defined as *"Esse in se subsistens"* has meant *God was beyond all essences* which are the one and only source of intelligibility for human beings, and so it rendered God incomprehensible to us. So, if God is "Being" and confined by the formal characteristics of the concept (i.e., one, non-generic, super-essential, infinite, unchanging, etc.), then the question arises: whence come the finite essences, the "World of Ideas" that were said to reflect God's perfections? God's Unicity (as derived from "Being") is so profound and exclusive that every "causality" of which God is author must be conceived as being identical to the selfsame Act of Existence and self-awareness that is the eternal and immutable Essence of God. That means "to be" and "to think" and "to create" are one and the same thing in God. Could such a God "think" (which in God is "to be") finite essences? In other words, how can God *be* the model of the finite essences (however infinitely multiplied) that supposedly comprise the "World of Ideas," the creative blueprints that allow the participation of the physical world of matter and form in the being of God?

This logical/ontological incompatibility revisited the ancient Greek dilemma that a physically immutable, unchanging God could not have been responsible for the cosmological movements

---

But, when not considered revelation, mystical experience has not been an acceptable starting point for western theology. Basing Religion on direct mystical experience would completely level the playing field and relativize Religion. It would forever eliminate the claims of any one religion to a unique objective superiority. It would also establish *experience*, and therefore the human being as the ultimate determining factor in doctrinal construction. This may explain why the authorities of western religious institutions have always discountenanced mystical experience and discouraged their followers from its pursuit.

— the antecedent and consequent events — that created finite beings. In the ancient world the "*Logos*-Demiurge" was conceived by the Greeks as a secondary deity not restricted by the immutability of the "One," precisely to account for this "movement" not compatible with the un-moved mover. The difficulty as it resurfaced in the context of mediaeval ontologism, however, had no such recourse. For in the meantime the *Logos* had been redefined at Nicea as *homoousion,* consubstantial with the Father, "God," the "One," the immutable *esse in se subsistens,* and was no longer available as a demi-god, a "divine" interface to account for change and finitude.

The Thomistic concept of analogy was developed to confront this difficulty. It was, in effect, an attempt to *dismiss the problem by claiming it was intrinsic to the very concept of being* itself and therefore to God. It said there were no incompatibilities to be reconciled. The only problem had been our failure to understand that *the contraries of finite vs. infinite were integral to being itself;* God embraced the finite within the infinite as being includes all finite essences. To my mind this amounted to sleight-of-hand. It re-defined the concept of being by attributing to it a content gleaned from the analysis of *other concepts.* That included everything being was capable of embracing, effectively retro-fitting the concept as a *quasi-genus* assigning it data that it did not originally possess. It was one example of the difficulties created by the ancient method of going from concepts to reality.

So it begged the question on a grand scale. The concept of *infinite being,* once it was re-defined by analogy as *internally composed* of the very incompatibilities thought to invalidate it, functioned to *internalize* finitude in God and eliminate the need for a semi-divine *Logos* to mediate between an infinite, immutable God and a finite world in motion. Analogy was a scholastic life-jacket fabricated to save the metaphysical anomaly created at Nicea.

The Ontological Argument

The perennial, distinctively western confusion between the logical and the real was responsible for other problems as well. For the mediaeval scientists "God" was the conclusion of a scientific syllogism based on the axiom of the necessity of being. In a world where *"if being is, being must be,"* "God" was considered *necessary* because *being* had to exist. We might add, at least the *idea* of God *had* to exist. But it is *unthinkable* that the *idea* of the Reality that sustained all of what did in fact exist, might refer to what did *not* exist. Therefore, it has been a perennial temptation in the West to draw from this subsequent "reasoning," the conclusion that God *must* exist. This came to be known, ironically, as the "ontological argument." Anselm, Descartes and Leibniz presented this argument in its most undisguised form where there was no doubt they were going from ideas to reality, from the logical to the real order. But others claim *every argument* based on the "axiom" of the necessity of being (*"if being is, being must be"*) is a version of the ontological argument, and suffers from the same flaw. Any necessity, they claim, is logical only, i.e., derives from the idea, not experienced reality. All these problems derive from the ancient Western claim to be able to discover reality from an analysis of concepts.

Defining God as "Being" has also been responsible for some of the peculiar vagaries of popular western religiosity. For the "concept of God" as the barren abstract conclusion of a rational syllogism, or as "pure Being," was too vapid to earn a place in the mind's eye of most people. Except for the philosophers, "God" remained adsorbed to earlier mythologies whose vivid hold on the imagination was far stronger, and therefore "God" was understood *anthropomorphically.* It was impossible to prevent it. It might not be unreasonably argued that the notion of "God" in the West has, in practice, *always been a metaphor* because, in spite of its perennial "scientific" imagelessness (or perhaps because of it) it has never been able to rid itself of anthropomorphism. This identifies but doesn't solve any problems. For being recognized as an anthropomorphism doesn't necessarily prevent a metaphor from being taken literally.

Against this background, it becomes completely understandable why the ancient Greeks would be drawn to accept the man Jesus as divine. It filled a vacuum of the imagination about "God" created by the airy abstractions of Greek rationalism. Yet, it was also

Greek rationalism that gave the divinity of Christ its ultimate significance. In various ways, the abstract Greek notion of God, the "One," was applied to Jesus, and eventually took precedence over the earlier identification of Jesus with the dramatic, death-conquering "god-men" of the mysteries. From very early on, Jesus became identified with the *Logos* of the One.

The Judaic notion of God, the other source of the Western idea of God, despite the Jewish abhorrence for idolatrous representations, was not anywhere near "imageless." Semitic poetry generated the anthropomorphic picture of a Yahweh who interacted "humanly," like a Father and Mother, or passionate warrior-lover, sometimes angry, sometimes tender, with the Hebrew People. It was that powerful Paternal image that Jesus made visible and alive by relating to it as "Son." "God" was not an ethereal philosophical concept for Jesus or the Jews. God was their "Father." But the Greeks were not Jews. For the Greeks the "divinity" of Christ filled a void that had been left in the wake of the rationalist discreditation of the traditional myths by the philosophers. Defining God as "Being," then as now, was too abstract to imagine.

The Greek philosophical concept of God as "Being" ultimately became the operative factor in the Christian conception of the divinity of Jesus. This is proved by the fact that its imagery came to reside in the notion of the *Logos* of the "One" along the lines explored by Philo (following Plato and the Stoics). The original association of Jesus with the kind of divinity found in the mystery religions soon became relegated to second place. The identification of Jesus with the *Logos* of God was made very early as seen in the gospel of "John." While it is undeniable that the Christian *Logos* (unlike the Platonic or Philonic) was a *person* and a human being claimed to have been known and touched by the witnesses, the divinity dimension in this conception was entirely of Greek philosophical origin. By contrast, the imagery derived from the mystery religions, clearly evidenced by early Christian iconography and sacramental rituals and the object of Paul's references in Corinthians, was never predominant in the writings accepted as canonical; and eventually came to be eliminated altogether.

- It might be relevant to note that these "contrasting" early Greek conceptions of the divinity of Jesus were *class-related*. The philosophical perspectives were the domain of the educated upper classes, while the mystery religions were, in general, embraced by the ordinary people, servants and slaves. The official association of Christian teaching authority with the ruling elite is thus shown to have begun very early.

- Another important point is that Greek philosophy, in spite of being focused on "God," was not strictly speaking "religion," but more properly "science." "God" in that genre was not primarily the object of awe and loving gratitude, but rather an item of intellectual enquiry, a *scientific fact* necessary to understand existence. As science, it was accepted as the "truth."

- It is instructive that, once awarded imperial status by the Romans, Jesus was redefined at Nicea as *Logos homoousios*, consubstantial with the Father. Since Jesus was the celestial counterpart of the Emperor of Rome; he could hardly be considered a secondary god. This fatally changed Jesus' religious role and significance. From the Jewish *rabbi-messiah* and then the Greek *Logos*, Jesus became the Roman *Pantocrator*, the All-Ruler, God-Almighty, the "Judge of the Living and the Dead." In my reading of history, the ultimate defining source of Jesus' "consubstantial" divinity, set in dogmatic stone in 325, was not God the Father, nor even the Council fathers, but rather the needs of the Roman Imperial Theocracy.

Pantheism and Panentheism

Defining God as "Being" also takes it very close to pantheism. This has been true of the western philosophical tradition since Plato and Plotinus. Many feel that, in spite of vigorous denials, the classic conception cannot be taken any other way. For in the traditional view, "being" comprehends all "essences," and the essence that is existence itself (God) is cognitively indistinguishable from anything and everything "else" that is. Besides, everything that exists, insofar as it exists, must partake of God's existence, since God is existence itself. By this definition God cannot be considered an "entity" apart from the rest of reality, and the existence of all other entities cannot be considered separate from God's existence. Finite reality does not have its "own" being. We are not permitted to imagine "being" as if it were "something" that God "has" and that now I "have" because God gives me some. In the traditional sense, "Being" is one, and all "being" is nothing less than God's very own Act of Existing. I exist only insofar as I "participate" in what God does, which is to exist. Like a sponge in the Sea, my existence is "part" of God-being-God. A term currently used to refer to this "participatory" existence is *"pan-entheism,"* which the Encyclopedia Britannica (1979) defines to mean "the view that the world is a finite creation within the infinite being of God."[142] For traditional theist theologians, the *immanence* of God in creation is as authentic a feature of divinity as *transcendence*.

This is the direct and unavoidable conclusion that follows from the "unicity" manifested by the "concept of being." *All being is one*. The fixed concept of being implies that there is *only one reality*, one changeless being. But our experience is *not* of one thing, but many, and *not* of permanence but change. Aware of this, Thomists tried to avoid pantheism by declaring the concept's predication "analogous" — by pure *fiat* as we mentioned earlier. So we impute changelessness and absolute simplicity to God as the unique proprietary subject of "Being," and to preserve "being's" absolute unicity, we allot creatures participation in the very same Being.

Furthermore, the "activity" imagined by a "common-sense" notion of creation *ad extram* would mean there was change in God, which was always considered impossible to "Pure Being."[143]

---

[142] EB 1979, 13: 975

[143] The *Logos* was originally conceived by the Greeks as a demi-god, — not "the One" but a "lesser divinity"— who could, without compromise to his nature, assume the role of *techné*, the craftsman who constructed the Cosmos. It was precisely this concept of *Logos* that Arius correctly identified as the original imagery underlying Jesus' "divinity." This Christology was unambiguously elaborated earlier in the adoptionism of Clement of Alexandria, and his inheritor Origen, in the Third Century. It was declared unacceptable at Nicea in 325 and resulted in the theology of the *homoousion* which established Jesus as absolutely equal to the Father. Arius was falsely condemned. Nicea must be recognized for the theological innovation that it really was.

By equating God and Being, traditional philosophical theology forces us to imagine that created things whose "forms" (from the World of Ideas) are generated in the One Necessary Act which *is* God's-self-knowing, then "emanate,"[144] or to use Thomas' evocative word, "proceed"[145] (as an element of the processions within the Trinity) into existence "*out of*" the exemplary mind of God and "*into*" participation in God's existence which is the very same Unique and Necessary Act. Please note: there is no movement possible here. For Aquinas, creation is not an *event*, it's a *relation* of dependency within the one all-embracing Act which is God.[146] *For classic theology, there is only one ontological "event," the Act of God existing.*

This unimaginable conception avoids pantheism only by some dazzling scholastic footwork like Aquinas' notion of analogy. As a matter of fact, this ethereal scholastic idea of God as "Being," however perennial among Western thinkers, always remained an arcane and esoteric doctrine, a "minority report" in Church circles, the province of a small intellectual elite. *It never functioned in general practice.* It was, in effect, rejected by the Church for mainline pastoral use. Those that preached it from the pulpit were routinely condemned as pantheists by the Inquisition, as in the case of Meister Eckhart, and the posthumous condemnation of the extraordinary 9th century Irish monk, John Scotus Eriugena.

Once Nicea had eliminated the idea of the *Logos*-as-demiurge and insisted that the *Logos* was itself as fully God as the "One," theology was denied its traditional solution to the problem of creation. This "internalized" creation (finiteness) within the Godhead, thus making the perennial classical world-view even more pantheistic — which forced Aquinas to adapt and utilize Aristotle's concept of analogy as an escape mechanism.

This didn't work. And when it fell apart early in the 14th century, the edifice Thomas built on Analogy collapsed into its two constituent and contrary directions simultaneously — the empiricism of the Franciscan, Ockham, who followed out Scotus giving priority to finite being, and the mystical panentheism of the Dominican, Eckhart, who perhaps more faithful to Thomas' own priorities, saw all reality as a manifestation of infinite being.

[144] ST. I, 45, 1 and passim
[145] ST. I, 28, 4;
[146] ST. I, 45, 2 ad 2

Creation: The Mask of God

So where do we stand? Clearly, we are no closer to a definitive answer to the question of "God" than our ancestors. All we've done in this chapter is to make an attempt to clear the air. We've offered a series of reflections on the source of the significance of the concept of Being especially as it has been applied to "God." If we challenged the validity of the traditional analyses and the conclusions that were drawn from them, it was not primarily to present other "answers" even though some were suggested; it was to assure ourselves that the ones we inherited are not, as once believed, *science*.

We record and cherish these ancient calculations, none the less; but not because they're science. They mean more to us than that. They represent eons of tireless tracking on the part of our tradition trying to follow the faint footsteps of God. Who can fail to be awed at the sense of the sacred, the love of life and yearning for immortality that these millennia of meditations evoke. They are the poem of our people. Whatever else they may or may not be, they are the treasure maps of those who were determined to find and drink directly from the Holy Grail that gave us life and this garden of delights. *They would kiss the very face of God.* No one can fault them for that. And no one can fault us for sharing their obsession.

The science of our times suggests to us that reality is our Universe-in-Process. Is there some way we can bring together the perennial poetry of our people and our science? God as elaborated by the traditional western cultural and intellectual project is "Being." If our science says that the Process is "being," does that coincidence also suggest that perhaps God is not distinguishable from this Universe? Even traditional theists who maintain that God is invincibly *transcendent* admit that God is also intimately and suffusively *immanent* in creation. So, if we dared project an image based on this hypothetical syncretism, it would look at least like *panentheism*. At least from a phenomenological point of view, it would mean God *is* this universe of things, including us. God *is* —

visibly, audibly, mathematically, and "conceptually" — indistinguishable from our universe and us as part of it. "God" is simply another metaphor for "being," meaning everything, this whole Universe of matter-energy in process, and "being" for "God."

The ancients said the essences of the life-forms that comprise our world were the very *ideas* that comprised God's self-knowledge. The "forms" of things mirrored the divine perfections. And they thought they knew both how and why that was. We may demur on the specifics of that vision but still find the overall identity between God and the universe acceptable. This is *at least* a functional, phenomenological, if not metaphysical pantheism; it's how God "appears." This echoes Eriugena who called created things "theophanies" — the self-manifestations of God. We are the "mask" God wears, he said. It's not only way we know God, *it's the way God knows Himself.*[147]

But many will find *panentheism* unsatisfying because it seems to offer us *no image for God except ourselves*. Our "conclusions" about an immanent God may account for our sense of the sacredness of reality, but it leaves unresolved our loneliness and our endemic perplexity about death. Panentheism means all things, including us, are "God" in some sense. Many of us are not easily convinced that *we are ourselves* what we have always thought of God: permanent existence, and the object of awe and loving gratitude.

But then again, our reflections suggest that "God" may not be the immutable permanence, the changeless "One" the traditional "concept of being" has projected, either. If *being is becoming*, might not "God" also be "in process"? Could it be that the real "God" whose "image and likeness" we have always claimed to be, is *emerging* from the latent possibilities of these lonely hunters, the "things-that-exist-in-time-and-change" as we forge ever more complex and intensely conscious forms of life? This conception is similar to what Teilhard de Chardin, Bergson, Whitehead, Sri Aurobindo[148] and others have been saying about the goal of evolu-

---

[147] John Scotus Eriúgena, *Periphysion*, III 689B, quoted in Deirdre Carabine, *John Scottus Eriugena,* New York: Oxford U. Press, 2000, p.36
[148] Sri Aurobindo, *The Essential Aurobindo*, Lindisfarne Books, 1987

tion. Perhaps our evanescent identities (our impermanent "selves") and the moral constructions we make through them are more important as contributions to that emergence than our tradition — or the Buddhist tradition — has prepared us to accept. *Perhaps the energy-field which is this evolving Universe is "God" in formation.*

It seems that, as the custodians of morality and finality, we have to live that way, anyhow. Would Pascal say it was worth a wager?

Buddhism

For its part, it seems to me, Buddhism makes sense only if you assume some kind of single substance or pantheism. But notice that Buddhism also requires a strenuous life-long asceticism to counteract what it considers the "illusions" that are contrary to its moral program. Original (Theravada) Buddhism believed enlightenment was impossible outside the monastery. The doctrine of *anatman* — that the "self" is an illusion — lies at the heart of the Buddhist vision and is quite contrary to our spontaneous sense of ourselves. This can only mean that Buddhists do not naturally embrace pantheism or panentheism either, just like us. Is our "natural instinct" in this case telling us something — or is it as deluded here as it is in so many other things?

I believe confusion over the reliability of "natural spontaneities" was also a problem that faced the ancient Greeks who opted for god-men, Dionysus, Mithra, Osiris, Jesus, rather than rely solely on the dry Saharan theorems of Platonic and neo-platonic pantheism. Greek philosophical speculation may have dispelled more illusion than people were able to handle.

Something similar may account for Buddhism emerging at about the same time in history as the first recorded ancient Greek Philosophers. Who could fail to be struck with the convergence? In both Greece and India, apparently worlds apart, there coincided a rationalist discreditation of the "gods" along with an unusual antipathy toward the body which took the form of communities of celibate ascetics interested in achieving an absolute quiescence of desire as the path to an ultimate immortality. In the West, this asceticism, characteristic of the Pythagoreans who had such a strong influence on Plato, came to be connected with the belief in the ultra-reality of *spirit* as the relevant factor in the human phenomenon and so retained an individualistic character. In the East, *anatman,* that the "self" is an illusion, came to prevail. Despite their contrary conclusions, each served as a logical ground to anti-body asceticism.

Among the Greeks, the first great debates about "being" took place in this context common in other respects with India. A transnational sharing of ideas must have occurred around 500 BCE sweeping across the fertile crescent from end to end, establishing the primacy of the "concept of being" in philosophical discourse. Buddhist scriptures report that the Buddha expressly rejected any validity to the division between "being and non-being"; so there is some evidence that they had become the terms of the debate in ancient India as well. If pantheism / panentheism offers a convincing interpretation of reality, the Buddhist perspective, philosophically speaking, would seem to be a logical response at least, in spite of the spontaneous "illusions" like the individual "self," that appear to challenge it.

Mystics of all ages and cultures, after all, have concurred with the sense of the sacred unity of all things. In any event, the alienated disdain for matter as death-bearing and corrupt, in contrast with an imaginary "spirit," is a European Christian inheritance. It has been at the root of some of the most irresponsible and abusive behavior — individual and collective — to be found in any culture, anywhere. We are well rid of it. The minimum conclusion to be drawn from our reflections is this: the material substrate of our lives is Sacred. Whether we concur with *panentheism* or not, we are invited to see the matter-energy of all things, including ourselves as somehow "divine."

Appendix to Chapter IV

Jean Paul Sartre

Right from the start, Sartre (*Being & Nothingness*, 1956, tr. Barnes) simply assumes the question of "being" is a relevant question. So he asks about the "being of the phenomenon" and its relationship to consciousness. He concludes that the consciousness of being is the being of consciousness.

But I have a basic question about the question itself. Does the fact that we can ask the question of the meaning of being make it meaningful? Is it possible that the *question* of being is itself an extrapolation from experiences that really have nothing to do with it and which do not require any "existential" analysis for their complete and satisfactory understanding? Again, the false assumption seems to be, "I can ask the question, therefore it must be relevant."

Of course one might argue, "it is relevant *to me*." But in that case the question could be asked *of my question* and not necessarily of "being." The question, "why do I ask the question?," may have a satisfying answer which may not necessarily be metaphysically significant. The answer may be, as we suggested in the main text, "I ask the question because I have falsely interpreted my death as the cessation of being and not only as change." Once the issue of death-as-*non-being* is eliminated, the question of the significance of "being" disappears, because *there is no non-being*. Everything is, always has been and never ceases to be. That is the "phenomenon of being."

One may then insist that the question of death, even if death is only change, is still dramatically relevant to me. I agree, but then it becomes a psychological or "spiritual" question (Sartre might say "existential"). It is no longer a "metaphysical" question. And, without the "metaphysical" question there can be no talk of "God" as traditionally conceived in the west — as "Necessary Being." The Source of the Sacred, or the question of my anguish over death, may continue to be pursued under another category, but not as "Being." The question of death is really the question of my *conscious self-identity,* not necessarily of "being." We have traditionally believed that they were one and the same precisely because we assumed the experience of "self" derived directly from the substantial (separable) existence of the spiritual soul. There is no other possible basis for belief in the independent, permanent reality of the "self."

Negation

Sartre then asks the question of the relationship between *negation and non-being*, and to my mind, he does not give a satisfactory answer. Any suggestion that verbal *negation* bears a necessarily *metaphysical* dimension, runs the risk of idealism — moving from the logical to the real. Bergson focused a large part of his repudiation of "non-being" on its unwarranted derivation from *negation*. When Sartre declares that the prior "existence" of *nothingness* (note the semantic contradiction, as well as the "substantive" word-form for "nothing") is the condition for the possibility of *negation*, he asserts the primordiality of non-being, as we have been accusing the western metaphysical project of doing all along. He suggests that *nothingness* or non-being "is the original condition of the questioning attitude and more generally all philosophical or scientific inquiry." (p.11)

Even so, if it were not done *metaphysically,* as Sartre does, I would have no problem with this statement. In other words, if it were rephrased to say, "the 'existence' of the *concept* of non-being *in us* is the original condition of the questioning attitude and more generally all philosophical or scientific inquiry," I would agree because I would understand it to include, as I have said, the possibility that this is a *false concept* that we generate because of a *false (metaphysical) interpretation of death*. I also believe, as I said above, that all western philosophy and science as well as religion, is built on this misinterpretation; and in that sense, Sartre is absolutely right. As descriptive of our local culture only, it holds true. But beyond that, it does not necessarily apply.

So much for the phenomenon of being.

The Song

With reference to the "being of the phenomenon," once we concede the possibility that "I," or any given "entity" (or phenomenon) may only be a mere modality of a substrate which is the true existent — once, in other words, the question is not necessarily about "metaphysical substance" — how do I ask it; what imagery can I use? Perhaps, a song? What is the "being" of a song? Does a song "exist"? When the song ends, does it's "being" end, cease? Does it fall into "nothingness"? What "exists," the individual notes, or the whole song, or none of the above? Is it a "song" if there's no human being to interpret these sounds as melody? If that's true, then is the "reality" of the song *as song* exclusively in its *being-perceived*? Is it only a modality of the perceiver or of the air on which it travels? Can we identify what "exists," i.e., what is metaphysically significant in all this?

I think this illustrates the elements of the "metaphysical" problem after "*essentia*-lism" and *"substantia*-lism."

When reality was identified with "essences" as it was in the world of Plato, what was real was the "seminal idea" as conceived and eternally present in the Mind of God. This corresponded to the belief that all being was God's being. Plato would have said that "song" was an *eternal idea* of God the creator, (and therefore a subsistent idea) and all songs were simply reproductions in matter, space and time, of that eternal idea. A material instance of "song," however, would have had only a *shadow existence*, secondary and derived, permitting a *glimpse* of the invisible but *really real* archetype of song which existed in the Mind of God.

When reality came to be identified with "substances" and "entities" in the days of the Aristotelian ascendancy (which includes early modern science), the individual sounds, or perhaps the individual harmonic components might have been conceded the quality of *real*, but only as modalities of the air or whatever medium bore the sound waves. The medium would have been considered the true "substance," the sound waves would have been called "accidents." Similarly, on the perceiving end, as far as the "song" as a totality was concerned, it would have been given *mental* existence. It would have been considered an accident of the perceiver who was the substance with being.

But for much of philosophy today what "exists" is the phenomenon alone. There is no invisible reality, no "essence" or "substance," hidden behind or beyond the phenomenon. "What you see is what you get." Similar to a song, the existence of *anything* is now conceived exactly *as it appears* in its condition of flux and change, along with the necessary presence of an observer and reporter. Also, the traditional assumption that there are "separate entities" has been called into question. An evolving reality, like a song, is not one fixed thing, but an unbroken sequence of phenomena changing continuously through time. Also, like a song, it may only be a "modality," an accident, like waves of some other "substrate," which in turn, may be only the "modality" of something else.

Corollary to this, the song's "existence," i.e., its coherence as phenomenal reality, requires that it be *perceived*. The presence of the perceiver-of-being actively perceiving is one of the *constitutive elements* of "existence" in a phenomenological world. What this means, of course, is that we cannot get out of the fact that "existence" is a human construct which is forged from the *experience of experiencing*. The very coherence we are accustomed to call "existence itself" is only available within the context of human experience. Being is itself a "phenomenon."

I want to emphasize: I am *not* denying existence, nor am I saying that reality is a projection of our imaginings, or created by our perceptions. I am rather trying to stress the active conceptual conformation (some may say *deformation*) imposed *by our perceiving* on what we perceive. The phenomenon as it comes to us for analysis is *already* a human product, anteriorly shaped and formed *by us*. Experience, even experience of something supposedly as simple as "being," is active and creative. It is not passive, as naïve realism claims.

Of course, the fact that human consciousness has *evolved from* the very reality it scrutinizes, suggests that the process and products of consciousness are integral to it. We suspect it's this integrity itself that leaves us unable to determine whether human knowledge is the result or the cause, derivative or creative (or both) of the congruence it experiences. This connatural identity with the reality around us is the unfathomable and always mysterious source of our sense of transparent clarity, but also of our perplexity, doubt and wonder — and inescapably, awe and gratitude which I for one, call "Sacred."

This leads us to conclude that what we say about existence is ... *a poem?*... or should we say, a *song*? Now, there is nothing shameful in this, in spite of what our scientific standards of objectivity and universality demand. What it does is to make clear that our cultural projects, which include not only our religion but also our science and philosophy, are just that, *songs* — local, relative, limited, contextualized historically, linguistically and ethnically — but, none the less creative, provocative, challenging, sometimes empowering, sometimes frustrating, always intoxicating*!* poetry*!*

Should it surprise us that our poetry is more humanly engaging, and therefore *more ontologically important* than the obsessive demand for an impossible absolute clarity, absolute objectivity, which we recognize is a function of our pathological lust for *absolute control*? What we do is supremely creative, that's what's most *true* about it.

Should it *ever* become acceptable to us that what is most relevant for "being" is *what we are actively creating*, not what we have "discovered" or "proven," and can control, then and finally, perhaps, we will allow ourselves to be satisfied that even our "scientific" projects are only expressions of poetic creativity, artistic insight and visionary daring. The Sacred Reality they discern, "as through a glass, darkly" may not reside in the past, but in the future.

Sartre and Nothingness

Sartre, after criticizing Hegel's essentialist conception of *non-being*, makes it clear that he believes "nothingness" is a *structure of consciousness* necessary to explain the possibilities of *negation,* which include *anguish* over future self-betrayal and the conscious rejection of past moral resolutions. This evidence, however, might not always exist. The structure could be simply explained, as I suggest, as a misinterpretation of the significance of death, and therefore, *possibly,* subject to suspension. In other words, the two phenomena might be so thoroughly linked that once the generally accepted interpretation of *death as non-being* is called into question, the "cleavages" (sic) that constitute *anguish* might disappear. The *separations* ("cleavages") that Sartre claims consciousness is able to place between the present "self" and either past or future "selves" are *possible* but not necessary, universal or invariable, and might actually be tied to illusion. In much of daily living the simple process of seeing, resolving and executing is an undistracted, interlocked, unitary sequence, possibly interrupted by external obstacles, but *not* by consciousness except under the rare circumstance when it confronts its own dissolution. But if dissolution is illusion, then it's a false consciousness ... and it proves nothing.

So if it's only *possible*, isn't that a problem? Shouldn't metaphysics *as a science* at least *begin* with the invariable, necessary and universal structures of reality?

Imagination and being

In this regard, the absolute necessity of the suspension of the judgment of reality, effectively *negation,* in the case of *operations of the imagination* seems a more compelling argument offered by Sartre. But it also has its weaknesses. He says consciousness knows clearly that two mental images, the same in every other respect, are supremely different when one is *imagined* and the other is *real.* The self awareness which is *imagination* utilizes a structure of consciousness which specifically recognizes non-reality, non-being. Given the fact that human childhood is characterized by imaginative conceptualization, either as a separate activity, or as ancillary to play, one is more inclined to see it as evidence of the presence of an invariable and necessary structure — this proves the existence of foundational "negation." He concludes that the *ability to deny existence implies the recognition of existence as existence.* Hence being and nothingness are correlatives.

But it doesn't goes as far as Sartre claims. For the phenomenon is as easily attributed to the awareness of simple *presence*, as to the so-called "experience of being." In other words, the ability to distinguish the "real" from the "un-real" does not necessarily imply a contrast between existence and non-existence but between presence and non-presence — which really means only experience and non-experience. He invalidly assumes that the judgment of experience is identical to the judgment of existence, thus betraying his own uncritical realism.

In this case as in all the others, I disagree with his traditional insistence on the primordiality of non-being. This insistence is at the core of the Western projections about "being" and Sartre continues that tradition. I have a problem with the elaboration of the "characteristics" of being, projecting being beyond simple *presence,* which assumes an *understanding* of existence, its meaning, its significance, and not just a recognition that *presence* is different from non-presence. This illusory "understanding" includes the unicity of being, the "improbability" of being, being as a positive quality requiring a "necessary cause" — all of these characteristics are derived from and corollary to the *primordiality of non-being*. For me this is evidence of the imposition of the structural characteristics of our *concept-of-being* onto reality, and goes far beyond the simple awareness of the difference between what is present and what is not. Hidden behind Sartre's over-extension of "negation" and "imagination" into structural *nothingness* is the ur-contradiction that *non-being exists*.

But being is all there is. There is no "non-being" to provide a horizon for being *ex machina*. The only other pathway to establish the kinds of "metaphysical" divisions within being requiring a relationship of ontological dependency would have to assume the existence of *metaphysically separate entities*, which is exactly what is at issue. The presumption of independent individual existence is what Buddhist *anatman* challenges as illusion. And the more we restrict ourselves to an analysis that is exclusively phenomenological, the more difficult it becomes to identify (or deny) a fixed and singular entity in a matrix world of flux and change. The entire universe may be one single "entity," responsible for its own existence. It may be "God." If you choose to reject this, as you very well may, please be aware that it's your choice, it's not *science.*

It's undeniable that all things are *phenomenologically individual.* This is clearly dependent on many things, perhaps even the *time-frame* in which we human beings currently are able to experience them; for a change in the sense of duration might radically alter the perception of individuality. It is a matter of choice and *fiat,* however, to claim they are *metaphysically individual.* This doesn't mean we are denying that they are the individuals we perceive them to be. It just means we have no basis on which *to know for certain one way or the other.* To a phenomenologist, anyhow, it is irrelevant. Traditional metaphysics *as science* terminates with the analysis of its possibility. Or perhaps it's better to say that metaphysics is the science of the known characteristics of the "concept of being," but that it doesn't tell us much at all. What it does do, however, is set the limits which prevent the mis-characterization of our culturally creative "philosophical" constructs as universal and objective. This reduces much of the detail in philosophy and religion to ethics and choice, preference and predilection — the art of living, the art of writing, not the science of being.

CHAPTER V
The Testimony of the Mystics I: Meister Eckhart

We have a host of witnesses from every religious tradition on the planet who have been willing to go on record about their direct experience of "God." What is truly remarkable is that from vastly different perspectives and separated by millennia of time, many agree on one fundamental feature of the God they have met: God resided within themselves. Some go even further and say that they experienced God *as themselves*.

The first one we'll look at is Meister Eckhart, a 14th century Christian. He was a Dominican priest and theologian from the Rhine Valley in Germany.

I. Eckhart's life and work

Born in 1260, Johannes Eckhart joined the mendicant Dominican Order in 1275 the same year its most famous theologian, Thomas Aquinas, died. Eckhart studied and then taught theology in Cologne in the Rhine Valley. He received his "masters" in Paris whence the sobriquet "Meister." He later taught there at the University that was the epicenter of Mediaeval thought. He was the provincial of his Order in Germany from 1303 to 1314.

Much of his work has come down to us in the form of sermons that appear to have been delivered in the Rhineland to groups of lay people who had an interest in contemplation and living the evangelical counsels without wishing to join a Religious order. Eckhart was the Dominican Prior at Strasbourg during the period after 1314. There seems little doubt that the authority structures of the Church were an issue for these people who were in fact part of a generalized movement.

These groups of lay people were closely associated with the Dominican Order and in all probability included members of a lay women's movement known as the Beguines that flourished in the Low Countries and the German Rhineland, dedicated to poverty and contemplative spirituality.[149] They were suppressed early in 1318 by the ecclesiastical authorities after they were declared "heretical."

The Beguines existed for two full centuries from about 1120 to 1318 and enjoyed ecclesiastical approval during most of that time. Commentators point out how intrinsically vulnerable the movement was, given the controls universally exercised over women in those times. Beguines were precariously situated between the household with its protective dominating male, and the convent, structured *by* and ultimately *for* the protection of celibate males in a society convinced that sexual activity was evil. Sex, the apotheosis of "sin," supposedly originated with the stimulation that came from women. This entire treatment of women was a predictable result of the Platonic definition of "matter," which we have dealt with extensively in these essays.

Heresy, Aristocracy and Revolution

In spite of solid academic credentials and a distinguished ecclesiastical career,[150] Eckhart was hounded by accusations of heresy for the last seven years of his life. A number of Eckhart's propositions were denounced by the local Inquisition in the Rhineland's Cologne in the 1320's. It seems hardly possible that the Meister's troubles with the authorities were unconnected with the contemporaneous campaign of the Inquisition to eliminate the Beguines. Smoldering disapproval on the part of the authorities for this "anarchic" feminist movement was made official with their condemnation in 1312 at the Council of Vienna and the publication of Papal decrees against them in that year and again in 1318.

---

[149]"Beguines" *Encyclopædia Britannica.* Ultimate Reference Suite DVD 2006

[150] Forman, *Meister Eckhart,* Element, Rockport MA, 1991 p.48, says that after the death of Duns Scotus in 1308 Eckhart had few rivals among Western Christian theologians.

Some Dominicans thought that since the original charges of "heresy" against Eckhart were made by a Franciscan, it was possibly an instance of the inveterate rivalry between those two orders. On that premise, the Dominicans had the case transferred to the papal court at Avignon. Eckhart wrote a defense and retraction of error which was subsequently rejected by the papal Inquisition and he was condemned again, this time by the highest authorities. Acknowledging the retractations, the pope, John XXII, published the condemned propositions in a bull of 1329.[151] It's not known how they planned to proceed against him. But Eckhart had already died of natural causes in 1327; he was 67 years old.

What seems clear in any case was that "heresy" was a catch-all category that did not necessarily explain the objections of the authorities, either toward Eckhart or the Beguines. Eckhart was a traditional Catholic Christian, which was reflected in his claim to strict orthodoxy. Most of what he wrote could hardly have raised an eyebrow. It was all there: Creation by God, the Trinity, Jesus the Lord, Church, sacraments, sin, repentance, heaven and hell. Except for a shift in emphasis, we would recognize all the usual elements. His belief in providence, for example, was indistinguishable from the version we criticized in the beginning of chapter 3. None of this could have been grist for the Inquisitor's mill.

It was rather in his attempt to express the experience of the presence of God in the depths of his own soul that he went beyond the ordinary terminology and imagery of his day. It drew the attention of the authorities. He identified the God he worshipped as the *existential core of his own personality*. His belief that sincere surrender to that Source would necessarily replace our finite selves with the Infinite Self of which we were only a pale reflective participation, was interpreted by the ecclesiastical establishment as much more than devotional *hyperbole* — they called it pantheism. When he said the human soul was "an aristocrat," they claimed that he didn't mean it as a metaphor. A universal aristocracy would be a threat to the stability of a traditional, highly stratified mediaeval Christendom.

---

[151] *In Agro Domenico* March 27, 1329

It made him the Father of Rhineland Mysticism and insured that he would be the target of accusations of subversion long after he was dead and gone. His revolutionary perspectives have led many to claim him as the "Father of the Protestant Reformation," though he never considered himself other than an orthodox Catholic. His "doctrine" certainly differed from Luther's; but all would admit the spirit of their theological innovations were similar and led to similar confrontations with authority. It's in that spirit, diffused throughout the Rhineland by Eckhart and followers, like Tauler, Suso, Ruysbroeck, that historians see Eckhart's connection to the Reformation.

The message of the Rhineland Mystics was so well rooted and so widespread in the region that a full two hundred years later it seemed the attitudes it had unleashed would become a thorn in the side of the German Princes newly liberated by Luther from Roman control. The "protestant" peasants of the Rhine Valley revolted in 1525 against the "protestant" Princes' failure to reform the system of serfdom. It was the spontaneous eruption of a revolutionary egalitarianism, a pervasive Rhineland belief that was reminiscent of what Eckhart called the "aristocratic soul," the divine core of every human being that put them on a par with their feudal lords.

In the aftermath of the betrayal by the German nobles who followed-up the peasants' voluntary capitulation with savage massacres, pacifist religious traditions like the Mennonites, Amish, Brethren, were born among the Rhineland peasants. These groups were all proponents of a similar mystical vision with its accompanying rural communitarianism and simplicity of life. Some have even claimed that Karl Marx, born in Trier in the same Rhineland, was an even more distant heir of that same spirit.[152]

Eckhart was Thomist to the bone. Thomas' residual neo-Platonism, often downplayed by later commentators, inspired Johannes Eckhart. It was as a convinced neo-Platonist that the existential insight of mediaeval philosophy became a missionary driving force in the Meister's life. Though recognized as an accom-

---

[152] Cf Matthew Fox "Meister Eckhart and Karl Marx," in *Understanding Mysticism*, ed. Robert Woods, O.P. Garden City, NJ; Image Books 1980, pp 541-563

plished academic, he saw himself primarily as a spiritual teacher. If the insight about being was true — if individual human existence is really God's existence — the implications for the ordinary person were huge. It signified nothing less than the total reconceptualization of the stony, pusillanimous, punitive god which the Western establishment, starting with Rome, had chiseled down out of the great-hearted loving "Father" of Jesus' open universalism. If God were not "other" than us, opposed to us, foreign to us, — if God, in other words, were one with us — then life was union, love, gift, generosity, abandon and the joy of self validation. Gone was congenital guilt, servile fear, groveling obeisance, and the grasping and hoarding spawned by insecurity. That to be one with God was not only *God's will* but God's own doing, *already and definitively accomplished in creation*, requiring only our acquiescence and surrender for its ultimate fulfillment, was, for Eckhart, heaven on earth. It stood in stark contrast to the Monster-God conjured by Augustine, Anselm, and later, Calvin — a God Who would blithely condemn all of humankind to eternal damnation, including newborn infants, for Adam's insult to the divine dignity. The God Eckhart glimpsed in Jesus, was not interested in defending his "dignity" by punitive violence ... and invited us to do the same.

The doctrine of Original Sin might have chilled this sense of abandon, but it didn't. While Eckhart never denied Original Sin, he ignored it. And well he could. For, in the 13th century the angry, insulted God imagined by Original Sin was theoretically no longer relevant to daily life. God had been rendered irreversibly benevolent by the almost universal erasure of "Original Sin" by Christian baptism.[153] What *was* relevant to Eckhart, however, was the existential relationship between Creator and creature; and it revealed an entirely different God, conspicuously like Jesus' merciful Father who was hopelessly in love with humankind. This was

---

[153] The existence of the Jews, of course, marred this cherished fantasy. The Jews were not baptized. According to the implications of Augustine's doctrine, they were still the object of God's wrath for the insult of Original Sin, and always a potential magnet for divine retribution, in the form of natural disasters in the region where they lived. This is why one of the responses to the Plague in the 14th century was the massacre of Jews.

the insight Eckhart transmitted to the simple people with whom he shared his message. God's creative immanence made them all "aristocrats," they were born of noble blood, their inner value was absolute and inalienable because they shared God's very being. The inquisitors were understandably upset. "He confused and mislead the ordinary people," they said.

Alienation and Justification in the Late middle Ages

Eckhart identified God as the creative source of his own personality in a manner that was intended to emphasize a primordial homogeneity with God leading to eventual fusion. That dynamic, that interrelationship of notions, is characteristic of mysticism. The *mystical perspective* typically starts with the *unity* of God and humankind; its premise is that the holy is already *given*. It then goes on to describe its development and full flowering.

In Western Christian culture the mystical perspective contrasts sharply with what I call the *moral-legal perspective*, which is quite the opposite. This latter attitude was always a strong current within mediaeval thinking and increasingly so during Eckhart's time. It ultimately came to dominate western Christian religious ideology. The moral-legal perspective starts with a presumed *opposition or separation* as the primordial status of the relationship between God and humankind. It assumes that God and we are hostile strangers. It believes that *connection* with this distant and forbidding God — grace — must be earned, achieved.

The notion that the primordial condition of mankind is an *alienation from God* which must be overcome by human labor, seems so fundamental to modern Christianity that we forget that it was not always so. It's interesting in this regard that original Christianity, in the mind of the New Testament author Paul of Tarsus, was born as a *mystical alternative* to *legalistic Judaism*.[154] As Paul saw it, the oppressive requirements of the Jewish Law were *annulled* by being pre-emptively fulfilled by the death and resurrection of Jesus, freeing his Christian followers from the obligations of the Law, what Peter described as the "burden neither we nor our fa-

---

[154] cf Romans chapters 5 through 8

thers could bear."[155] Four hundred years after the writing of the New Testament, Augustine's fantasies elaborated the doctrine of Original Sin which would eventually obviate the mystical unity that early Christians claimed was forged *hapax,*[156] once and for all, by Jesus' death and resurrection. Augustine's personal projections newly reinstated *alienation and separation* as the primordial condition of human life. In my opinion it was an extension of his own obsessive guilt about his past, generated to justify his betrayal of his lower-class marriage partner in the pursuit of his upper-class career, which required her dismissal.[157] Unfortunately it resulted

---

[155] Acts 15:10

[156] Epistle to the Hebrews: 9:26

[157] The interpretation that follows here, to my knowledge, is mine. It is based on the patent fact that Augustine dismissed his mistress (whose name we are never given), the mother of his son Adeodatus, well before his real "conversion," in order to accommodate his mother's arrangement for his "marriage" with a 15 year-old Christian girl of noble Roman birth. He promptly took a concubine to "tide him over" until the betrothed came of age, apparently a compromise entirely acceptable to the great "saint" Monica. One suspects Monica's desire to convert Augustine to Christianity, later touted as a traditional model for the mothers of "sinners," had less to do with his "salvation" than his political future in embracing the religion of the Emperor.

In my opinion, Augustine's subsequent "conversion" was a subconscious self-manipulation designed to extricate himself from that sleazy arrangement in order to recuperate his lost integrity *without* returning to the dead-end life and wife he had abandoned. Celibacy was the price he was willing to pay for that liberation. He was never able to integrate his lower-class married life with his career aspirations, for one thing because his upper-class status would not tolerate it. But I emphasize: his conversion was subaltern to his career decision. His admission in the *Confessions* that sending his partner away was the hardest thing he had ever done, is for me the giveaway. Please note: he made that "supreme sacrifice" *before* his full conversion. Apparently he had plenty of "free will" for that career choice even in the "absence of grace." Augustine was at least honest about what happened and thorough in his description, and so we can interpret the events. Thus does "career" make cowards and monsters of us all. He never recognized the whole episode as a knot of betrayal, in my opinion, because he was invincibly upper-class. He was not able to overcome his conviction that Imperial Christianity was a sacred community designed by Providence for the salvation of the world. One joins the Church, in Augustine's view, in order to *become* holy. The sinner is not holy, he is helpless. The perhaps *only* moral choice he *can* make is to join the Church. The presumption is that the sinner is trapped in his sin, not free, exactly what Augustine claimed about himself (folin one of the most damaging archetypal ruling notions of Western culture. Once this difference between the legal and mystical perspective is recognized, it's not difficult to situate the revolutionary phenomenon of Eckhart's mysticism and its suppression by the Inquisition in the 14th century.

By the high Middle Ages Christianity was regressing into a moralistic legalism that worked hand in glove with the repressions of a feudal agrarian "Christendom," dominated by the Papacy, besieged and crumbling before an emerging national Europe that was increasingly town-centered, commercial and middle-class. Augustine's Roman reformulation of the Christian message under the over-arching fantasy of Original Sin, took on ever more oppressive features through these mediaeval centuries as one vain attempt after another to reform the venal and corrupt Church hierarchy failed. Those attempts at reform — part of the birth pangs of a modern Europe — elicited repressive counter-measures which always operated in the authoritarian, legalistic-moral mode.

Reform and Original Sin

This bi-polar spiral afflicting post-Mediaeval Christianity culminated in 1517 when Luther nailed his challenges to the Church door at Wittenberg. The reforms of the protestant revolt sought to apply an antidote for legalistic moralism, but what they came up with to take its place was not classic mysticism.

The Lutheran proposal validated human life and freed oppressed believers from the demands of obedience obsessed authority. But it did so with an ironic twist. For Luther said that we were "justified by faith, not by works." "Justification" was still uppermost in his mind, because justification was still in doubt.

---

lowing Paul). This is entirely consistent with all the elements of his battle against the Pelagians: on free will, original sin, baptism, predestination, the *ex opere operato* function of sacramental ritual, and his theory of history. Becoming Christian is not an act expressing personal integrity, because, in his view, without Christianity there is no integrity possible. It is rather a declaration of impotence and a surrender to the integrating, sustaining power of the community — like a "powerless" alcoholic joining AA. In this case, conveniently for Augustine's career, it was the Imperial Community.

The Doctrine of Original Sin was so firmly established in Christian ideology by Luther's day that the neo-platonic primordial unity that was so natural to Eckhart's mediaeval vision, allowing him virtually to ignore Original Sin, was no longer available to Luther, just as it was no longer available to the counter-reformers at Trent. For 16th century Christians, Catholic as well as Protestant, God's love came refracted through the prism of *permanent ontological alienation*, and thus for all, "justification" hung in the balance. Original Sin meant Permanent Hostility. It was believed to have created such an insurmountable barrier to God's union with us that it could *never* be erased, it could only be *inactivated* by an arbitrary divine decree, *voluntarily ignored* by a merciful God, and hence salvation (justification) was a matter of a forensic pardon and from there "salvation," but never real unity.. Many claim that all Christian theories of redemption from Original Sin effectively reproduce this paradigm, no matter what the mechanism of reconciliation proposed. Alienation is primordial and irremediable. Every new baby born inherits the hostility of God.

Luther said that humankind pardoned by grace was like a "dunghill covered with snow." Even the sacrifice of the cross, while it achieved pardon, was ultimately powerless to erase the original enmity between God and the human race. The power of the cross functioned "after the fact." According to Luther, we remained always guilty, though forgiven. God, out of sheer goodness, simply chose to not impose due punishment upon the *unforgivable crime* of Adam's original insult, and save individual humans because of the intervention in their lives of Christ and the Church. We were always simultaneously reprobate and reprieved. This must be recognized for the schizoid palliative that it was. It apparently worked for that era in practice, but its negative significance was too overwhelming to remain innocuous. Humanity was now confirmed as intrinsically and irreparably evil. We become God's friends only through the appropriation of the power of the cross.

This "solution" was not exclusive to Luther. It was common to the Christianity of the day. Catholicism, for its part, argued for a more mechanical (and supposedly more secure) justification guaranteed through *ex opere operato* effects of the sacraments. But it was also an extrinsic justification focused on avoiding an imagined imminent damnation; it did not re-establish original creation as the basis for mystical union. Thus, *alienation was institutionalized by Western Christianity* across the board. The Reformation and its Catholic reaction made it a permanent and general feature of modern European Culture.

Pre-Modern Mysticism

In the early 14^{tha} century, however, Eckhart didn't have such obstacles to contend with. The neo-platonic mysticism that dominated his thinking and held sway in the monasteries, it appears, through the end of the century,[158] seemed impervious to institutionalized guilt. Eckhart, like Luther, went straight to the heart of the matter: God's indisputable love. But, unlike Luther and his Catholic colleagues two centuries later who were forced to find mechanisms to circumvent a permanent "original" alienation, Eckhart was able to ground both the possibility and the actuality of God's love on what the "science" of his day had asserted about the very nature of reality itself. No by-pass mechanism was necessary. For creation was not only God's *doing*, it was God's *very Being*. Union with God was organic and primordial, permanent and inalienable.

Eckhart's spiritual message to his flock was based almost exclusively on the insights generated by philosophical theology. Scripture for him was ancillary: parables and stories apt for the illustration of the "scientific" truths of philosophical theology. Thus, for Eckhart, the Genesis Myth would have been taken figuratively, symbolically, in a way that did not contradict "science." His era believed that critical religious information — what we needed to know — was made available to us by God through various paths, some for the erudite, some for the uneducated; but they all said the same thing. They had to; there was only one "truth."

---

[158] This refers to the writings of late 14th century mystics, like the author of the *Cloud of Unknowing* who were clearly in the same neo-platonic tradition as Eckhart.

Eckhart's worldview: Participation in Being

As a neo-Platonist, Eckhart understood both creation and spiritual transformation to be a function of *participation in being*, not of separated, individual existence. In other words, in a manner somewhat strange for us today, he conceived of reality as a series of concentric overlaps or interpenetrated strata where one reality "nested" metaphysically inside another — the one deriving its own qualities from the other. Reality was structured according to the paradigms of logical classification. Fixed as we are today on the primacy of the individual entity or existing substance as the locus of metaphysical *act* (i.e., existence), it is difficult for us to grasp the Platonic pattern of locating existence *primarily* in the conceptual "genus" or over-class (the idea) and in the individual *only derivatively*. In this case the super-essential or super-generic *idea of being* — which was taken, in fact, to be God — defined and characterized the individual.

This overlap or nesting is called *participation*. Essence (form), the Greek category, translates to *species* as the modern category, and is intrinsically participatory. In the *species* many individuals share the same nature, they *participate* in the same "reality.". They are what they are by reason of their common essence or form — humanity for example. So in Platonic terms, I am said to be a human being by *participation* in the "form" or essence of humanity, which by the fact that it provides this reality to many of us simultaneously, *must be more real than any of us*. There are not multiple "humanities." There is only one.

It's this notion of shared reality and the inclusions it implies that separates our world from Eckhart's. It can place an obstacle to understanding what it meant for him to "share being" with God. For us in our times, both we and God are thought to have each our "own" separate being. But that wasn't true for Eckhart. In his world no one had their "own being." The shared *concept* was the precise mirror-image of the shared *reality*. There is only one "being," and it is not only owned by God, it is God's own. It is not only God's; it is God.

This "sharing" of being does not obliterate the receptive pole of the creature-Creator relationship; quite the contrary, it's what makes the creature "to be." It means the two poles — Creator and creature — are *intrinsically* not extrinsically related. Relationship to God, therefore, is not a personal choice for us nor is it in any way dependent on our consequent behavior or God's. It is not a human achievement. It cannot be alienated. It cannot be lost. It is not created by redemption, merely "upgraded." It is not voluntary on our part. It comes first; it's our very existence itself.

The act in which we exist is God.

The Concept of Being

Much of what Eckhart says about the relationship between God and Creation and God and "the soul" is built on the implications of the *reification* of the concept of being. For him, *God was Being*; the concept was *real*. He thought the analysis of the concept of Being would give him accurate information about God and God's world. It revealed a *pan-en-theist* universe.

That God was Being itself might be called the seminal idea of the scholastics — not because they were the first to identify it, but because their particular angle on it had such a creative effect within their system. The unique contribution of the middle ages to the *philosophia perennis* was to focus on the notion of *being in itself*, abstracted from the actual entities that existed, as a source of insight and reflection into the relationship between Creator and creature. Meister Eckhart went the furthest in drawing out its practical implications for Christian spiritual exploration.

This "scientific" notion that God was Being confirmed a fertile misreading of the Hebrew name for God recorded in Exodus — *Yahweh*, "I am who am" — erroneously taken in a metaphysical sense. It translated to the *esse in se subsistens* of Thomas Aquinas. The scholastics developed the perspective that, beyond the physical causalities of antecedent and consequent in the cosmos, the sheer continuance in being of the realities around us — existence itself in the here and now — revealed a dependency that required the active presence of an ontological force of infinite power and self-possession.[159] For them, of course, that ontological force was God. But it was this *vertical* dimension, this *necessary* ground for the existence of "unnecessary," i.e., contingent being in the here and now, that characterized the mediaeval innovation in the understanding of God as Being. It emphasized the *ontological* rather than the *cosmological* nature of the creative relationship — *that* things are, not *what* they are.

As a corollary, they identified the existence of creatures (taken as *existing*) as *participatory*. Since Being is One, whatever exists does not have its "own" separate existence, but rather shares *God's,* which is God's very essence. It was this grounding doctrine that inspired Eckhart and provided him with the philosophical context for his mysticism. It was pan-en-theist to the core.

Eckhart is often read as a poetic preacher whose striking turns of phrase have inspired many people in their quest for a more intense "spiritual life." But our interest goes further. We want to know how his mysticism was fed by and in turn fed his view-of-the-world ... and how it may help guide our own search.

Eckhart's Fundamentals

There are a number of foundational ideas that circumscribe Eckhart's view-of-the-world. They repeat the central tenets of scholasticism. They are the basis for the understanding of his mysticism.

(1) *God is Being.* All created things subsist metaphysically *within* God's very Act of Existence which is God's essence. The Godhead is *eternally* emanating created participatory existence in the Eternal-Now.

(2) *God is Triune.* The Godhead's absolute self-possession of being produces an internal convulsion (a "boiling" and an "overflow")[160] of recognition and joy that results in a unity with an inner relational structure. God is absolutely one; the dynamism of self-awareness and self-embrace generates internal subsistent relations that are entirely subordinate to the absolute unity of the Godhead.

---

[159] SCG Bk II, ch.37 [3]
[160] Robert Forman, *Meister Eckhart,* Element, Rockport MA, 1991, pp 198-199

These relations — metaphorically called "persons" and named in Christianity as "Father," "Son," and "Spirit" — are the necessary dimensional elements of God's inner being. They are of the very essence of God. This inner tripartite relational dynamism, since it is constitutive of Being as such, is also necessarily *constitutive of created participatory existence* in every creature and in every instant of the Eternal Now.

(3) *The human "soul"* as created being and the *imago Dei,* exists in the context of these two antecedents, God as Being and God as Triune. As created being, the human individual exists by participation in God's Being in the Eternal-Now, and this means it is simultaneously borne along in the dynamic Trinitarian "convulsion" that is the innermost characteristic of Being. It exists in that *phase* of God's relational interiority that corresponds to the *expression* of God's Self, the Word. The human person, the finite self, in other words, is a *participatory* element of the generation of the Trinitarian Word, The Son, the *Logos,* the Infinite Self. Our *self* is a finite participation in the infinite *Self* which is the *Logos* — God the Son.

(4) The *personal appropriation* and *concrete activation* on the part of the human individual of this generation of the Word constitutively present in the depth of the soul, is accomplished by the conscious and purposeful eradication of "self-will" with a corresponding total ascendancy of the will of God. Once the clamorous "will" of the *false human "self"* is stilled, the "birth" of God's "Son" takes place in the depths of the soul, Eckhart says, *necessarily*. The Father *has* to generate the Son, like it or not, says Eckhart, just as God *has* to love. This necessary Trinitarian aspect of Being is palpably experienced in the "soul" under the aforementioned conditions of human surrender. The Trinitarian "being" which is at the "core" of the finite self, has been there all along,[161] waiting for its full potential to be activated. This full activation is conceived as a *withdrawal of obstacles*, not as an achievement of the human self.

---

[161] ibid., p.106

This intimate divine contact is *unconscious,* however, because it occurs in the very "core" of the soul, where the soul's being and God's Being mesh in the embrace of immanent participation, which is beyond the reach of the intellect. You don't *know* it, Eckhart says, you only *know about* it.[162] The elimination of "selfishness," the de-mystification of personal knowledge and the quiescence of personal desire affects the *erasure of the human "self"* and results in its automatic replacement by the *Self* that is the *Logos* of God.

This sketch is sufficient to give us an idea of where Eckhart's experience fits into his scheme of things. The features that interest us most are, first, the "functional pantheism" that we identified in the last chapter as a characteristic of mystical experience across time and across traditions. Then, the human individual and the Creating, Indwelling God are specifically identified by Eckhart as the components of mystical experience — one experiences God as *the "core" of one's own self.*[163] Third, the "transformation" of the contingent (perishing and therefore illusory) human self into the real absolute imperishable Self, the Godhead, the Being in which we live and move.

We have to admit that Eckhart's manner of speaking doesn't seem to limit this transformation merely to the "soul's" upward enhancement into the fullness of Being, but goes further and implies the *obliteration* of the human self entirely and its replacement by the Divine Self. This apparent difficulty tends to disappear, however, when we take seriously his philosophical understanding of *participatory existence*: to Eckhart the finite self and the Infinite Self were never "distinct existences" to begin with. To call the transformation "obliteration" or "upward enhancement" are only terminological differences; for Eckhart considers the *independent* finite "self" a phenomenological illusion without any real metaphysical depth. Its "obliteration" is simply the dissipation of a fantasy, not a metaphysical destruction. The finite self separated from

---

[162]Eckhart, *the Aristocrat*, Blakney tr., *Meister Eckhart*, Harper Torchbook, 1941, p. 79f.

[163]Forman, op.cit., p. 204, quotes from a sermon he identifies as W 2:333: "You should wholly sink away from your you-ness and dissolve into His His-ness, and your "yours" and his "his" should become so completely one: "mine" ..."

God, as far as the Meister is concerned, does not exist. It is "nothing." Eckhart uses this word often for the human being, and it was one of the "propositions" singled out for censure by the Inquisition.

Should this "nothingness" which is the finite self, then, attempt to assert itself as having *being* in its own right, it sins. Sin, of course, since the days of Augustine, was itself classically defined as "non-being." This neo-platonic notion helped Eriugena in the 9th century explain how God, in spite of being immanent in created things, cannot be held responsible for evil in any way; for *God cannot create non-being.* This was a classic difficulty because as the "Primary Cause" of all things, the Being in which everything participates, God would logically be responsible for evil. Indirectly, it confirmed human freedom. Sin is the attempt of the creature to stand in the place of God, to deny finite dependency and to arrogate absolute independent being to what exists only contingently and by participation. It is a form of idolatry.

Eckhart as Guide

At this point, someone may object to this trend of thought. Am I simultaneously criticizing conceptual *reification* as fantasy and then using it under Eckhart's aegis to support the notion of the Sacred Totality and functional pantheism? I reply: Seeing how it was used by Eckhart to explain his inner experiences does not imply philosophical subscription on our part. These experiences, correctly understood on their own terms, help us to identify and situate the same or similar experiences in our own context — with our own peculiar "metaphysical" categories, priorities and angle of vision. Eckhart's thought serves us as a guide, not a recipe.

As the case begins to build for a new doctrine of God, we shall find, I believe, that there is less opposition between our vision and that of the 14th century Rhineland Mystics represented by Eckhart, than there is between him and the "orthodox views" of his contemporary inquisitors. Given the massive shift created by 600 years of philosophical development since those turbulent years in the 14th century, this agreement across the centuries is itself a remarkable phenomenon. It suggests the homogeneity of the experience of the Sacred.

On the other hand, the rejection of Eckhart's potentially universal vision by his contemporary religious authorities resembles similar rejections of other mystical visionaries in other times and traditions, and that includes Jesus'. These rejections speak to the purposes of social stability to which religious energy is normally harnessed. Society is invested in preserving that function. It is a commonplace, at least for us, that religious rebellion will engender a violent reaction from religious authorities. And while Eckhart may not have anticipated the consequences of his thinking, he certainly felt the brunt of it.

II. Eckhart's Relevance to Our Times

Interesting? Perhaps. But what does all this have to do with us? If we claim that Eckhart understood his experience in terms of the science of another era what interest does this have for us besides historical?

As a metaphysical model, *none*. Even for that era, its long-familiar world-view changed rapidly after Eckhart's time. It is noteworthy that his younger contemporary, the Franciscan William of Ockham rejected Platonism entirely. He would not have permitted Eckhart to use the reasoning process that we've been examining in these pages. For it was Ockham who definitively challenged the practice of *reifying* human concepts. He invalidated the conclusions about reality deduced from conceptual analysis alone. For Ockham, there was no "humanity" to share; there were only individual humans. "Humanity" was an arbitrary mental construct that did not exist outside the human mind. The only things that existed were existing things.

We are searching for a doctrine of God that is relevant to our times and our view of the world, not to the few people who are still willing to view the world through the lens of the Platonic Paradigm. In this section, instead of trying to understand what Eckhart thought his experiences meant within the neo-platonic cosmos he believed existed, we will look at Eckhart's descriptions and try to see how they may correlate with the way we, in our times, conceive the structure of the universe, and how they may help us form for ourselves a more adequate idea of God.

Eckhart's "Stages" of Spiritual Transformation

Like all Spiritual teachers, Eckhart claimed that spiritual growth went through certain stages which, while not clearly separated from one another, served as descriptions of progressive development.

The following is a description of the stages as Eckhart understood them described in an Encyclopedia Britannica article on Eckhart written by Reiner Schurmann:

> (1) *Dissimilarity:* "All creatures are pure nothingness. I do not say they are small or petty: they are pure nothingness." Whereas God inherently possesses being, creatures do not possess being but receive it derivatively. Outside God, there is pure nothingness. "The being of things is God." The "noble man" (the spiritual "aristocrat") moves among things in detachment, knowing that they are nothing in themselves and yet aware that they are full of God — their being.
>
> (2) *Similarity:* Man thus detached from the singular (individual things) and attached to the universal (Being) discovers himself to be an image of God. Divine resemblance, an assimilation, then emerges: the Son, image of the Father, engenders himself within the detached soul. As an image, "thou must be in Him and for Him, and not He in thee and for thee."
>
> (3) *Identity:* Eckehart's [sic] numerous statements on identity between God and the soul can be easily misunderstood. He never has substantial identity in mind: but God's operation and man's becoming are considered as one. God is no longer outside man, but he is perfectly interiorized. Hence the statements: "The being and the nature of God are mine; Jesus enters the castle of the soul; the spark in the soul is beyond time and space; the soul's light is uncreated and cannot be created, it takes possession of God with no mediation; the core of the soul and the core of God are one."
>
> (4) *Breakthrough:* To Meister Eckehart, identity with God is still not enough; to abandon all things without abandoning God is still not abandoning anything. Man must live "without why." He must seek nothing, not even God. Such a thought leads man into the desert, anterior to God. For Meister Eckehart, God exists as God only when the creature invokes him. Eckhart calls "Godhead" the origin of all things that is beyond God (God conceived as creator). "God and the Godhead are as distinct as heaven and earth." The soul is no longer the Son. The soul is now the Father: it engen-

ders God as a divine Person. "If I were not, God would not be God." Detachment thus reaches its conclusion in the breakthrough beyond God.[164]

The last stage, what Eckhart call's "the Breakthrough," *der Durchbruch,* is particularly interesting. It should be noted that this extraordinary terminology is found mostly in Eckhart's German sermons and other teachings, and not in his Latin treatises. The linguistic adventurism of Eckhart was highly prized by the great German wordsmith, Martin Heidegger, as a model and in some cases a direct source for his own thinking which was frequently based on the radical re-interpretation of German words. Eckhart was a great favorite of Heidegger and influenced his thought, some say seminally.[165]

Eckhart's descriptions of *"the breakthrough"* are truly untraditional. He speaks of the experience of wanting *nothing* at all, not even God. He specifically likens it to the experience that one had *before birth, while still in the womb.*[166] It is something one strives for by means of the most radical detachment imaginable. It represents a state in which affect of all kinds has been definitively quelled. This is not achievable by ascetical practice alone, but one must wait for it because it is a "gift of God" and "God's doing." I would also associate this "doctrine" of Eckhart's with the suggestion of Raimundo Panikkar — which we will look at in more detail shortly — that the experience of the modern atheist, *precisely in his atheism,* comes closest to the experience of God identified by the mystics.[167]

The "ONE"

We have said that in this section we want to examine Eckhart's experiences directly. But his descriptions of the character of the "Breakthrough" are so bizarre that it requires that we return to his philosophical vision, briefly, or his statements become incoherent for us.

---

[164] EB 1979, article "Eckhart," macropedia vol 6, by Reiner Schurmann
[165] cf John D. Caputo, *The Mystical Element in Heidegger's Thought,* Ohio U. Press, Athens, OH, 1978
[166] sermon on poverty
[167] Raimundo Panikkar, *The Silence of God,* Orbis, Maryknoll NY, 1991

Eckhart's sense of the Triune God was dominated by *Unity*. He thought of God's tri-unity as structured in a certain logical, not metaphysical or chronological order. Raw absolute Being-in-Itself was *undividedly One*; Eckhart called it the "Godhead" and distinguished it from "God," which was the Trinity. He saw the "Godhead" as the absolute principle whose internal "boiling" and "overflow" instantaneously and internally emanated, as if it were a *second moment*, the Trinity of persons. This Trinity, then, represents the "Godhead's" full ecstatic awareness of having absolute self possession of being. In this instantaneous self-recognition which generates the subsistent relations of Father, Son and Spirit, the created universe is spawned as a finite participation *within* the generation of the Son, the *Logos,* the Word. Creation is part of the divine expression which is the Word. There is a certain sense in which Eckhart's descriptions of this "Godhead" seem to imply a pre-conscious primordiality. But since the sequences involved are "logical" only, in theory it has no bearing. However, in our search for hints for a modern formulation of the doctrine of God, it's important to make note of it.

For Eckhart, the ultimate source of all things, therefore, is not the Father, but "the One," the "Godhead" beyond "God," the Reality *anterior to the Trinity* that stands as principle before all, the source of all, the goal of all — *Pure Infinite Being.* The soul's return to the "Godhead" is part of the Son's (the *Logos'*) constitutive expression of the Godhead together with the Father and the Spirit. It's important to maintain the tri-unity or Eckhart's conception deteriorates into a sequence of emanations. They are not. The Trinity is the necessary intrinsic efflorescence of the "Godhead" in the "Eternal Now," the Universal Act of Existence, the Essence of God, the "processions" within the Godhead which represent God's self-recognition. Finite creation, then, participates in this "eternal overflow" by evolving, unfolding, flowering (*becoming*) in the here and now of sequential time. For Eckhart, as far as God is concerned, it is all *One Single Thing, One Single Event, One Eternal Now* — the Godhead, the Trinity and the material Universe.

There are no sequences for God; but there are for us. We who live in time, express these "Eternal now" realities in sequential "here-and-now" time. Through the time-borne transformations which are the moments of our lives we "become" the Word Itself and so we "become" *one* again with the Godhead, borne back to the source of all *within* the Returning Word. As we "become," by choice after choice doing God's will, one with God ... as we withdraw from attachment to anything but pure absolute being — the "Godhead" beyond God — we eventually "*break through*" all separations, divisions, oppositions and individualities and we become one with and within the One in which all things subsist.

Eckhart's sense of the Divine Unity is a unique feature of his theology. His own terminology about the "Godhead" is even more challenging than our descriptions of it. He says the "Godhead" is

> "... a non-God, a non-spirit, a non-person, a non-image, rather ... He is a pure, sheer, limpid One, detached from all duality.
> ... If the soul sees God as He is God, or as He is an image, or as He is three, it is an imperfection. But when all images are detached from the soul and she sees nothing but the One alone, then the naked essence of the soul finds the naked formless essence of divine unity, which is superessential being ..."[168]

Eckhart scholar Robert Forman comments:

> Eckhart stressed the absolute desert-like silence of the Godhead ... beyond even the bare threeness of Father, Son and Holy Spirit. ... beyond all distinctions, those between creatures and God, ... and even the subtle distinctions between the Trinity and the Godhead. Most importantly, all creatures come to be cognized as non distinguished from the divine expanse which has been (since the Birth) encountered *within myself.* The peculiar oceanic feeling is hence encountered not only internally but externally, ... It is to find oneself amidst the ontological core of the cosmos.[169]

Forman continues: "When Eckhart speaks of the 'Breakthrough' in the first person he suggests that it involves perceiving the unmoved mover which stands at the source of both "myself" and the world. This entails the perception that self and other are One. [He quotes Eckhart]:

> When I flowed forth from God, all creatures declared: "There is a God"; but this cannot make me blessed, for with this I acknowledge myself as a creature. But in my *breaking through*, where I stand free of my own will, of

---

[168] Walshe, M. *Meister Eckhart, German Sermons and Treatises,* London, Watkins, 1979 vol 2: p. 331
[169] Forman pp.178-180

God's will, of all His works and of God Himself, then I am above all creatures and I am neither God nor creature, but I am that which I was and shall remain forevermore ... this *breaking through* guarantees to me that I and God are one. Then I am what I was, then I neither wax nor wane, for then I am the unmoved cause that moves all things."[170]

This is truly extraordinary language for a mediaeval scholastic. But it is even more remarkable when we see its resemblance to the projections of the "process" philosophers like Whitehead, who sees an unconscious primordial deity as the basis of all cosmic development. The Meister's notion of *"spiritual becoming"* on the "time side" of the "eternal-now" equation, can be easily expanded and understood to include a cosmic unfolding in the evolutionary terms of the process philosophers. Cosmic becoming would recapitulate the emanations *from* and the return *to* the "One" on the "eternal side" of the equation. The divinization of the "individual soul" would then be a sub-routine of this cosmic becoming.

Beyond God to the Godhead

The famous sermon of the Meister given on the text "*Blessed are the Poor in Spirit*" from Matthew's gospel, is especially strong in its insistence that the God of religion and of religious spirituality *must be transcended and effectively shed* before the authentic connection with the ultimate Source of the Sacred can occur.

Others say virtually the same thing. The detachment of the "dark night" of John of the Cross in which blind, empty trust alone, beyond all knowledge or clarity, beyond all consolation or assurance, is similar in that it insists that all concepts and images are transcended when authentic mystical contact occurs. In this same regard, the Buddha was particularly trenchant against "religion" and the gods. He was so uncompromising in refusing any religious alliances that his enlightenment has come to be considered "atheist."

Here is more from Eckhart on the issue from the same sermon, on "*Blessed are the Poor in Spirit*." It should be easy to discern when Eckhart uses the word "God" to mean the object of our reli-

---

[170] Walshe, op.cit. vol.2: p.275

gious understanding, and when he intends the "Godhead" which is beyond all understanding.

... If one wants to be truly poor, he must be as free from his creature-will as when he had not yet been born. For by the everlasting truth, as long as you will to do God's will and yearn for eternity and God, you are not really poor; for he is poor who wills nothing, knows nothing and wants nothing.

Back in the Womb from which I came, I had no God and merely was myself. I did not will or desire anything, for I was pure being, a knower of myself by divine truth. Then I wanted myself and nothing else. And what I wanted I was, and what I was I wanted, and thus I existed untrammeled by God or anything else. But when I parted from my free will and received my created being, then I had a God. For before there were creatures, God was not God, but rather, he was what he was. When creatures came to be and took on creaturely being, then God was no longer God as he is in himself, but God as he is with creatures.

Now, we say that God, in so far as he is only God, is not the highest goal of creation, nor is his fullness of being as great as that of the least of creatures, themselves in God. ... *Therefore we pray that we may be rid of God,* and taking the truth, *break through* into eternity, where the highest angels and souls too, are like what I was in my primal existence, when I wanted what I was and I was what I wanted. Accordingly, a person ought to be poor, willing as little and wanting as little as when he did not exist.

. . .

The authorities say that God is a being, an intelligent being who knows everything. But I say that God is neither a being, nor intelligent and he does not "know" either this or that. God is free of everything and therefore he is everything. He then who is to be poor in spirit ... knows nothing of God, or creatures, or himself. ...

Thus far I have said that he is poor who does not want to fulfill the will of God but who so lives that he is empty of his own will and the will of God, as much so as when he did not exist. Next we said that he is poor who knows nothing of the action of God in himself. ... But the third poverty is the most inward and real ... it consists in that a man *has* nothing.

... If it is the case that a man is emptied of things, creatures, himself and God, and if still God could find a place in him to act, then we say: as long as that exists, this man is not poor with the most intimate poverty ... since true poverty of spirit requires that man shall be emptied of God and all his works, so that if God wants to act in the soul, he himself must be the place in which he acts ... he would himself be the scene of action, for God is the one who acts within himself. It is here in this poverty, that man regains the eternal being that once he was, now is, and evermore shall be.

... *Therefore I pray God that he may quit me of God,* for unconditioned being is above God and all distinctions. It was here that I was myself, wanted myself, and knew myself to be this person, and therefore I am my own first cause, both of my eternal being and of my temporal being. To this end I was born, and by virtue of my birth being eternal, I shall never die. It is of the nature of this eternal birth that I have been eternally, that I am now, and shall be forever. For what I am as a temporal creature is to die and come to nothingness, for it came with time and with time it will pass away. In my eternal birth, however, everything was begotten, I was my own first cause as well as the first cause of everything else. If I had willed it neither I nor the world would have come to be. If I had not been, there would have been no God. ...

It's not my intention to promote Eckhart's neo-Platonism or his Platonic theories of the pre-existence of the soul. But his sermons are not only theoretical doctrine. They are the records of his mystical experience. This means to me we should examine Eckhart's experience as the experience of being human — mystically human.

What I hear from him is that his experience of connectedness with the Sacred deepened progressively over the course of his life and eventuated in an awareness that goes *beyond religion and religion's "God,"* and meshes with the reality at the core of all things. He senses himself to be one with everything, and one with the source of all, which he defines in the only terms that he understands: he calls it "Godhead" and distinguishes it from religion's "God." His neo-Platonism is an interpretative tool of his experience. His experience is what interests us; and his experience took him "beyond God."

It seems to me that his fidelity to his experience comes highly recommended to us because he chose to express it in ways that got him into inextricable trouble with the religious authorities.

Detachment and "Atheism," Darkness and Faith

Transcending God for Eckhart, is a function of "detachment." When I look at the development of "detachment" as Eckhart describes it, I spontaneously relate it to the universal disillusionment that the process of living brings to every human being in every culture and in every historical epoch. I believe the process of progressive detachment is an unavoidable part of everyone's life. It begins for all of us as an element of character formation, as we learn to delay gratification and discipline ourselves to the common goals of our society. Inevitably, for all of us in one way or another, whatever dreams we had about controlling life — making it secure and permanent — are soon dissipated in the all but universal condition of suffering, privation, frustration and loss that ultimately characterizes human existence. I'm not offering this as parallel to Eckhart's stages, I'm simply pointing out that the kind of growing detachment Eckhart identifies as the return path to the One, may be a normal by-product of a life-time of daily living and ultimate dying for virtually everyone, and is not reserved for the neo-platonic spiritual elite or other ascetics, religious and non-religious..

Going a step further, it seems to me that the *religiously detached* mindset that he speaks of is a much less difficult achievement for a *modern atheist* than for a superstitious mediaeval Christian who was culturally immersed in a world of ghosts and goblins, visions and revelations, and the personal rewards, punishments and "leadings" of "divine Providence." Without such a religious God dominating the cultural imagination, getting "beyond God" is not nearly the epic achievement it was for Eckhart. Eckhart unequivocally counsels his followers to get beyond religion. For the people of his era, his message was counter-intuitive and it required a lifetime of asceticism to achieve. For us in our era, however, without those religious "supports" it may come more naturally.

But I suspect there's more to it than just detachment. Eckhart doesn't even mention (perhaps because he took it for granted) what John of the Cross, two centuries later, will repeat endlessly: *Faith*. It's not just that one is *blind* and in darkness; but that one clings to God in *blind faith*. If you didn't know it was a 16th century Spanish contemplative, you might think you were reading a 16th century German reformer. But in each case there would be no doubt it was the 16th century. The 14th century, however, was different. Faith, trust in God, was taken for granted; it was the air they breathed. It was rather "spiritual detachment" — a separation from the mystifications of religion — that challenged them and had to be counseled, pursued, practiced, embraced. Detachment from religion needs no encouragement in our case; it is the air *we* breathe. It's trust in the Love that spawned us that needs to be re-kindled.

But the "vision," what is "seen," is the same in either case: *We see nothing.* Whether or not there is faith, the intellectual and volitional conditions for connecting with the "One" are the same — total darkness, true emptiness, complete detachment. The mystics testified to the validity of the dual-formula of detachment and faith. No one in the West has credibly[171] said that detachment alone would do it. Some have tried. But their efforts have been termed a "slippery slope."

For a philosopher like Martin Heidegger, for example, emptiness itself is "nothing." But for him "nothingness" is *a critically important factor* in the authentic understanding of reality. It brings back a lost transcendent vitality to the question of being. We may question the validity of that conception. But Heidegger feels that it is precisely the mystical dimension that he found so vibrantly alive in Eckhart that serves as a model to rescue "being" from the dungeon of forgetfulness into which rationalist "objective" thinking has imprisoned it. But one must be careful. One false step and atheist "emptiness" is suddenly metamorphosed into the One of Plotinus, by definition unknowable, inconceivable and therefore indistinguishable, *as a phenomenon*, from other forms of "absence." This transformation may serve as a welcome corrective for the hidebound traditional theist, but it seems to spell the end of any but the most symbolic atheism. Perhaps that was Heidegger's intention, after all.[172]

But is it possible that total detachment may usher in an invincible "unknowing" or "knowing nothing" that is truly beyond all the determinations heretofore associated with a naïve theist "God" that was considered metaphysically "other" than my being? Might this very "ignorance" of what is "out there" bring me into *non-conceptual contact* with Something beyond them all, Something that does not correspond to any intellectual objectification and is expressible only as *the silence of my own subjective self-validation* which is

---

[171] I intentionally omit the East. One may think of Westerners like Nietzsche or Schopenhauer. Perhaps they did achieve a mystical oneness with all things. But, clearly in the case of Nietzsche in his madness, people have tended to distrust it as a mystical path even while admiring it as "thought."

[172] Cf Caputo, he says this is the focus of the "later Heidegger."

my own inalienable possession of being — my person as an expression of the Sacred?

Inclusive self-validation? Inalienable possession of being? Is this pantheism — again? Or is it, in a contemporaneous sense, the recognition that I am, we are, it is, *all* simply divine?

Could it be that the progressive theological "purifications" applied by the subsequent history of western thought, have actually brought modern westerners to the plateau of an *intellectual detachment* long-ago discovered and settled by spiritual pioneers like Eckhart, whose fidelity to this experience forced him radically to rethink what he meant by God? Modern non-religious people may be ironically privileged to have been served up by their modern non-religious culture an *intellectual poverty* that a mediaeval religious Meister Eckhart had to achieve through a lifetime of ascetical practice and a fatal confrontation with the Papal Inquisition. Are modern Westerners, in their very atheism, potentially closer to the "Godhead" of Eckhart than any mediaeval Rhineland mystic could have hoped for?

Raimundo Panikkar: Atheism and Mysticism

Raimundo Panikkar is a contemporary Catholic Theologian and Hindu Mystic, the son of a Catalan mother and Indian father. He is a Catholic priest and focuses on the correlation between Christian and Hindu mysticism. He taught for many years at UC Berkeley. He has written more than thirty books.

Panikkar examines the predispositions of modern atheism in his book, *The Silence of God*,[173] and finds them not incompatible with mystical experience — similar to Eckhart's — known as *apophaticism*. The term "apophatic" means "ineffable" and refers to the traditional doctrine that God is completely incomprehensible. Panikkar's paradox points up the commonplace that much of what is called "atheism" in the modern world is in large measure a reaction to the puerile irrelevance of the standard religious doctrine of God, and not necessarily a rejection of the Sacred "in which we live and move and have our being." For Panikkar, atheism can

---

[173] Raimundon Panikkar, *The Silence of God*, Orbis, Maryknoll NY, 1996. pp.122-134

represent exactly the kind of conceptual suspension and existential emptiness required for the full experience of the Sacred that dwells, as Eckhart would say, "at the core of the soul." The following extensive quote from Panikkar elaborates this idea.

> ... atheism is an attitude characterized by the negation of a particular *Presence*. ... Human beings are alone. Nowhere have they any superiors, for human beings "are" in the measure that they make themselves what they are. The Presence is alienation: it leans upon another. The Presence is interference by another. ... human beings find themselves alone, solitary, without company. The Presence is cowardice, the projection of one's fears, a negation of the human condition. God, for the atheist, is the Great *Absent* One: God is nowhere, God is not. We are not far from mysticism.[174]

Then he presents the mystical position:

> Long before atheism introduced a set of basic correctives in the idea of God, a whole orientation of thought ... consistently maintained that the best knowledge to be had of the Incomprehensible is to know that we neither know, nor can know, that Incomprehensible. It even defended the dimension of *absence* as God's most fundamental characteristic. ... God is the one who is *absent*. ...
>
> God is always absent. ... Any Presence of God is a presence only, a veil, a manifestation, and thereby a disfiguring. ... A God who is not absent will be a simple idol. ... Strictly speaking, God is nowhere, in no place. God is pure absence, non-existence. The presence of God is only for making God's absence noticed. ... Strictly speaking, God neither has nor is *esse,* but is an absence, a non-being from which beings take their origin. ... It should be clear that we are not dealing with a strategic absence, a divine self-hiding for the purpose of attracting and purifying us. ... It is an absence of being, of essence ... [This perspective] takes an antecedent stand, from which any affirmation or negation of God loses all absolute, definitive signification — hence its recourse to nothingness, the void, and non-being.[175]

While I present these extraordinary statements because they coincide in fundamentals with the spiritual doctrine of Eckhart, I would also like to comment on one or two aspects of Panikkar's way of expressing himself that make them problematic for me.

First of all, his characterization of the "atheist" smacks of a kind of muscular existentialism. A phrase like, "the Presence is cowardice," is a caricature of a Sartre-like position that, to my mind,

---

[174] ibid., p.129
[175] ibid., pp.129-134

does not have much depth or openness. Panikkar's generation was Sartre's, and was perhaps noted for that kind of atheism. I find that atheists today have a more organic, earth-mystical point of view. It's revealing that they tend to call themselves "non-theist" instead of "atheist."[176] Frankly, given Panikkar's pallid description of the atheists' position, his triumphant exclamation, 'We are not far from mysticism,' seems a gratuitous overstatement. I don't think his premises support it; but as a conclusion I fully agree.

Also, Panikkar's constant reference to God as "non-being" in the elaboration of the mystical position should be explained to the reader as corresponding to a classic neo-Platonic usage in which the word "being" refers to "beings," entities, and therefore immediately implies a finite, conceptualized, comprehensible object. Eriugena uses "being" in the same way and like pseudo-Dionysius whom they all follow, says that God is "beyond being" and they therefore they call God "non-being." It is traditional neo-Platonic terminology. The more rarified use of "being" characteristic of the scholastics would claim higher metaphysical ground and hence distance itself from such statements without contradicting their import. Aquinas would totally agree that God is incomprehensible; but I am inclined to think that calling God "nothing" would not be his preferred way of saying it.

Incomprehensibility: Being is No-Thing

It is most interesting and in fact, ironic, that one of the first qualities about God yielded up by an analysis of the "Concept of Being" is "incomprehensibility." The reasoning goes like this: God is Being. But to be pure being is not to be "this" or "that." It is not to have an essence the way other beings have essences that are "defined" by genus and specific difference. The essence of God is "super-essential"; it is existence itself. There is no genus here, no difference by which to distinguish and identify the "entity" in question. Being is not an "entity" because it is not opposed to any other entity; it is the being of all beings. Being is one. Being is beyond all opposition, classification and therefore beyond all definition.

---

[176] Ursula Goodenough, *The Sacred Depths of Nature,* Oxford U. Pr, NY, 1998, p.140

Now, without the ability to "define" and conceptualize, human knowledge is neutralized. It has no "object" on which it can focus, no definition which it can predicate. The human mind cannot know pure Being. Therefore, if God is Being, God is incomprehensible.

In defense of Panikkar's atheist mystics (and my own position) I would say that once you admit the principle of incomprehensibility, then *all human concepts applied to God* — and the concept of being is no exception — fall under the axe.

I recognize the possible circularity in play here, so I won't justify my argument on the basis of this Western theorem alone. The fact is that God's incomprehensibility is one of the remarkable congruences attested to by Religious traditions from all over the world. We can accept it as a premise here because under any circumstances we will insist on sustaining it as a conclusion. Its corollary is that the concept of being is a limited human construct like any other and we have no right to declare an exemption for *being* and claim that it reveals the inner nature of an incomprehensible God. What ultimately lies at the root of this statement is the invalidity of the transcendent characteristics that have been traditionally but inappropriately assigned to the concept of Being itself, and then applied to God.

Referring to that more thorough critique, then, if God is incomprehensible in principle, then we may not even say "that" God exists, except metaphorically. The point is not to deny the existence of God but to question the appropriateness of the term "to be" as used for God in any way remotely resembling that of any other existent, no matter in what "analogical" sense we claim for it. [177]

---

[177] "Analogy," is simply a rationalization that substitutes for what is patently univocal. "Existence" means only one thing for us, the "being-here" of an entity, a substance; we mean exactly the same thing in everything that we apply it to — from protons to primates. Insofar as they exist, everything is doing the very same thing. Since we do not know God we cannot say the same for God, though we claim we can. Does God "exist" in the same way we do? Can we say God "is here" in the same way we mean it for everything else? If not, what can it possibly mean? Could it mean, for instance, that God "is here" only in and through the "being here" of everything we see around us? Would that also be pantheism?

So, we cannot apply "Being" to God. That means, therefore, we say nothing at all. We can't even deny it, for that would also be a groundless predication. What this really means is, as with all the so-called divine attributes, *we have no idea what it means for God to exist.* All we know is that God sustains our immense Universe — somehow, in a way our tradition has chosen to call "immanent," for better or worse — in each successive "now" of time. How do we know that? Because creation exists; and what we mean by God is the source of that existence. *The Created Universe is the only "being" we know* and therefore the only "being" we have a right to say anything about. We cannot speak about God outside of Creation. The "being-here" of creation is the only part of God's "being" we will ever encounter — *and we are it.* Is that all there "is"? Perhaps we can go no further. Eriugena calls us (created being) the "mask" that God wears, and mask it truly is.

Pantheism?

You may ask again: isn't this Pantheism? My answer would be yes and no. Yes, because I am speaking about "being" — yes, even my very own — for which "I" (whatever "I" may be) am not responsible, for "I" had no hand in its appearance and I have no way to prevent what seems to be its disappearance. I cannot guarantee my own existence. I do not "own" my own existence. Therefore it must belong to "Someone or Something" else. It is Someone else's "being." My being is God. God is my existence. In that sense, "I" "am" "God."

But then, and starting from the very same premises, I would also answer, no, it is not pantheism. I do not know who or what God is aside from God's action in sustaining me. And since "I" had no hand in my origination and cannot guarantee its perdurance, I know that "I" am not the God whose being I most certainly bear.

We seem to have great difficulty keeping in focus exactly what we know and what we can say. And that runs in both directions. We should not say *more* than we can legitimately know, but at the same time we cannot say *less* than what undeniably compels our assent. We cannot *dismiss being* simply because we are limited to its dependent side and have no discernible access to its independent side, which we know must be there, somewhere. Being, in however evanescent a form it comes to us, must be taken seriously — and by that I mean *sacredly*. We cannot disregard the *significance* of existence.

Being *matters*. ... It is undeniably *good* to be here.

But the being that we know, "being-here," is what we experience, not something beyond our experience. What we are limited to knowing and saying, however, does not prejudice what may "exist" in a way that we can neither know nor say. When we reach those limits we have to respect them. We cannot say we know what we do not. But neither can we dismiss what we know and experience. And we have to live with the implications of both those limits. What they imply, minimally, is the identification of *the sacred* with ourselves.

The Sacred as Ground

Our existence, "being-here" such as we are, is the only "being" we know; but it *is divine*. I propose that the Sacred is a raw, primary datum of experience, not the conclusion of a syllogism. *We infer the existence of God from the sacredness of reality, we do not deduce the sacredness of reality from the existence of God.*

How is this possible? How can we begin with the experience of the Sacred?

We are the ground of that possibility. It springs from us, and is reflected in the way we ask the question of being. For, it is we who decide whether to ask, "Is being sacred?" or, "Why is being Sacred?"

Does this sound at all familiar? Do we recognize the significance of the dichotomy illustrated here? Isn't this just another expression of the starting point we saw shifting in western history between the perception of primordial friendship or the perception of primordial alienation as the original state of the relationship between God and humankind? We are facing here an ultimate *point of departure* which has no prior basis for its determination than our *instinct* — which some say is our *choice* — or, in other words, *how we perceive ourselves*. How we perceive ourselves determines how we ask the question of the Sacred.

Is it, or is it not, good to be here?

Who do we think we are?

There may be no way out of this impasse, scientifically. The only indisputable datum we have to go on as justification for choosing between these two alternatives is the natural predisposition of humankind, that is to say, our instinctive response. Isn't this a major begging of the question? What else do we have to fall back on once we realize that *we cannot think outside the box,* for our thinking is the box, we are the box. There is no "outside" source of evidence or knowledge. It is either good to be here or not. Is this, once again, too simple?

I said that some call it "choice." But do we really have a choice? How do we explain the ecstatic joy that wells up in our hearts at *being-here*, and correlatively, the anguish and despair that wrack us at the thought that someday we won't? Does it tell us anything about who and what we are, and therefore how we are primordially related to existence? This doesn't take away our freedom. We can still choose to be offended at the impermanence of it all. But if we are at all inclined to trust, do we really need more proof?

In a world in which *trust*, as the precondition for everything we do in life, has been elicited from us at every turn — trust in our parents, trust in the benevolence of the earth whose creatures become the food we eat, the air and water we consume, trust in the genetic forces that bring us infallibly from birth to adulthood, trust in the diaphanous perfection of our bodies and minds, trust in the process of healing, trust in our teachers, our doctors, our neighbors, our friends, trust in the fertility and solidity of love — why should trust all of a sudden become counter-indicated when it comes to "Being," which, after all, embraces all of the above?

As these issues become clearer in the light of the simplest and most available of evidence, it appears that Eckhart's vision was nothing but a restatement, in the terminology of mediaeval scholasticism, of the spontaneous perceptions of the joy of life and the continuance it augurs. If we accept Eckhart's way of approaching things, our questions are reduced to silence. We can begin to imagine, as he suggests, a state like that time before we were born, which Eckhart says was the "home" from which our "souls" came and to which they long to return — when what we wanted we were and what we were we wanted — Being in Itself, pure, limpid, One and eternal.

CHAPTER VI
The Testimony of The Mystics II: An Historical Overview.

This next chapter is an attempt to review the religious import of the five previous chapters but from an entirely different perspective. It examines the decisive impact of the 14th century on christian experience, and tries to show how the transcendent events in that unique century, coupled with latent foundational elements embedded in christian theology, began shaping the view of the world and the spirituality that our generation was formed in.

Part I: The Background

A. The Historical Context

We're in England. The year is 1385. Common opinion would say it was the darkest of the dark ages. Many dispute that. No one would ever argue, however, that it was lifeless. The age roiled with ferment as people sought new lamps to light their way.

Let's contextualize. The most salient event of the age was the Bubonic Plague, better known as the Black Death. The first and worst wave of the plague had swept over Europe only thirty-five years earlier, slaughtering between one third and one half of the entire continent's population. It returned periodically thereafter, about every dozen years, though with less severity. Nothing on that scale had ever happened before. Christians were shaken to the core by what seemed an unmistakable sign of God's wrath. In an age that saw in natural events the direct intervention of "God," it seemed to confirm Augustine's theory that Original Sin had made our relationship to "God" one of Original Hostility.[178]

But even more, the plague cast doubt on the Church's claim to be "God's" unique agent on earth, "God's" partner who "knew" God intimately and had the unquestioned power to guarantee divine benevolence. For not only had the priests obviously failed to prevent the disaster despite their pricey rituals and official prayers, but there was a growing belief that it was, in fact, clerical venality and corruption that had brought it on.

The Schism of Rival Popes began just seven years ago in 1378 and it has sharpened Christian cynicism about the Church. Three Popes now vie for power, one under control of the King of France and one loyal to the German "Emperor." Disaffection with papal abuse of power is even now spawning a revolutionary Conciliar Movement that will threaten to put an end to the autocratic papacy that has defined Europe since the fall of Rome. For the better part of the next century, the popes will be subjected to humiliating control by a series of ecumenical councils which will claim to exercise ultimate authority in the name of God ... even over the pope. Eventually the movement will not be able to sustain itself against the inevitable reassertion of papal power, and conciliarism will be condemned.[179]

The plague also challenged faith at a deeper level. By casting doubt on the credibility of the Church's understanding of the way "God" worked, it rekindled the classic questions about divine justice and the existence of evil in the world. These questions had perplexed the philosophers before Christianity. Faced with such a stark reminder of the fragility of life and the randomness of natural events, bedrock traditional beliefs were no longer taken for granted. Providence and predestination**Error! Bookmark not defined.** once again became everyday topics of conversation. The very foundations of the religious world-view were subjected to skeptical and sometimes cynical review. It was an "Age of Faith" in mortal crisis.

---

[178] Peter Brown, *Augustine of Hippo,* U.of CA Press, Berkeley, 1967, new ed. 1999. p. 397-98, with fn to *De Civ.Dei,* XXI, 24,78, "for mortals, this life is the Wrath of God.",
[179] Pius II. Bull, *Execrabilis,* 1460 and 5th Lateran Council, 1513-1517

Thomas Aquinas has been dead for over a century at this point and the mediaeval tapestry woven by his generation of philosopher-theologians is beginning to unravel. The English Franciscan, William of Ockham, who died on the continent during the first onslaught of the plague in 1348, had spent his last twenty years in the employ of the Emperor in Bavaria attacking the French-controlled Pope in Avignon. He provided an early theoretical foundation for Conciliarism. His academic assault on the vestiges of Platonism, however, challenged the philosophical underpinnings of the mediaeval Catholic synthesis and, in the long run, may have been even more damaging to the heretofore unchallenged power of religious authority.

French wealth and power was the dominant political factor throughout the century. The French king was able to subject the Papacy to unprecedented secular control as evidenced in the Avignon "captivity" in which eight French Popes ruled the Church starting in 1309 for the next 70 years, eventuating in the Great Schism dividing Christian loyalties among three rival Popes.

The Valois drew the fire of the English and German princes clawing for power in this time of the disintegration of feudal Christendom and the emergence of the new nation-states of Europe. The internecine struggles of the aristocracy over boundaries and territory managed to keep Europe at war for a hundred years, alternating bloodbaths with recurrent outbreaks of the plague. The working poor, who were expected to supply their "Lords" with food and foot soldiers, were the ones who paid for it all, and well they knew it.

Piers Ploughman

The plague engendered guilt and perplexity. In England, William Langland voices the opinions of the common man in this "Age of Faith:"

> For God is deaf nowadays and will not hear us;
> And for our guilt he grinds good men to dust.

In 1385 Langland is revising, probably for the second time, his *Piers the Ploughman,* an elaborate allegory denouncing the failings of Christian practice and the oppression of the poor by the rich in a society that, because it was Christian, claimed to be congenitally egalitarian. Even 35 years after the plague, it was prominent in his musings. For him it was social injustice that was the cause of the plague. He never doubted divine providence, nor the truths of Christianity. He deplored the cynical questioning of providence and the will of God that had become rampant among Christians:.

> Since the Plague, friars and other imposters have thought up theological questions ... so that folk are no longer confirmed in the faith. ... among the rich and the poor throughout the whole realm, pride has spread so much that all our prayers are powerless to stop the pestilence.

He cites an example of their impertinence::

> "Why," they say, "did our Saviour allow the Serpent into the Garden of Eden to beguile first the woman then the man and to lure them to hell? And why should all their seed suffer the same death, for their sin alone?" [180]

The complaint, articulated here by Langland and deplored, was repeated endlessly through the latter part of the century and encapsulated the universal perception of the illogicality of the explanation for suffering: if suffering was a punishment for sin, why did God permit "sin" to enter the world with Adam and Eve in the first place? Sound familiar? This was also the gist of our penitent Fidel's take on the problem that we saw in Chapter III. It's endemic to the naïve understanding of providence. For if "God" micro-manages our lives, then it is "God's" fault for not preventing us from sinning. ... and plagues of the virulence of the Black Death, are at least permitted by God, and therefore "his will."

The "friars," i.e., Franciscans with the vow of poverty, were the particular object of Langland's venom. And as we'll see, he wasn't the only one to question their integrity. Nor had he any kind words for Popes whose interest in secular power and financial accumulation was as crass and undisguised as any secular prince.

Judging from the number of copies extant, Langland's poem must have been widely read in its time and in the following century, an indication of its impact among the general population.

Langland was a commoner. But his training for a clerical career, arrested apparently for lack of patronage, had given him suf-

---

[180] Langland, *Piers Ploughman,* B, Book X, c.65 & 105 Penguin, p.152f.

ficient literary skills to be spokesman for an agricultural proletariat mutating from feudal serfdom into paid labor and finding its voice for the first time. And it was a voice of protest.

Peasants' revolts

There had been an English Peasants' Revolt, quashed treacherously and brutally by the king's men just a few years before in 1381. The main grievance was the Statute of Labourers of 1351, still in force thirty years later, which had attempted to fix maximum wages during the labor shortage immediately following the Black Death.[181]

The revolt was the first of its kind recorded in England, but it was not by any means a singular event. Europe was peppered with uprisings of the lower classes, all occurring in the latter half of the century — after the plague.[182] In France peasants had gone on a rampage of systematic slaughter of the aristocracy in response to the continued institutionalized plunder levied on them by the warlords under the pretext of feudal obligation. Known as the *Jaquerie,* a word derived from the leather jackets used by common foot soldiers, the uprising occurred in 1357 during one of the episodes of the century's war. But the decimation of the working population by the plague had worn thin not only peasant resources but also their credulity in the threats of the Church which preached submission to feudal authority under pain of sin and damnation.

Uprisings occurred later in city after city, sometimes joined by the artisan and commercial classes. This growing bourgeoisie, just beginning to exercise the power that wealth brings, were still gallingly subjected to feudal service imposed by an aristocracy quick to resort to violence in the maintenance of its privileges. Revolts directed at the elite took place in Florence, Ghent, Bruges and Ypres in 1378. In Laon and Paris in the same year riots instigated by oppressive taxes spilled over into pogroms of Jews and ignited similar actions in Chartres and other French cities.[183] These re-

---

[181] "Peasants Revolt" *EB* 1979, micropedia, Vol VII, p.824.
[182] Barbara Tuchman, *A Distant Mirror,* NY, Knopf, 1978, pp 372-378.
[183] The Jews were always an open target that could be attacked with impunity. "God's" anger evidenced by the plague was assumed always to be directed at the Jews for "mur-

volts in many cases exhibited an irrational fury that purported to exterminate the aristocrats physically. They revealed an unsuspected class hatred fed by years of simmering resentment.

The Upper Classes

The poor, however, were not the only ones to express their discontent. The elites were equally restive. John Wycliff, a highly educated Oxford theologian and a favorite of the Court had been criticizing the Church in a most daring manner right up to his death last year in 1384, protected by powerful members of the English royal family whose political interests against Papal control and ecclesiastical tithes he openly served. He challenged belief in the magical sacraments, rejected transubstantiation, priestly orders and called for dogmatic renewal based solely on the authority of the scriptures (which he was the first to translate into English). He was condemned by a synod of British Bishops at Blackfriars in 1377 but was never punished or silenced. His "heretical" ideas were carried forward by followers called *Lollards* who came from every level of English society. After their violent suppression at the end of the century, these harbingers of a future Protestantism continued as an underground movement and emerged into the light of day a century and a half later when the Lutheran revolt reached the shores of England.[184]

Meanwhile, Geoffrey Chaucer, another member of the upper class, is writing stories for the entertainment of the elite that recapitulate the generalized uneasiness of the times. Chaucer's famous work, *Canterbury Tales,* was obviously inspired by Giovanni Boccaccio's *Decameron,* a collection of stories written in Florence in 1349 in the immediate aftermath of the plague. Boccaccio's setting: ten people, self-quarantined in an isolated rural location to escape the Black Death, tell ten tales each to relieve their boredom. In his introduction, Boccaccio repeats the accepted wisdom that the

---

dering God's Son." Killing them and other infidels was always considered a way to please God and avert future wrath. That "God" himself, according to the western theory of redemption, required that Jesus die to assuage "His" insulted divinity, seems to have been omitted from the analysis ...

[184] EB 2006, CD Rom version, "Lollard"

deadly pestilence was "... sent upon us mortals by God in His just wrath by way of retribution for our iniquities." Though Chaucer doesn't refer to the *Decameron* in his own work, it was well known that the plague was the setting for the Florentine's tales, and would certainly have been taken as the precursor and context for Chaucer's.

Against the background of the symbolic orthodoxy of a pilgrimage to the shrine of martyr-bishop Thomas à Becket, one after another of Chaucer's fictional pilgrims tell their tales out of school: of lecherous friars and adulterous wives, of the depredations of war and the fatalism given lip-service as "Providence." The *Canterbury Tales* were laced with a cryptic criticism of the Church and the society the Church had forged.

Censure of the aristocracy, however, so prominent a feature in Langland's work, is not surprisingly absent from this courtly poet, the recipient of royal commissions, sinecures and favors. But, what is remarkable is that in spite of his class loyalties, Chaucer displays a skepticism concerning religious matters that run much deeper than we have been accustomed to expect from an "Age of Faith." In the "Knight's Tale," for instance, Palamon complains about the dire fate of humankind, abandoned by "the Gods:"

> ... O cruel Gods, whose government
> Binds all the world to your eternal bent, ...
>
> what more is man to you than to behold
> A flock of sheep that cower in the fold
>
> For men are slain as much as other cattle,
> Arrested, thrust in prison, killed in battle,
>
> In sickness often and mischance, and fall,
> Alas too often for no guilt at all.
>
> Where is right rule in your foreknowledge, when
> Such torments fall on innocent, helpless men?

Put into the mouths of "pagans," Chaucer is able to get away with such a challenge to common beliefs, but what he meant was clear to all.

In the "Franklin's Tale" another "pagan" speaks her mind. Dorigen's bitter issue with God, on which she almost shipwrecks her marriage, is her perplexity over the presence of coastal boulders — created and placed there by God — whose only purpose seems to be to cause shipwrecks and kill people.

> "Eternal God that by Thy providence
> Guidest the world in wise omnipotence,
>
> They say of Thee that Thou hast nothing made
> In vain; but Lord, these fiendish rocks are laid
>
> In what would rather seem a foul confusion
> Of work than the creation and conclusion
>
> Of One so perfect, God the wise and stable;
> ... I know it pleases scholars to protest
> In argument that all is for the best,
>
> Though what their reasons are I do not know."

These expressions of doubt in divine providence show that it was obviously not confined to the poor. The plague is never directly mentioned by Chaucer, but the use of Boccaccio's format and the conspicuous introduction of speculation about ultimate questions supposedly settled and secure like providence and evil in the world, reveals its festering presence.[185]

B. Late Mediaeval Mysticism and Modern Spirituality

But the rancor and dark misgivings of the times ironically correlate with a new mysticism. The loss of confidence in the official public and liturgical project of the Church has driven people to look for God *on their own and within themselves.* In the German Rhineland, the direct inheritors of Meister Eckhart radiate his influence throughout the region.

Johannes Tauler, like Eckhart a Dominican priest, born in Strasburg in 1300, where the Meister had worked from 1315 to his death, is proposing a mystical spirituality that includes elements of the individualist piety that we associate with a later era. Tauler was never sent for higher studies by his order, and even exhibits a certain suspicion of "book-learning" in his writings.[186] That such a man would have been steeped in mystical spirituality — and written extensively about it — was a sign of changing times. Martin

---

[185] M.E.Thomas, *Mediaeval Skepticism and Chaucer,* Cooper Square, NY, 1971
[186] Oliver Davies, *The Rhineland Mystics,* London, SPCK, 1989, p.63

Luther read Tauler and was greatly impressed by him. Tauler was a casualty of the second outbreak of the plague and died in 1361.

Jan van Ruysbroeck, a Belgian priest also in the lineage of Eckhart, founded a forest-dwelling community of simple living, not unlike the Beguines, in Groendaal near Brussels before the outbreak of the plague. He emphasizes a religious individuality and pursuit of personal experience that does not conform to the Church-centered practices of his day.

> " ... I have told you how all the saints and all good people are united with God through an intermediary [*the Church, the sacraments etc.*]. Now I want to go on to tell you how we are united to God *without intermediary*."[187]

"Without intermediary" might be taken as the religious motto of the age. The preference is for individual experience. There is exploration everywhere — and on the part of lay people a desire for personal spirituality and direct, unmediated contact with God bypassing official ecclesiastical practices. This spirit would later evolve into the doctrinal challenges nailed to the Church door at Wittenberg.

In England, the cloistered anchoress Juliana of Norwich, recognized now for reconceptualizing the Trinity with a feminine dimension, in 1385 is writing *The Revelations of Divine Love*, a record of her mystical experiences. For her, "God" is unquestionably good. So she is asking almost *verbatim* the question that Langland disapproved: how could a good "God," knowing that Adam's sin would introduce death and all manner of suffering into human life, ever have permitted the tempter, Satan, entry into paradise. Her response was silent acceptance of what she flatly declared she could not understand.[188]

Around the same time, Walter Hilton, an Oxford cleric trained in law, becomes a monk and turns his attention to mystical questions. He writes the *Ladder of Perfection*, a manual of traditional mystical doctrine for those seeking direct experience of "God."[189]

---

[187] Jan van Ruusbroeck, *The Little Book of Enlightenment, 122*, quoted in Davies, *op.cit.*,
[188] M.E. Thomas, *Mediaeval Skepticism and Chaucer*, NY, Cooper Square, 1971, p.79

[189] "Ladder" is what Hilton's title means to translate. The image is from Pseudo-Dionysius. But Hilton called his book *The Scale of Perfection*. It is translated from the Middle English with notes by Clark & Dorward, Paulist Press, NY, 1991.

The Ladder comprises two "books" which appear to be two separate essays on the mystical life, the second written in 1390, some years after the first. A comparison between the two is illuminating because it records Hilton's personal transition from belief in the necessity of a contemplative community and program (a monastery), to acknowledgement that mystical experience is available to all, in every walk of life. It was the key transition that characterized the entire era.

The Cloud of Unknowing

Not far away, in the same British Midlands, a nameless monk, probably Carthusian, an acquaintance if not a correspondent of Hilton's, is writing *The Cloud of Unknowing* and other letters to disciples laying out the ground rules for the contemplative life. The author of the *Cloud* is also convinced that contemplation need not be confined to the monasteries. This development was a product of late 13th century theology and had an historical impact far beyond its theoretical trappings. Some see it as the central insight that underlay the protestant reformation.

How the language and notions of the English author of the *Cloud of Unknowing* came to resemble those of Johannes Eckhart and his followers in the German Rhineland is anybody's guess. One observer attributes it simply to the spirit of the times; mysticism, he says, was in the air.[190] Others point out their common connection to Pseudo-Dionysius, the sixth century neo-Platonic Syriac monk whom mediaeval Christians believed a contemporary of St.Paul.[191] But there may have been a more direct influence that followed the flow of the Rhine as it dumped continental goods, people and ideas onto the Flemish delta, positioned for easy transport across the few miles of water to England. There is undoubtedly a line of historical influence that moves in an arc from Germany through the Lowlands and across the English Channel.[192] In any event, it's clear that Ruysbroeck, a disciple of Eckhart's, was

---

[190] Oliver Davies, *The Rhineland Mystics,* London, SPCK, 1989, p.17
[191] Clifton Wolters, tr., *The Cloud of Unknowing,* "Introduction," Penguin, 1978. p.20f.
[192] G.G.Coulton, *The Mediaeval Scene,* Cambridge, 1930, p.157. Quoted in M.E.Thomas, *op.cit.,* p.69

known and read in England at the end of the century. Davies says that "extracts from two of his works were circulating in England in English translation, primarily within the Carthusian order."[193]

We've already explored Meister Eckhart's thinking in Chapter V. Like Thomas Aquinas, Eckhart was a Dominican. He was assigned by his order to the same chair of theology at Paris warmed by the "angelic doctor" himself thirty years earlier. It's not surprising that Eckhart the disciple would have focused on those elements of Thomistic doctrine that supported his own spiritual interests. Aquinas' position on the *universal vocation to mystical union* provided Eckhart with what he needed. Thomas believed that the highest reaches of Christian spirituality were not reserved for the monastic elite, but were the natural flowering of religious life for all Christians. We've seen how the English mystics shared these notions. The Meister developed a mystical doctrine with an egalitarian character applied to all Christians, no matter of what class or condition and regardless of education, gender, age or status. In a society characterized by rigid social stratification, this was truly revolutionary. Eckhart, not surprisingly, was accused by the Inquisition of "confusing the common people."

Eckhart's connection with the English mystics of the late 14th century, however, runs much deeper than their shared respect for the common man. There is a similarity in the *Cloud* to the writings of Eckhart and his followers that speaks to the wide diffusion of the mystical ideas, philosophical assumptions, insights and methodology of Christian neo-Platonism. In 1385 this ancient mystical spirituality was in vogue in the Midlands monasteries, just beginning to be affected by the transformations that would later become a sentimental piety focused on an imagined personal relationship with the suffering Jesus. The spirituality in *The Cloud* shows tendencies in this direction, as do the Rhineland mystics, but *The Cloud* was still fundamentally based, like Eckhart, on the imageless mediation of a Cosmic Christ, the *Logos* of God. Our anonymous monk believed that this "God" in Whom all things "lived and moved and had their being," who would forever escape the grasp

---

[193] Davies, *op.cit.*, p.89

of our intellect and imagination, dwelt at the core of the "soul" and could be lovingly embraced by our will in a "cloud of unknowing."

> He [God] cannot be comprehended by our intellect or any man's. ... But only to our intellect is he incomprehensible; not to our love.
>
> ... So, for the love of God, be careful, and do not attempt to achieve this experience intellectually. I tell you truly, it cannot come this way. So leave it alone.
>
> ... The higher part of contemplation — at least as we know it in this life — is wholly caught up in darkness, and in this cloud of unknowing, with an outreaching love and blind groping for the naked being of God ...[194]

This conception of religious experience — an "unknowing" immersion in the *Logos*, the creative Word that "spoke" a Sacred Universe — bears on the question of God's suffusive presence in Creation. It is the belief in divine *immanence,* suggesting precisely that Creation (including the human being) is the outward display of the Indwelling God, that correlates to the religious imagery we have been discussing in these many chapters. Creation was the material dimension of "God." It is what impelled Eriugena in the 9th century to call created things "theophanies."[195] His conception of the divine immanence-in-creation required that he express himself in ways we are not accustomed to:

> God is both above everything and in everything, since He, who alone truly is, is the Essence of everything; and although He is whole in everything He does not cease being whole outside of everything; whole in the world, whole around the world, whole in sensible creation, whole in intelligible creation, whole He makes the universe, *whole He is made in the universe,* whole in the whole of the universe, whole in its parts, because He Himself is both whole and part, and neither whole nor part.[196]

Such a vision was derived from the Platonism that had "explained" Christianity since ancient times, until Aristotle, applied with surgical effectiveness by master logicians like Duns Scotus and William of Ockham early in the 14th century, changed the west's view of the world — permanently.

---

[194] Anonymous. *The Cloud of Unknowing,* ch 4 & 8, tr. Wolters, Penguin, 1978, p.63ff.
[195] Eriugena, *Periphyseon,* V [23] Indianapolis: Bobbs-Merrill, 1976. ... emphasis mine. The discussion is at the end of this remarkable chapter in which Eriugena says that the whole universe will participate in the general resurrection which is a *natural event* enhanced but not created by grace. Classically neo-platonic.
[196] *ibid,* IV [5]

A new "vision"

As Ockham's demolition of Platonic assumptions deepened and widened, confidence that the created universe was a reliable guide to "God's" presence and therefore where authentic relationship could be established, evaporated. Nature's implacable hostility displayed in the Great Plague of 1348 appeared to confirm the general disillusionment. Along with the Church, traditional Philosophy was losing its trusted status. Creation could no longer be embraced as a "theophany," the Sacrament of God. If anything it had become the instrument of torture, the tool of divine punishment, a sign of a hostile "God's" real feelings toward us. We were no longer at home on the earth.

The traditional signposts disappeared, and people searched for new assurances. The Plague was not a passing occurrence. The enormity of the event traumatized the European psyche in a state of religious fear. God was angry. Nothing could be more threatening. Christians needed to know what would assuage this "God's" fury. It seemed that in the absence of reliable intelligence about "God's will," once provided by the Church, only some form of *direct revelation* could give them that certitude. This translated, in the northern or Protestant solution, into an insistence on the authority of the scriptures, and for Mediterraneans, an increasing mystification of the official pronouncements of the Pope. Recourse to direct religious experience — already underway early in the century — was also a part of this disaffection with the claims the Church made of its ability to please and appease God. But in all cases, since neo-Platonism had defined created existence as the Sacred epiphany of an Indwelling God, its philosophical discreditation cast doubt on the reality of God's intimate presence in things, including us. So a feeling of distance from both God and material things was spawned by this new vision, this nightmare of divine wrath. *For us in our times, the sense of separation from God, derived from the now long forgotten catastrophe of the Plague of 1348, has grown to rule the Western view of the world.* The world is no longer our sacred home, because "God" is no longer believed to live there. Amicable relations with such a far-off and thin-skinned Deity in our era came to be considered an almost impossible moral achievement rather than the natural flowering of our inmost reality.

In the aftermath of the Plague, universally believed to be punishment for sin, emphasis was understandably placed on "works," i.e. what people were required to do — as revealed in Scripture or Papal Bulls — to avoid antagonizing a very sensitive God. Christians reasoned that a "God" so angry with them as to unleash an earthly fury of this magnitude, could hardly be expected to save them from eternal punishment without some major changes in behavior. But what was it they were doing wrong? And what did they need to do to set things right?

The obsession with damnation, personal sin and personal morality, along with ecclesiastical gimmicks (like indulgences) "insuring" salvation, increasingly characterized Christian practice on both sides of the Alpine divide. It is also easy to understand how a Church that had always supported itself by the sale of its sacramental products might be quick to capitalize on the marketing opportunities provided by the new calamities. Luther's revolt 130 years later would address both these distortions of Christian life. Given the paranoia about "God" that had come to dominate Christendom by Luther's era, however, his "reformation" did not get at the root of the problem. It was a band-aid, stop-gap solution: *"trust in the mercy of an Insulted God."* It did not challenge Augustine's "Doctrine of Original Hostility," i.e., that God was irreparably insulted.

Martin Luther was a child of his times. He was culturally conditioned against visualizing "God's" relationship to humankind as the unlimited loving overflow of a created universe borne within God's own being, as intimately one with God as the *Logos* itself, — "the apple of God's eye." It was not an option for Luther to think that "God" was too big to be insulted. Had he painted such a picture, no one could have believed it, so far had "God's" reputation deteriorated from the mediaeval synthesis that dominated Eckhart's vision. Juliana of Norwich in the 14th century would hardly have recognized the "God" the reformers had to wrestle with in the 16th.

The "God" of *The Cloud* vs. *The Imitation of Christ*

But in 1385 the English Midlands monks had not drifted far from that earlier mediaeval vision. In the mind of the cloistered author of *The Cloud of Unknowing* "God" was still "... his own being and yours, too."[197] It was the classic neo-platonic view, inherited from the ancients, of "participation-in-being." God dwelt as much — or more — in created theophanies,[198] and in people, as in the scriptures or the eucharistic host ... or Papal Bulls. This is important to remember. Otherwise we will not understand how this quiet monk could have so much confidence that the Indwelling God was not only accessible but even *eager* for intimate contact with each and every human being. "God" for him did not first come with the sacraments or with forgiveness and "grace." God was already here with us, in creation, the material world, sustaining all things in both *what and that* they were. It is the key insight of *The Cloud* and its central connection with Eckhart: We not only *have* but ARE God's "being," and only intentional refusal could prevent that "metaphysical" connection from growing naturally into intimate loving experience — contemplative union, the palpable precursor of the beatific vision, to which all humankind is called. The religious universalism implied here is too obvious for comment. "Salvation" does not need to be "won;" and to be lost it would have to be consciously rejected.

The *Cloud's* perspective is quite foreign to the paranoid religiosity which formed later generations and in which our own generation was brought up. The "modern" world-view is for us in our times the default conception of Christian practice, but only because the more ancient, which had existed for 1300 years, has been totally forgotten.

The transition to this "modern" spirituality is exemplified clearly in a Rhineland religious of the very next generation. Tho-

---

[197] Anonymous (the same author as the *Cloud*...), *Letter of Privy Counsel*, written probably around 1390, in *The Cloud,...* tr.Wolters, op.cit, ch.4 p. 170
[198] Eriugena, *Periphysion*, V[23} cites the Areopagite from ch.4 *On the Celestial Hierarchy*: "So all existing things participate in His being, for the being of all things is Superbeing, Divinity."

mas à Kempis is familiar to many of us as the author of *The Imitation of Christ*, one of the best-known Christian books on prayer, devotion and spirituality, used widely right up to Vatican II. Born in 1380 at Kempen, Germany (40 miles northwest of Cologne) in the same Rhine valley where the Beguines were rooted, Eckhart worked, and the late mediaeval mystics who followed him flourished, young Thomas Hemmerlein received his early training at a school in the Netherlands run by a religious community called the *Brethren of the Common Life*.[199] The Brethren were the direct descendents of the Rhineland mystical tradition, from Eckhart and the Beguines, but their spirituality had been transformed by the events of the previous century.

These mystics were scattered along the Rhine from Switzerland through Strasburg and Cologne and into the Netherlands. The communities that sprung up from this movement became the principal promoters of a spirituality known as the *devotio moderna* — the Modern Devotion.[200] It was a phenomenon of the 15th century — a hundred years before the Protestant Revolt.

Devotio Moderna

The "modern" (i.e., post-mediaeval) view looks like this: God is Pure Spirit and therefore Holy, and because of Original Sin, which corrupted our bodies and matter, *we are not*. Adam's sin insulted God, irreparably and contaminated us all, making our love of material things, inordinate. We have forgotten our spiritual origins. We are *sinners by birth,* "wretches," and naturally alienated from "God." Therefore from the moment we are conceived, "God" is angry with us and morally demanding, and because of Original

---

[199] CF *Wikipedia:* "The Brethren of the Common Life." ... "The Confraternity of the Common Life resembled the Beghard and Beguine communities which had flourished earlier and were by then in decay. Its members took no vows, neither asked nor received alms; their first aim was to cultivate the interior life, and they worked for their daily bread."

[200] "devotio moderna." *Encyclopedia Britannica.* 2006 Ultimate Reference Suite DVD 27 Nov. 2006: "a school and trend of spirituality stressing meditation and the inner life and criticizing the highly speculative spirituality of the 13th and 14th centuries. ... The *Imitation of Christ*, traditionally attributed to Thomas à Kempis, is a classic expression of the movement."

Sin, our souls have become dominated by our corrupt flesh. We are constantly failing in our compliance to His commands. Christians are trying to save their souls from eternal damnation by suppressing sinful flesh and declaring their faith in the saving power of Jesus, whose death on the cross is the only thing capable of averting this hostile "God's" abiding wrath. Motivation for this titanic effort is had in contemplating (imagining) both the horrors of hell and the sufferings of Jesus on the cross, borne for our sake to save us from eternal punishment. Catholics differed from later Protestants only in the relatively minor matter of the "assistance" coming from the proper (i.e., juridically valid and ritually correct) performance of the "sacraments." These sacraments did not in any way change the common Christian view of an alienated world, or of "God's" angry attitude or of our chances for salvation. They simply offered an automatic assistance brokered exclusively by the Church.

In such a world, by early in the 15th century, the view that dominated Christendom is that the spiritual "God" is anything but friendly toward us. The most we materialistic wretches could ever hope for is that "God" would be merciful and not damn us for our sins, our "material" concerns and addictions. The emphasis was pervasively negative.

By 1950 when I was growing up the scene had not much changed. My generation of Catholics spent our life avoiding (mortal) sin and eternal damnation. "Good works"? They were of value only because they built up "merit" which would stand us in good stead on judgment day. Prayer became almost exclusively petition for salvation and penitence for sin. Salvation was forgiveness. In general christians sought assurance in the "feeling" that "God" had forgiven their sins i.e., their love of material existence. The Catholic Church elevated confession into a mechanism that "guaranteed" pardon, thus keeping the feeling of forgiveness dependent on the rituals of the Church.

The entire edifice was constructed on the base of fear, guilt and the individual's moral "achievement" of salvation for him / herself. It was "modern" western culture. It formed personal character that was grasping, pusillanimous, selfish and afraid. It was alienated to the core — a fitting human counterpart to a hostile and insulted "God."

The Imitation of Christ illustrates these attitudes and proposed remedies. Listen to the fundamental vision that percolates not far beneath the surface of these words:

- ... *Living on earth is truly a misery. The more a man desires spiritual life, the more bitter the present becomes to him, because he understands better and sees more clearly the corruption of human nature.*
- ... *Remember that because all flesh had corrupted its course, the great deluge followed. Since, then, our interior affection is corrupt, it must be that the action which follows from it, the index as it were of our lack of inward strength, is also corrupt.*
- ... *This is the greatest wisdom — to seek the kingdom of heaven through contempt of the world.*
- ... *the Apostles, martyrs, confessors, virgins, and all the rest who willed to follow in the footsteps of Christ ... they hated their lives on earth...*
- ... *woe to those who love this miserable and corruptible life. Some, indeed, can scarcely procure its necessities either by work or by begging; yet they love it so much that, if they could live here always, they would care nothing for the kingdom of God. How foolish and faithless of heart are those who are so engrossed in earthly things as to relish nothing but what is carnal! Miserable men indeed, for in the end they will see to their sorrow how cheap and worthless was the thing they loved.*
- ... *if you had never to eat, or drink, or sleep, but could praise God always and occupy yourself solely with spiritual pursuits, how much happier you would be than you are now, a slave to every necessity of the body!*

It promoted an attitude of personal friendship with Jesus that would displace and substitute for all other relationships:

- ... *Your Beloved is such that He will not accept what belongs to another — He wants your heart for Himself alone.*
- ... *It is a great art to know how to converse with Jesus, and great wisdom to   know how to keep Him. Be humble and peaceful, and Jesus will be with you. Be devout and calm, and He will re-*

> *main with you. You may quickly drive Him away and lose His grace, if you turn back to the outside world. And, if you drive Him away and lose Him, to whom will you go and whom will you then seek as a friend? You cannot live well without a friend, ...*

Mental states and inner feelings are ascribed to God's actions:

> *... It is God's prerogative to give grace and to console when He wishes, as much as He wishes, and whom He wishes, as it shall please Him and no more.*

> *... remember that the light which I have withdrawn for a time as a warning to you and for My own glory may again return.*

> *... Fear the judgments of God! Dread the wrath of the Almighty! [Those that do] constantly long for everlasting things; they are unwilling to hear of earthly affairs and only with reluctance do they serve the necessities of nature. These sense what the Spirit of truth speaks within them: for He teaches them to despise earthly things.*

This gives us a sense of the direction things were going in.

Part II: Divine Immanence In a World of Matter

The foregoing was an admittedly quick look at the historical developments that nourished the view of the world that has prevailed in Western Europe since the 15th century, right up to our time. Hopefully, despite its cursory character, this sketch is sufficient to help us understand the mindset in which we were formed, and which formed the default cosmogony and corresponding "modern" (post-mediaeval) personality throughout Western Europe.

If there is one central idea that I want draw from this overview it is that the conjunction of factors, historical and philosophical, that accumulated in the 14th century, served to create a distorted image of God. And while the paranoid picture of an angry, implacable "God" had been theologically prepared by Augustine much earlier, and therefore was always alive and ready to spring into action in Western Christianity, it wasn't until the unique conflation of factors occurring in the 14th century that this destructive view of "God" and the world came to predominate to the exclusion of all others. In the crucible of the sufferings of the 1300's, what had been elaborated by Augustine as a theoretical explanation for evil in the world, became the guiding imagery of daily life and ordinary christian spirituality. The 14th century awakened a dormant potential in Western thinking — an insuperable mistrust of "God" and a terrified obsession with moral behavior focused on the avoidance of the attractions of the flesh.

Providence and Original Sin

I contend that the traditional notion of "providence" in conjunction with the doctrine of Original Sin was at the root of this distorted image of "God." An angry "God" was a grotesque fantasy of the elderly Augustine's guilty mind, abundantly confirmed by the disasters of the 14th century. There was a tragic inevitability about this development. If you believe in a traditional providence micro-managed by a "personal God," then sooner or later you will attribute to "God's will," (intention or permission) the most heinous and inhuman of occurrences: cataclysmic natural disasters (like the

Plague), tortuous debilitating mental and physical illnesses, intolerable personal and social crimes. A "God" that would not prevent these things from happening to us would have to be a vindictive and punitive "God." Juliana could never have accepted that. How western Christians could ever have believed it is an anomaly worth trying to understand. For whatever the source of such universal paranoia — doctrine, culture or pathology — it is our special demon.

The great mediaeval theologians, like Aquinas, knew "providence" did not function outside the natural order, what they called "secondary causes." In fact, Thomas' very definition of providence is "to order things to their proper end."[201] He explained that this meant that "God" created a vast ordered universe in which the divine will (providence, the "primary cause") is carried out by created agents (secondary causes), acting autonomously, each in its own way — not by "God" acting alone.[202] *Providence, in other words, is indistinguishable from the natural order.* The theologians, however, were not in a position to challenge the popular concept of an interventionist "providence," preached by the Church (to this very day), the source of its income and its power over the minds of men. Aquinas tried to balance this by constantly warning against anthropomorphism in his writings. But to no avail. In practice the Church promoted the ancient naïve view, and lived off it.

Personally speaking, following Juliana of Norwich, I refuse to accept any notion that would effectively deny compassion or "goodness" to "God." We went through this analysis in chapter III. But it means changing our anthropomorphic imagery about providence. "God" does not micro-manage the universe. There is no evidence whatsoever of any divine effort to alleviate suffering (or punish wrongdoers) except what may be provided through us. If there is a "divine providence" that functions after the initial equations of the big-bang — i.e., that goes beyond the normal operations of nature, — it is offered exclusively through human agency. I consider the common version of "providence" not only disin-

---

[201] ST, I, 22 passim
[202] SCG, III, 77

genuous in the extreme, but ultimately blasphemous, an insult to the goodness of "God." For there is only one way to interpret the personal disposition of the "God" of popular providence. Given the horrors we suffer, "God" can only be implacably hostile toward us. This was Augustine's conclusion. We have to admit, Augustine was both honest about life and uncompromising in his logic. His mistake was to believe "God" was "personal" as we are, and acted like we do in our history and in our lives.

On the other hand, if "God" is benevolent and *really wants* to save us from these awful things, then we'd have to say "God's" persistent *inaction* proves "he" is impotent (or at least permanently immobilized) in precisely the ways we have traditionally defined as "providence." This is just a more elaborate way of restating the old cynical paradox:

If God is good He is not God; and if God is God, He is not good.

Against this I claim that to say "God" is *both good and God* requires a radical change in our understanding of God's presence, character and "action" in the world. My adjustment of the imagery surrounding providence does not affect my conviction of the existence of "God," or "God's" presence in the world, as often happens when people awaken to the absurdities of the naïve notion of providence. But it changes, in a major way, my image of the "face of God." So we're back to our question: What is "God" *really* like?

What is "God" like?

If, as the evidence indicates, "God" does not act in those particular ways that the doctrine of providence has perennially declared he does, and yet is the source of the development and creation of things, it can only be as an immanent creative *presence.*

By *presence*, I mean physical, material. *Presence* is what Eriúgena meant when he said, "... *whole He is made in the universe, ...*" For, to say that God exists in any form requires knowledge. If God's presence were *not* physical, we could never know it. Our universe, after all, is entirely material and so are we. And if "God's" presence were not physical, "God" could have no role whatsoever in the physical effects, the observable entities and events, of the material world. "God's" existence would be of no interest to us — an academic fact of the most irrelevant kind. I believe it was this intuitive requirement for *relationship to the physical world* that has been traditionally translated into "omnipotence," and its derivative "providence," against all the available evidence.

If "God's" presence is physical it is therefore *empirical*, it can *be experienced* either directly as an entity immediately observable in itself apart from its effects, or indirectly, as an entity with a capacity for physical action resulting in palpable effects from which an active presence, even though not observable, can be validly inferred. In this latter case such "causative" action is itself *necessarily physical* and stems directly from a physical power in the agent. Therefore, again, "God" must be physical ... *"God" must have a material dimension.*

That God might be *more* than physical, as this latter case may be taken to allow, I believe is not only unknowable it is also irrelevant. The claim that our "reasoning" can resolve that impasse and actually give us new information, — for example, that "God" is spirit — is the traditional western escape mechanism. The attempt has always led to positing the existence of "spirit," i.e., what is *not* physical. It has led to our proclivity to define ourselves as spirit and locate ourselves *outside* the material world. Such an extraction is contrary to nature. It has historically entailed the destructive misunderstanding of our *selves* as bodies as well as the catastrophic exploitation of the earth, its macro systems and living species.

There are assumptions driving that ancient spiritual "solution" that are unacceptable. For an inference such as the existence of "spirit" to function, what is *not material* would have to be inferred from what could only be material effects. To presume to know that a particular material effect points to a source that transcends materiality is contradictory on its face. No material effect, as such, can be non-material or point to something non-material as its essential source. Conversely, the evidence for what is not material must be had in what is not material. But what is not material cannot be known by our cognitive apparatus. Traditional western philosophy has accepted both those fallacies as axioms.

Furthermore, the claim that certain material effects validly imply the existence of something *beyond materiality* is necessarily based on the entirely unsubstantiated assumption that we know *what the limits of materiality are*. Such an assertion is made by "philosophers" who in all other respects are willing to leave the description of the characteristics of "matter" to the physicists. But, I contend, *no one, philosopher or physicist, knows what the limits of materiality are, or even if it has any limits at all. It is my belief that what we, historically, have been calling the evidence of "spirit" is simply a manifestation of a capacity of matter that we had not suspected was there.* The assertion that there exists anything other than matter is entirely gratuitous. There is no effect, heretofore assigned to the operations of "spirit," which can at this point in time be said definitively to transcend the capacities of matter. There is nothing to prevent "God" from being physical — and if physical, empirical. Being is entirely homogeneous.[203]

---

[203] The contradictions involved in the traditional understanding of a "spiritual" God creating a material universe were not lost on the ancients. And they were honest in their admission that a resolution was not rationally possible. The following is from Gregory of Nyssa (Fourth Century CE), On *The Making of Man*, XXIII, 3 and 4:

> *"3. ... they [who challenge the possibility of matter being created by an immaterial God] employ in support of their own doctrine some such arguments as these: If God is in His nature simple and immaterial, without quantity, or size, or combination, and removed from the idea of circumscription by way of figure, while all matter is apprehended in extension measured by intervals, and does not escape the apprehension of our senses, but becomes known to us in color, and figure, and bulk, and size, and resistance, and the other attributes belonging to it, none of which it is possible to conceive in the Divine nature, — what method is there for the production of matter from the immaterial, or of the nature that has dimensions from that which is unextended? For if these things are believed to have their existence from that source, they clearly come into existence after being in Him in some mysterious way; but if material existence was in Him, how can He be immaterial while including matter in Himself? And similarly with all the other marks by which the material nature is differentiated; if quantity exists in God, how is God without quantity? If the compound nature exists in Him, how is He simple, without parts and without combination? so that the argument forces us to think either that He is material, because matter has its existence from Him as a source; or, if one avoids this, it is necessary to suppose that matter was imported by Him ab extra for the making of the universe. (cont'd)*
>
> *4. If, then, it [matter] was external to God, something else surely existed besides God, conceived, in respect of eternity, together with Him Who exists ungenerately; so*

"God's" presence, therefore, because it is material, is able to be experienced. I believe this is the philosophical implication, the ground of the phenomenon we call mystical experience.

The "God" of Mystical Experience

"God's" *personal presence* has always been the premise for traditional mysticism in the West. But we're trying to answer the question: What is this "God" really like? ... and therefore what does "God's Presence" mean concretely? The "God" of *traditional* mystical experience was the same "God" who (1) created heaven and earth and (2) hovered providentially over everything that happened, including (3) the psychic states of the human soul because (4) "He" was a person, just like us.

None of this, I claim is true as stated.

First, "God" did not create heaven and earth . One of the reasons why we, in our times, cannot accept the traditional image of "God" is our understanding of evolution. Our science has identified the adaptive self-modification of organisms to new environmental conditions as the source of the diversity of species. "God" is not separately involved in this process in any discernible way. Evolution is reducible to *an energy* at the core of physical reality — we can call it "the drive to survive," the insistence on existence — as the source of all development. As far as our sciences are concerned, there is nothing beyond the presence *and self-directedness* of this foundational energy. I think there is enough evidence that biological evolution utilizes the same processes that are in integral continuity with those of pre-living entities to allow us to extrapolate validly to all aggregations and development in the universe, atomic, molecular, organism, personal. This self-

---

that the argument supposes two eternal and unbegotten existences, having their being concurrently with each other — that of Him Who operates as an artificer, and that of the thing which admits this skilled operation; ... Yet we do believe that all things are of God, as **we hear the Scripture say so; and as to the question how they were in God, a question beyond our reason, we do not seek to pry into it**, *believing that all things are within the capacity of God's power — both to give existence to what is not, and to implant qualities at His pleasure in what is.*

organizing energy for continued existence is *the* primordial datum of the physical universe.[204]

Evolution, therefore, immediately severs the oldest and most venerable connection between the traditional "God" and the material universe: *cosmogenesis*, by which I mean the design and production of the entities made of matter that populate the world around us. "God," we now know, considered as an independent entity or agent, *did not do this* — neither in production *nor design*.

(Design is a key concept in the derivation of the traditional notion of "creator." We cannot attribute the "design" of things directly to intelligence and from that infer an intelligent designer. Evolution has revealed that things were designed by incremental adaptations to environmental changes, driven by the *thirst to survive*, not for any other purpose. Therefore *what* they are was not designed by "God."[205] We are thereby forced to say, once again, that "God" can only be either the very energy of matter itself, or the proximate and ever present source of that energy. *The agent of creation is material energy.* But please observe: in either case, "God" is material and therefore directly or indirectly empirical — "God" as *matter's-energy* can be experienced.)

Second, "God" does not hover "providentially" over creation. "Providence" would logically involve the use of the same interventionist powers as Cosmogenesis. Our conclusion that "God" did not directly design and produce the things we see around us, therefore, is consistent with the assertions we have been making about naïve providence. If "God" did not directly *create* the natural order, God does not directly *provide* by manipulating the natural order, either. But that is nothing new. The rejection of a naïve providence has, in fact, also characterized the best of our intellectual history. We can cite in support our greatest philosophers and theologians, even those who lived in the high middle ages, like Aquinas, for whom "providence" was to be found in the operation

---

[204] CF the work of Stuart Kaufman et al.
[205] ... unless you are prepared to see the drive to survive as "God." This would be pantheism. For a pan-entheist, however, the "vital impulse" is the "congenital self-embrace of being," the primary display of the divine presence, and the determining force in all creation.

of secondary causes, the natural order. "God" does not micromanage the universe, nor did "he" design it and form it.

It's not what "God" is like.

Mystical Experience and The Character of "God"

Well, then, what *is* "God" like? — the "God" of mystical experience.

I offer an image: God "breathes" me into existence. This is obviously a metaphor, *not* a "scientific" statement. But it is a metaphor for something I can actually experience. I'm not the first one to find this image appropriate. The great Eriúgena used it in the 9th century:

> ... *we believe the soul was created by the breath of God, or rather that it IS the very breath of God,* ....[206]

But what do I directly experience? What the ancients, like Eriugena, called the "soul," we call the *self*. *I experience my self.* It's my metaphysics (or my beliefs) that interpret this experience for me and tell me that the *existence* I palpate as *me*, the *self* that emerges in time, is an energy that is "God's" very own. It is not a spiritual entity, a "soul" apart from my body. It is the energy that enlivens the cells of my body and every other organism in the universe. It is existence, *matter-energy. Therefore I know "God" (and all things) in knowing my self.* God is at the core of my inmost self, the source and sustainer of my physical "being," and must similarly be at the base of everything else that exists. Because I can experience my *self,* when I listen to myself in deep silence — when I'm no longer talking, when all the words have stopped — I can hear "God" "speaking" my existence, my *self.*

I don't believe this is some kind of extraordinary supernatural or visionary event. I concur with what the Buddhists have said for 2500 years: that contemplative experience, *nirvana,* is the result of *ascesis* — an exercise, a studied, strenuous and repeated attempt to achieve mental and volitional quiescence mediated by a focus on the reality (sufferings) of life. Contemplative experience is not due to the "movings of divine grace."

---

[206] John Scotus Eriugena, *Periphyseon,* Book IV, [9].

A personal "God"?

So, **third**, "God" does not manage our psychic states. "Movings of grace," is an important phrase for christians, historically. One very strong and persistent current in Western mysticism has attributed the initiation of contemplative experience to the almost whimsical gift of a personal "God" who related and interacted episodically with the "soul," revealing "Himself" in acts of love. We saw this functioning in the *Imitation of Christ*. Mystical experience was considered something of a miraculous event — beyond the normal operations of nature. "God," who was believed to be pure spirit and beyond the reach of human consciousness "revealed" "him" self to the "soul" in an event that was believed to be unequivocally *supernatural*, uniquely possible only to those who enjoyed the privileges that came exclusively with Catholic Christianity, viz., access to "sanctifying grace" through the sacraments. No "heathen" (or even "non-Catholic") could ever hope to experience any such thing.

And this implies, **fourth**, that "God" is not a "person" as we are persons. That means "he" does not "interact" with us personally. There is no dialogic relationship with "God." Because the traditional "God" was considered a "person," the experience I speak of was traditionally characterized as relational, a loving interchange established on the unpredictable initiative of "God," which subsequently followed the rules of all interpersonal relationships: it was exclusive; it required absolute fidelity, in all respects a "love-affair." It's instructive that Christians have classically called this contemplative contact "union," "espousals" and "marriage." Today we admit these terms are *metaphors*, but the Christian ascetics of the not very distant past took them quite literally, and many still do. One of the historic roots of the celibacy required of the spiritual elite in the Catholic tradition is that holiness means a personal psycho-erotic union with a personal "God," involving all the privileges and obligations of matrimony.

This was, I believe, an invincible anthropomorphism. Of course, it is completely understandable, and some would say, inevitable. Humans cannot "love" the impersonal *or* what is not-physical. The fact that such an interactive personal relationship could *not* in any way be validly said of the traditional immutable "God" of western philosophy was ignored. The scriptural "God," presented in the Song of Solomon (and later applied to Jesus) was an intense personal lover. That was the image that dominated. This "personal" description has proven to be another of the contradictory elements in the western view of "God." Both providence and predestination fall under the same anthropomorphic categories that have been used to describe mystical experience ... and they present similar anomalies. ... but, that's *not* what "God" is like.

Even discounting the erotic imagery of *the Song of Solomon*, I believe the West was culturally predisposed to treat mystical experience as a dialogic "love affair" with "God" because the classic religious Western world view, inherited from the Hebrew scriptures, is grounded on an omniscient and omnipotent *personal* "God" who providentially micro-manages each and every event in the universe, including our psychic states. One would think this an outlandish idea on the face of it. But it has been traditionally maintained from ancient times because it's a necessary corollary to saying that God was "our Father" who gives us rules to follow and will reward or punish us for the quality of our compliance. This kind of "God" could hardly be expected to reward and punish our behavior if "he" was not minutely attentive and occupied with everything we did, said *and thought*. This was the Judaic tradition onto which Christianity was grafted.

This "God" as Father could not easily mesh with the Greek philosophical image of "Being," the "One," conceived as a self-absorbed unchanging supra-cosmic force. But in practice, at the pastoral level, the anthropomorphisms of the Hebrew imagery dominated the imagination as one would have expected. They were concrete and personal. The Greek philosophical projections — pallid, cerebral syllogisms, devoid of concrete character — were effectively subordinated to it, if not abandoned altogether. This generated even more anomalies. For it made the divine "self-absorption" of the philosophers operate in the service of the personal whim of the Biblical Yahweh, "Father." Connect that with the "unforgivable insult" of Original Sin conjured by Augustine and it produced the absurd image of a selfish, infantile and unpredictable "God," a monster-Father, eternally obsessed with the primordial insult to "his" dignity therefore eternally angry with humankind, and yet amorously available to his chosen favorites.[207]

Even where such a pathological amalgam did not coalesce, at the popular level the image of "God" has changed very little since the days of the Psalms which unapologetically prayed for economic prosperity, victory in battle, curing of disease and revenge on enemies. Yahweh is believed to act in our lives and in history as we do, only infinitely more powerful and all knowing. The psalmist was perfectly comfortable with asking "God" to punish his enemies by "dashing their children's' heads against the stones." Needless to say, we, in our times, cannot do that!

The "Old Testament" Book of Job, which wrestled with the contradictions of an omnipotent, micro-managing "God" who allows horrors to befall innocent people, is as relevant, challenging, and controversial today as the day it was written more than 2500 years ago. This is no surprise; for the image of "God" it set out to question so long ago, has not changed in the least, and reigns to this day. It's what reigned when the Black Plague decimated Christendom in 1348. And it's what confused our penitent, Fidel, and left him feeling betrayed by a "God" he thought loved him.

The Testimony of the Mystics

It's ironic that the projection of a "personal relationship" breaks down among the very mystical writers that propose it, *because they attempt to systematize the experience.* Christian mystical writers have traditionally claimed to be able to explicate the exact process by which "God" would relate intimately with the "soul." Systematization, it hardly needs to be said, would seem to run directly counter to the spontaneity of interpersonal relationship. So by insisting on it, the mystics were, I believe, implicitly admitting to the organic nature of the presence of "God" in the "soul" and our ability to relate to it. They knew "God" was there, permanently, stead-

---

[207] C.G.Jung, analyzing the Book of Job, characterized the "God" presented there as "infantile." Archibald MacLeish, in his play *J.B.,* a take-off on the Book of Job, has "J.B." *forgive* "God."

ily, reliably. "God" isn't going anywhere or doing anything unpredictable. Any sequence of experiences that took place had to do with the changes in the human partner alone. If the mystical counseling was accurate, the "movements of the soul," i.e., the experiences of "God's" presence, were predictable, even if not linear, and depending on the moral disposition, astuteness, hard work, and fidelity of the human subject, inevitable. This concurs with the general teachings of the Buddhists through the millennia. *Nirvana* was not a divine gift; it was a human quest, the result of insight and hard persistent ascetical practice.

A very revealing though somewhat obscure component of the advice of mystics, is that mystical experience requires *physical health*. Aquinas says *sanitas corporis* is one of the essential components of the contemplative life. And the author of *The Cloud*, for his part, is unexpectedly urgent about its importance:

> Sometimes illness or some other upset of body or soul, or natural necessity will prove a real hindrance, and often prevent you from contemplating. ... beware of illness as much as you can ... I tell you the truth when I say this work demands great serenity, an integrated and pure disposition, in soul and in body.
>
> So for the love of God treat your body and soul alike with great care, and keep as fit as you can.[208]

This unexpected emphasis of the mystics for a "material" integrity in what is supposed to be an entirely "spiritual" phenomenon is not surprising once we realize they are talking about an organically based experience of *self* through which contact with "God" is mediated. If contemplative experience were, as traditionally believed, truly a "spiritual interaction" with a personal "God," the presence of illness should have no adverse effect. Quite the contrary, one might even expect "God," as a loving parent or partner to be even more attentive and "present" to the "soul" that was suffering a bodily illness.

Another item that suggests that the mystics had a different conception of "God" than the popular one, is the Thomist doctrine of the universality of the "call to perfection." In the middle ages, this was an issue of some controversy and Thomas took an untradi-

---

[208] *The Cloud ..., op cit.* ch.41

tional and historically important position with regard to it. The accepted wisdom held that the heights of union with "God," sanctity, required a *special vocation*, community and intellectual program of life. Only highly educated monks (almost always, members of the nobility) and those *called and educated* to the practice of prayer and meditation within a structured life-style approved by the Church (monasteries) could aspire to such achievements. But Thomas disagreed. By insisting that sanctity resided exclusively in the possession of "charity," i.e., the habit of love, he said the heights of sanctity were accessible to all.[209] And since all people are capable of the beatific vision *because of their nature as human beings,* it followed that mystical union was simply a foretaste of the beatific vision, and all are equally capable of that as well. There is nothing in Thomas to suggest that the universal call to Christian perfection would somehow *not* entail all the privileges and prerogatives traditionally associated with that state; and that included mystical experience. If mystical experience were accessible to all because of "God's" presence in the *caritas* of the Christian, then mystical experience was, in a very real sense, *dependent upon the interior disposition of the Christian,* not "God's" "personal" whim or initiative, much less on the structures of monastic life

This was historically more significant than it first appears. By opening the heights of mystical experience *to all,* it had the effect of freeing ordinary people from the limitations imposed by their "state in life" in the middle ages. It eliminated one of the ideological props of the stratifications in feudal society, with the educated elite nobility at the top in every category, including "spirituality." It challenged the hierarchical order and hence it was potentially socially destabilizing. Aquinas' position was picked up by disciples like Johannes Eckhart who preached a radical egalitarianism he called "christian aristocracy," a status acquired by *birth and baptism alone* that qualified everyone for the great achievements of religious life. Eckhart used this "new" thinking to support the

---

[209] ST 2-2,23-24 passim; cf SCG III, 57

Beguines in the Rhine Valley where he worked.[210] Many see this as an important step in that *leveling* of mediaeval social structures that led to the formation of the modern world.

If, as is proposed in these reflections, we consider "God's" generative presence to be, in fact, *existentially constitutive of all the components of the human person*, then the awareness of *self* is, in fact, the contemplation of the divine presence. Human consciousness is simply attending to the fundamental energy of ongoing, emergent existence sustaining the whole organism, the *self*. This is what we in the West have traditionally called the "God" of mystical experience. I believe the human experience of the existential origination in the here and now of one's own personality, one's *self*, welling up from the primordial energy of life, the driving force of being's "congenital self-embrace," is what the mystics have been calling the experience of "God." That presence, i.e., that existential energy and drive, is always there. It is *physical, material and entirely empirical*; but it is none the less Sacred. It is *transcendent* in the sense that it is both beyond my capacity to create or control (though not beyond my capacity to experience) and it is the sustenance in existence of everything else that *exists* as well — i.e., things beyond me that owe nothing to me for their existence. The absolute invariability of the energy of existence and its homogeneity throughout the universe as well as its complete identification with all things *as they are,* has fooled us into thinking it was not "God." Naturally. For we had naïvely preconceived of "God" as a separate entity rather than as *the existence of everything that exists*. The divine presence, however, is stable and continuous, homogeneous and universal. Even though it may be more than, *it is not distinct from,* the being of all the things that are. So in experiencing existing *things-in-process*, one is experiencing "God."

---

[210] The Beguines were communities of lay women in a movement that had begun early in the 12th century. Dedicated to celibacy, poverty and a life of christian service, the Beguines consciously tried to avoid either of the two traditional male-dominated lifestyles open to women in the middle ages: the family under a father or husband, or the convent under the tutelage of the all-male hierarchy. We know the Thomist doctrine had its impact because the Beguines were suppressed in 1317 for 'heresy" and Eckhart was condemned 10 years later.

And insofar as all things, just by existing, are doing exactly the same thing, "God's" presence does not vary. Duns Scotus in the early 14th century would say that for this reason "being" was a *univocal* concept. For it denoted the same phenomenon wherever it was found. The only possible source of variation is our experience of it. And that has to do with the psychology of the human individual — his / her capacity to eliminate any distracting focus on the "ordinary" objects of intentionality (what we "want"), achieve a state of ideational and affective quiescence in order attentively to rest, in absolute stillness, in the non-conceptual, connatural, cognitive awareness of the primal energy of existence itself as it emerges continuously in time producing my *self* and all the things around me.

The *self.* Eriugena called it the breath of "God."

Please do not misunderstand. I am not trying to "reduce" the experience of "God" to its material components in order then to dismiss it. Entirely to the contrary, I believe the material components are the primordial and determinative expression of the Sacred. I'm trying to understand a mystical phenomenon that is common to people from diverse cultures around the world and at all times throughout the millennia of recorded history. We in our culture have unfortunately only been willing to acknowledge true mystical experience in those people involved in orthodox Christian practice and in line with the elite educational status currently established by Christian society. But I believe that the mystics of all traditions have encountered what we are seeking. Christians happen to call it "God;" some others do not. Hence the word "God" must always remain in a state of active deconstruction. Since "God" is unknown, even the use of the term runs the risk of resurrecting the old personalist, activist, anthropomorphic designer imagery for us. Especially in the West we need to remind ourselves constantly that "God" is not like us at all … even while we ourselves are the gate that opens to contact with "Him," or as Eriugena says, we are the "mask that 'God' wears."

In the descriptions of their experiences, I trust the mystics — all of them, christian and non-christian. *What the christian mystics have called "God," I am convinced, is the simple, silent perception of emerging existence as the elements of my organism maintain their "presence" successively through time.* In experiencing *my presence* I experience "God's" presence. I personally believe that what we have called "God" IS the energy of this very physical presence which we experience in its dimension as Sacred Source. According to the mystics, if we can become still enough, quiet all desires and "listen" to existence emerging in the depth of our being, we will experience what they experienced: the breath of the Sacred on our cheeks, Elijah's gentle breeze.

This existential presence is *passively generative,* allowing all us creatures to drink from the bottomless cup of existence, the true Holy Grail. It can only be put in terms that describe a *maternal* love that is primordial, universal, unchanging and entirely non-interventionist. This mother "God" does *nothing* but simply allow "Herself," i.e., "Being", to be used by "her" children in whatever way they decide. Once the human being realizes the overwhelming and invincible Love that is at the source of his / her palpable, empirical *self,* the experience of self becomes the basis of mystical experience. It provides a "profound and available sanity," as one Christian poet put it.

Read what they've written, East and West. The conceptual emptiness, the existential "darkness," the loving trust, the resulting confidence — the sense of ultimate security and personal value, the utter tranquility and quiet joy — are all there in each one of the world's mystical traditions. And yet their "theologies," the roster of their beliefs, are all different. In the East there is little talk of "God;" and even among the Hindus where there is belief in the "Absolute," it is not "personal." Brahma is a suffusive creative presence, but it is not a "person." How is all this possible if the traditional theological claims of the Christians about "God" are literally true?

For me, and for many others who come from a Christian background, mystical experience is not exclusively due to "sanctifying grace" channeled through the Catholic sacraments. But it is a full and authentic experience of the Sacred nonetheless, shared and confirmed around the world. It is an unmistakable marker pointing to the ultimate source of our existence. I would have no problem with Christians calling it an experience of "God," if it weren't for the fact that they insist on taking "God" as an anthropomorphized *person,* made in *our* image and likeness. They have given the object of that experience an interactive personal and interventionist character — consistent with their anthropomorphic image of the Almighty Father "God" of naïve providence, who is also the "Intelligent Designer" of the Cosmos — that I am convinced is just not there. Before you dismiss me as a refractory atheist, however, please note: *the great Christian theologians, like Aquinas, agree with me.* Their notions of providence are universally non-interventionist. That should be no surprise. Otherwise, if "God" were a person as I am a person, and micro-manages the universe, "he" must be held accountable for the horrible things "he" allows to happen. In practice, based on these anthropomorphic premises, Christians in fact *do* get angry at "God." This is patently absurd, and is the source of an unnecessary anguish added to the suffering in question. "God" does *not* micro-manage the universe, and the sooner we acknowledge it the more comprehensible life becomes. Anything that seems personally interactive with "God," either in history or psychic states, is supplied entirely by the human subject's imagination.

The Abrahamic Tradition

The personalist and activist "God" of the early Christians is a legacy of those ancient near-Eastern people, the Hebrews, responsible for the Scriptures that created the Abrahamic Tradition which the present-day Jewish, Christian and Islamic currents have all inherited. It has traditionally been called the "Old Testament" by Christians who appropriated the text and promoted its "God" as their own. That "God" of the Hebrews was in every respect the heavenly counterpart of an ancient near-Eastern Sheik. He was Father, Warrior, Lover, Protector. He was jealous and demanding, and by turns angry and forgiving, punitive and compassionate, ferocious and gentle. But above all He was jealous. He was the same as all the gods that represented their people in the pantheon of the Fertile Crescent: like a lover, "He" wanted to be the *only one* — the only god of the Hebrew people. [211]

But this "love-affair" meant, like matrimony, that the god became identified with the historical fortunes of his partner. All the other gods in the Near East neighborhood disappeared, swept into the "dustbin of history" when their people lost military power, political autonomy and national identity. The god of the Hebrews avoided that fate. But it was not because "he" prevailed over his rivals. The fact was that "he" was lucky enough to find favor with the world conquering *Greeks* and through them acceptance into the new pantheon of the emerging Hellenic Mediterranean Empire ultimately managed by Rome.

The Greeks inherited Palestine in the conquests of Alexander the Great. They became enamored of the Judaism they discovered there. They had great respect for the monotheism recorded in the Jewish Scriptures. The Hebrew "God," Yahweh, refused either to be named or allow any images to be made of him. This paralleled the developments in their own Greek religious thinking espoused by the Pythagoreans, Plato and the Stoics and most recently, Aristotle, tutor and advisor to Alexander. The Greek philosophers came independently to the conclusion that the all-too-human antics of the gods of Olympus were absurd. "God" was, as the Jews suggested, "One," nameless and imageless. The Jewish Scriptures, enjoying the prestige of antiquity and the weight of an independent source, corroborated these new directions in Greek thought and gave the Greeks courage to pursue the terrifying task of dismissing their traditional gods. They were so impressed with the Jewish Scriptures that they had them translated into Greek. The sponsors of the Septuagint, Philo tells us, were none other than the Ptolomys of Egypt, the regional kings and heirs of Alexander the Great.

The Greek philosophers saw "God" as an immutable source of "being," oblivious to the vicissitudes that attended life for any of the creatures that flowed from the "One's" existential superabundance. It was of less concern to them that the anthropomorphic imagery describing the Hebrew "God" of the Scriptures would not

---

[211] Cf especially the prophet Hosea (Osee).

jibe with either the ethereal conceptions of the philosophers' "One" or even the Hebrew Yahweh's own demand for a nameless and imageless worship from his people. But, they considered the Hebrew imagery harmless at any rate, and it satisfied the needs of the ordinary people who required something concrete and could not relate to the empty conceptuality proposed by the philosophers.

Emptiness — the Dark Night

But for mystics, conceptual emptiness was not a problem. It was the very air they breathed. In the Hindu East ascetics exhilarated in the rarified atmosphere at the mountaintop of the Absolute. In the Christian West, however, the search for the quiescence of all imagery and desire that was the condition for "contemplative union," was more problematic. Given the belief in a personal "God" who might be expected to engage the "soul" in dialogic interaction — minimally giving commands and punishing disobedience, often warm and revealing and then turning cold and hidden — the quest ironically included efforts to transcend the ups and downs of the "relationship." In the 16th century, the explicit and most emphatic counsel of Carmelite mystic John of the Cross was *to reject those aspects of the relationship that resembled the satisfactions (or frustrations) of personal (human) contact.* Forget all such things, advised John. The contemplative was to pursue "God" in the darkness and emptiness of "faith alone," — in a "Dark Night." Even the sensations that "God infuses," John says, the "soul" must

> set no store by them; it must set them aside and take up a passive and negative attitude with regard to them. ... all the soul has to endeavor to do with respect to all the sensations that come to it from above ... — it matters not if they be visions, locutions, feelings or revelations — is to make no account of [them] ...[212]

These counsels were traditional in the Christian mystical writers throughout the centuries. What Dionysius the Areopagite, and the author of *The Cloud* called "unknowing," John of the Cross called the "Dark Night." The mystics of the West universally claimed that sustained contact with "God" was a work of one's own self-management directed precisely at getting beyond any imagined

---

[212] John of the Cross, *Ascent of Mount Carmel*, Bk III, ch XIII, 4 & 6 (Penguin p.293-4)

"personal" interaction. It meant entering into a humanly unimaginable "relationship" *that was not personal at the level of human experience,* and therefore was like walking in darkness. To call it "personal" was a statement of imagination based on belief, not fact, that sustained the "love" from the human side. This is a very revealing paradox. The personal "God" of the mystics in the West is declared by their very own counsels to be a stable interior presence which became the object of contemplation *only through the programmed negation of all the imagined feelings of interpersonal exchange.* The "God" that the mystics knew by experience was akin to the "One" of Plotinus and very different from the "God" preached by the Church. It brings up the same old question: "What is 'God' really like?"

The goal for the mystics was absolute quiescence. They attempted to attune themselves, by a process of progressive detachment, to the almost imperceptible hum of "God's" unchanging and non-interventionist presence at the core of the "soul" providing *nothing* but existence.

"God" does nothing to the soul and that's for two reasons: first because the "soul" has everything it needs to live out and fulfill its human destiny, and second because "God," having everything, wants nothing for "herself," not even obedience, not even love. "God's" presence is pure unmixed *gift*, the sheer overflow of a superabundance of being. By failing to emphasize this, the traditional religious imagery implied *some sort of need* in "God" which only the compliance of the human individual could satisfy. How else could they claim "God" was angry with them, or pleased ... or in the case of the mystics, "drew close" or "moved away"? This is obviously impossible. The mystics knew that "God" who needed nothing, *wanted nothing and, in fact, did nothing.* "God" was at the core of the soul, silent and un-demanding. "God" was neither enhanced nor diminished by anything the human individual did or did not do. And to perceive this absolutely silent presence of "God" one had to be as empty of all needs and as fully at peace with oneself as "God" was. One had to learn to be silent, just as "God" was silent and to love oneself unreservedly in "God," as "God" loves herself — and us in herself — unreservedly.

This may not sound traditionally "Christian." But of course, we've not been taught the doctrines of the mystics. Aquinas' doctrine of contemplative egalitarianism was shelved in practice. For even in our time the Catholic Church continues to promote a bimodal spirituality: one for the ordinary people, and one for the religious elite.

Mystical spirituality has ideological social implications. It impacts conventional *mores*. For it means everything else besides "God's" presence becomes secondary — not eliminated but secondary — morality, politics, "social skills," education, marketability. It is the ultimate basis of socially independent human self-esteem. To hear such a faint and inaudible whisper means to ignore the imperious call of every huckster in the psychic marketplace, even those considered spiritually refined, like honor, reputation, "integrity," esthetic sensitivity, "self-fulfillment," success. Don't get me wrong. These things are good. But they are not ultimate. They are not "God." For the mystics, to hear "God" meant to *need,* hear, see, want and have *nothing else.* It wasn't even enough to say that to have "God" was *to allow oneself to be given, to let oneself be loved, to be "breathed" into being*; for the positive component of each of those correlatives was itself a *desideratum*, the object of a definable desire. *And you could not hear the silent melody of existence while you were invested in having anything else.* To have or know "God" was, therefore, to be content not to have, not to know, not to speak ... simply to be. And to be for a human being is to be one's self. To learn how *to simply be oneself* was the exercise of a lifetime.

Now the irony is that the exercise required here is not to exercise at all. It is to *do nothing* to achieve or accumulate an experience, since trying to have the experience militates against it. The goal, in the final analysis, is simply to re-enter the unchanged stream of life and work within it with a new awareness, an attunement, a sensitivity, an alertness to the background sound of existence, the Sacred, which we in the West call "God". It is to remain in a condition of passive receptivity with regard to existence that does not project itself, organize itself or assert itself in any way. It is a state of non-pursuit, particularly with regard to the mystical experience one was after. Indeed, what one was after was precisely *not to be after anything*. This cessation of striving, desire and even concept formation was "emptiness," *sunyata* for the 2nd century Buddhist Nagárjuna. In general, Buddhists called it *nirvana*. The Western tradition is in every respect the same. Here's the way 14th century Johannes Tauler put it:

> " ... all the energies of your soul must be silent. It is not a question of learning to *do*, but of learning *not to do*.[213]

Mysticism and Metaphysics

I believe there is a nexus here between practice and theory that is very important. The experience of the mystics points to an underlying metaphysical reality that I am convinced can best be described in the terms I have been using throughout this analysis — that phenomenal existence is *matter-energy*. "God," I propose, is the name that we of the Abrahamic lineage have traditionally given to the source of our existence. I conceive of that source not as the historical "initiator of being" but rather as the very inner energy of the outpouring existence of what actually exists *now*. In other words, I don't look for "God" at the beginning of time but rather *in the here and now*. This is not new. It is a traditional statement for philosophical theology. *"God" is the source and core of phenomenal existence in the present moment.* The "source" that I'm speaking of produces a necessarily palpable effect, viz., *here and now existence as we know and experience it*. (Here and now existence can have no other definition for us than "what we can experience as present.") Experience, therefore, ordinary, everyday, mundane experience is at the very center of the definition of the "Source of Being" and therefore "God," or "the Sacred." We can only experience what is material. "God" dwells in the core of the self as emergent existence and can be experienced.

The mystics not only knew it, they knew *how* it worked.

As human beings, we are in a unique position with regard to being, because our cognitive apparatus nor only experiences existence, but we can reflect on it. We know that things *are here*.

---

[213] Johannes Tauler, *Sermon 31*, in *The Rhineland Mystics*, ed. Davies *op.cit.* p.71

Moreover, since we ourselves exist, we "understand" existence, not conceptually but *connaturally*, from within, *as interior experience*. This is the basis of mysticism. Mystical experience, I submit, is the interior, connatural, cognitively transparent *co-dwelling with one's own existential energy, one's self,* as it emerges continuously producing the flow of time. It is a material experience. Such experience is not immediately conceptual, and for the mystics there is no necessity for it ever to move to the conceptual level, though obviously it can because it has for those mystics who have written about it. They wrote about it to share it, and to invite others into it. That experience of the *self* emerging into (or being sustained in) *presence, existence,* from moment to moment, for the Western contemplative is the experience of "God." And I leave open (because I believe irrelevant) the question whether that energy *is itself* "God" or only the un-mediated effect of "God's" active presence. In either case, presence, existence is "God's Presence." "God's" presence *IS* the human organism experiencing its own existence. The *self* is the palpable breath of "God."

Taking it a step further: this interior experience of "emerging being" is validly extrapolated, as a conclusion of analysis, to all things. Since we know ourselves interiorly and immediately as "*matter-energy* emerging into existence" through the moments of time, we can rightly claim to know all things, even the most unfamiliar and unrelated, residing in the most remote corner of the universe. For, however alien in other respects these far off entities or aggregates of entities might be, they, like us, *are material energy that exists in time*. We, our *selves,* are THAT — that very same *energy of matter.*[214] This provides the conceptual basis for our metaphysics, our speculative understanding of all things, the whole of existence, cosmo-ontology. Our science has discovered that everything that exists is *materially homogeneous*; existence itself is homogeneous.

What I experience of my existence emerging in time I realize is a progressive event, *a process* that I project to be true of every-

---

[214] This intentionally alludes to the famous Hindu phrase, *tat tvam asi*, traditionally rendered "Thou are That." It evoked the unity of all things. It was said that Beethoven kept it prominently displayed on top of his piano.

thing that exists, right now, everywhere, even where I will never be or ever be able to imagine — galaxies at the limits of the reach of our instruments or the deepest, densest "singularity" of the darkest black hole in the universe, wherever it may be. It is all emerging into existence progressively creating time, NOW, exactly as "I" experience it in my *self*. I am no different from any of THAT. I am a "thing" among things, or better, a process among processes. The "me" that spontaneously thinks of itself as a different kind of "thing" from all the things around me — a "thing" that has existence on its own — is deceived. What *has* existence is the substrate, a potential called *matter-energy*, combining and recombining, composing, decomposing eternally, but in my case, temporarily gathered as "me." "I" realize that there is no "me" with it's own independent existence, being, substance or "stuff"*!* My existence is composed of the "stuff" of the universe. Similarly I understand that everything out there is conditioned in exactly the same way. The illusion the mystics dispel is not that there are things "out there" with special characteristics and manner of surviving; the illusion is rather that these "things" exist *on their own, in their own right, independently.* Substantial, "stand-alone" existence is the illusion. What exists, in fact, is the primal energy of which all things are made. These "things" condition one another universally so that the character and "stuff" of each enters into the character and stuff of every other. The experience of the mystics is that being is a constantly emerging gift, as a current from a spring, one shared homogeneous thing, given, received and given back — a metaphysical recycling.

Existence is a property of *matter-energy*, or matter's energy is a property of existence; it doesn't matter which way you put it because wherever you find the one, you find the other. Some have identified it with *vibrating strings* thought to underlay sub-atomic particles. Or perhaps there is an even more elemental building block out of which even the strings are formed. It doesn't matter. But please be advised: it is both concrete and scientifically specific.

This energy base, whatever it is, is the ground in which all existence is rooted, even our cognitional existence. This energy temporarily re-arranges itself as "me." "I" am merely a momentary concrescence of *matter-energy* that dismantles itself in time, permitting its sub-atomic components to be re-used in other modalities and other entities endlessly. I cannot *cling to* this special configuration called "me." In a real sense "I" am not really there. The Buddhists called it *anatman*, the illusion of the substantial *self*, i.e., the illusion that the self has stand-alone existence. This makes the self, like all other things, an *empty* phenomenon. *Emptiness* is the Buddhists' favorite word for the way they believe we should look on reality. Eckhart said it a slightly different way: he said we were *nothing*. He equated the illusion of stand-alone existence with "sin." Sin, he said, was behaving as if we had existence from ourselves — as if we were "God." The *self*, he said, was *nothing*. The paradox for us is both galling and apparent. For it is this evanescent *self* that is the gateway to our direct experience of *matter's energy*, "God."

The point of these final reflections was to let mystics describe their experience of "God," and try to understand it. We focused on the 14th century because it was the time when contemplative prayer moved out of the monasteries and into the lives of ordinary people. And thanks to the erroneous imagery associated with "divine providence" it also represented the beginnings of a paranoid, alienated Christian world-view in which we ourselves were formed and are right now in the process of reforming yet again. I think that at this point in time we are turning back to our roots; and that is giving us a new perspective on other traditions as well as on science. The mystics through the ages and across cultures tend to describe their experiences in similar terms. Their observations corroborate the discoveries we made about *existence or presence*, arrived at through a kind of physical / metaphysical or cosmo-ontological enquiry. It is our perennial search for the Sacred Source of our being, what we have traditionally called "God."

So what seems to be a sequence of disparate topics is really an interrelated history-conscious exploration of the anatomy of our spirituality, grounded in our view of the Sacred world. These connections — historical, scientific, philosophical-doctrinal, mystical — are organic and integrally related. We arbitrarily turn them into separate "topics" to concur with our (equally arbitrary) separate academic disciplines. But our prayer-life is one integral whole with our belief system and our scientific view of the world. Mysticism — Religion — Cosmology / Ontology — the physical and biological sciences — our "spirituality." It's all one thing.

In this vision, our intellectual, academic divisions are finally overcome. There is "consilience;" we can think and live in awe with one undivided mind in this Sacred world.

Bibliography

Abbott, ed. and Gallagher, tr. *The Documents of Vatican II,* New York: Guild Press, 1966
Anonymous, *The Cloud of Unknowing and Other Works,* tr. Clifton Wolters, London: Penguin, 1961
Aquinas, Thomas, *On the Truth of the Catholic Faith, (Summa Contra Gentiles),* tr. Anton Pegis, Garden City NY, Image, 1955
-----------, *Summa Theologíae,* Madrid, Bibl. de Autores Cristianos, 1961
Arendt, Hannah, *The Human Condition,* Garden City NY: Anchor, 1959
Augustine of Hippo, *The City of God,* tr. Walsh et al, Garden City NY: Doubleday Image, 1958
Aurobindo, Sri, *The Essential Aurobindo,* Gr. Barrington MA: Lindisfarne Books, 1987
Becker, Ernest, *The Denial of Death,* New York: Free Press, 1974
Bergson, Henri, *Creative Evolution,* Mineola NY: Dover, 1998 tr. Mitchell 1910 from the original published 1907
Berry, Jason and Renner, Gerald, *Vows of Silence,* NY, Free Press, 2004.
Blakney tr., *Meister Eckhart,* Harper Torchbook, 1941
Borg, Marcus, et al. *The Search for Jesus,* Bib.Arch.Soc. 1994
-------, *Jesus,* HarperCollins, NY, 2006.
Brown, Peter, *Augustine of Hippo,* U. of CA. Press, rev. ed., 2000
---------, *The Body and Society,* New York: Columbia U. Pr, 1988
Carabine, Deirdre, *John Scottus Eriugena,* NY: Oxford U. Press, 2000.
Caputo, John D., *The Mystical Element in Heidegger's Thought,* Athens, OH: Ohio U. Press, 1978
Church et al. tr, *Complete Works of Tacitus,* New York: Random House 1942
Copleston, Fredrick, *A History of Philosophy,* Westminster MD: Newman Press, 1962
Coulton, G.G., *The Mediaeval Scene,* Cambridge, 1930
Cozzens, Donald, *The Changing Face of the Priesthood,* Collegeville, MN: Liturgical Press, 2000
Davies, Oliver, *The Rhineland Mystics,* London, SPCK, 1989
Diamond, Jared, *Collapse,* New York: Viking, 2005
Enchiridion Symbolorum, Denzinger-Schönmetzer, Rome, Herder, 1963
Encyclopaedia Britanica, 15th ed, Chicago: Benton, 1979
Encyclopaedia Britanica, Ultimate Reference suite DVD, 2006

Eriúgena, Juan Escoto, *División de la Naturaleza (Periphyseon)*, Barcelona: Folio, 2002
----------, John the Scot, *Periphyseon*, tr. Uhlfelder, Indianapolis: Bobbs-Merrill, 1976
Forman, Robert, *Meister Eckhart*, Rockport MA, Element, 1991,
Fox, Matthew, *Passion for Creation, the Spirituality of Meister Eckhart*, Rochester VT: Inner Traditions, , 1980
Freud, Sigmund, *Civilization and its Discontents*, Vienna, 1930
Funk, Robert W, *Honest to Jesus*, Harper Collins, 1996;
Geisler, Norman, reproduced in *The Intellectuals Speak Out About God* Ed. Varghese, Regnery, 1984
Goodenough, Ursula, *The Sacred Depths of Nature*, Oxford U. Press, 1998
Haight, Roger, *Jesus the Symbol of God*, Maryknoll NY, Orbis, 2002
Harnack, Adolph, *The History of Dogma*, tr. Buchanan, New York: Dover, 1904
Hilton, Walter, *The Scale of Perfection*, Clark & Dorward, tr., New York: Paulist Press, 1991
Holy Bible, Revised Standard Version, New York, Thomas Nelson & Sons,1953
John Paul II, "Address" To The Commission Of Episcopates Of The European Union (Comece), 30 March 2001.
Jones, C A.H.M., *Constantine and the Conversion of Europe*, New York: Collier, 1962
Jowett, B., tr., *The Works of Plato*, New York, Tudor, undated
Langland, William, *Piers Ploughman*, London: Penguin, 1959
Maimonides, Moses, *The Guide for the Perplexed*, (1175), Dover, NY reprinted 1956 (orig. translation 1904)
Marcuse, Herbert, *Eros and Civilization*, New York: Random House, 1955
McKeon, Richard, *Introduction to Aristotle*, New York: Random House, 1947, rev and expanded, 1973
Milgrom, Mordehai, "Does Dark Matter Really Exist?" *Scientific American Special Report*, (undated)
Nolan, Albert, O.P., *Jesus Before Christianity*, Maryknoll NY: Orbis 1976
O'Murchu, Diarmund, *Quantum Theology*, New York: Crossroads, 1999
Panikkar, Raimundo, *The Silence of God*, Maryknoll NY: Orbis, 1990
----------, *The Trinity in the Religious Experience of Man*, Maryknoll NY, Orbis, 1973
Pasachoff & Filippenko, *The Cosmos*, Harcourt College Publishers, 2001

Patterson, Stephen, "Sources for a Life of Jesus," *The Search for Jesus*, Washington DC: Biblical Archaeology Society, 1994
Pelican, Jaroslav, *The Emergence of the Catholic Tradition*, U. of Chicago Press, 1971
Rahner and Vorgrimler, *Theological Dictionary*, New York: Herder and Herder, 1965
Rahner, Karl, S.J., *On the Theology of Death*, tr Charles Henkey New York: Herder, 1961
Ratzinger, Joseph Card., "Instruction On Christian Freedom and Liberation," March 22, 1986,
Richardson, Cyril, ed., *Early Christian Fathers*, New York: Macmillan, 1970
Sartre, Jean Paul, *Being and Nothingness*, New York: Philosophical Library, 1956
---------, *Nausea*, tr. Alexander, New York: New Directions, 1969
Tattersall, Ian, "Once We Were Not Alone" *Scientific American Special Edition*, June 2003
Teilhard de Chardin, Pierre, S.J., *The Phenomenon of Man*, (1955) tr. Wall, Harper & Row, NY, 1959
Thomas, Mary Edith, *Medieval Skepticism and Chaucer*, New York: Cooper Sq. 1971
Tuchman, Barbara, *A Distant Mirror*, New York: Knopf, 1978
Walshe, M., *Meister Eckhart, German Sermons and Treatises*, London: Watkins, 1979
Whitehead, Alfred North, *Process and Reality*, (1929), New York: Free Press, 1957
Wills, Gary, *Papal Sin*, New York: Doubleday Image, 2000
Woods, Robert O.P., ed. *Understanding Mysticism*, Garden City, NJ; Image Books 1980
Yonge, G.D., tr., *The Works of Philo*, Hendrickson, 1993

Index

14th century, 145, 274
20th century physics, 149
5th Lateran Council, 61
abortion and euthanasia, 108
Abrahamic Tradition, 309
absence, 267
Absolute, 69, 308, 311
absurd, 190
Act of Creation, 202
ad extram, 199
Adam, 289
Adam and Eve, 277
Adeodatus, 246
adoptionism, 227
Alexander the Great, 310
alienation, 79, 150, 193, 245, 248, 249, 286, 290
all-Cosmic existence, 88
Almighty, 157
Alpha, 151, 158, 179, 180
Ambrose, 99
analogy, 211, 215, 223, 228, 269
anatman, 86, 219, 231, 238, 317
animals, 74
annulment, 28
Anselm, 221, 224
anthropocentrism, 79
anthropomorphism, 5, 132, 135, 140, 141, 224, 225, 294, 302
Apocalypse, 98
Apologists, 71

apophatic, 266
Apostolic Succession, 36
Aquinas, 180, 183, 193, 202, 211, 228, 240, 251, 268, 276, 284, 294, 299, 306, 313
aristocracy, 306
Aristotle, 64, 146, 202, 205, 285, 310
Arius, 227
Ascent of Mount Carmel, 311
atheism, 266, 267
atheists, 264
Athenagoras, 71
Augustine, 18, 20, 21, 22, 23, 24, 25, 32, 96, 98, 99, 100, 124, 127, 130, 140, 159, 174, 187, 193, 244, 246, 247, 255, 275, 287, 293, 295, 303
authority, 35
Avignon, 242, 276
Bavaria, 276
beatific vision, 288, 305
becoming, 28, 92, 144, 151, 154, 155, 167, 169, 171, 172, 177, 178, 180, 183, 184, 185, 186, 188, 200, 201, 203, 205, 206, 209, 218, 230, 257, 259, 261
Beguines, 241, 282, 289, 306
being, 184, 207
Being & Nothingness, 233
being and non-being, 232

Being as such, 207
being of the phenomenon, 233, 234
beliefs, 30, 38, 59, 61, 66, 67, 80, 91, 95, 96, 108, 113, 116, 134, 135, 146, 275, 280, 300, 308
Bergson, 75, 76, 93, 110, 173, 174, 185, 208, 214, 230, 234
beyond God, 261, 263, 264
big-bang, 294
Black Death, 147, 274, 277, 279
black hole, 316
Boccaccio, 279
Book of Job, 303
bourgeoisie, 278
Brahma, 308
breakthrough, 258, 260
breath of God, 300, 307, 308, 313, 315
Brethren of the Common Life, 289
Bubonic Plague. *See* Black Death
Buddha, 86, 119, 194, 196, 203, 232, 261
Buddhism, 212, 231
Buddhist, 194
Buddhists, 300, 304, 314, 317
C.G.Jung, 303
Calvin, 244
Calvinism, 128
Canterbury Tales, 279
Cardinal Law, 34

Carmina Burana, 150
Carthusian, 283
Catholic Catechism, 67
celibacy, 4, 10, 11, 12, 16, 17, 24, 25, 26, 31, 32, 33, 43, 46, 55, 58, 231, 301, 306
Chaucer, 279, 280
chimpanzees, 72
Christendom, 247
Christian ideology, 71
Christogenesis, 154, 188
City of God, 159
Clement of Alexandria, 99, 227
Cloud of Unknowing, 182, 283, 284, 285, 288, 304, 312
Cologne, 241, 289
concept of being, 207, 223, 251, 269
conceptual suspension, 267
Conciliar Movement, 275
concupiscence, 22, 23, 99
congenital self-embrace, 299, 306
conquista, 147
conscious self-identity, 233
consciousness, 62, 63, 72, 74, 75, 78, 80, 83, 88, 93, 94, 95, 109, 110, 113, 153, 154, 155, 160, 161, 167, 168, 169, 170, 171, 179, 191, 208, 233, 236, 237, 301, 306, 317
consequent nature of God, 154, 175, 188

contemplative spirituality, 241
contraception, 26
Copernican Revolution, 148
core of the soul, 254, 257, 285, 300, 312, 315
Cosmic Christ, 285
cosmogenesis, 299
Council of Vienne, 242
creation, 93
creationism, 188
cult of the Roman gods, 96
damnation, 290
dark energy, 185
dark matter, 149, 185
Dark Night, 311, 312
darkness, 6, 116, 264, 265, 285, 308, 311, 312
Darwin, 145, 148, 152, 188
death, 64, 77, 81, 212, 233
death as a change in modality, 212
Decameron, 279
Deists, 125
Demiurge, 223
demons, 96
denial of death, 82–85, 134
Descartes, 88, 224
devotio moderna, 289
Dionysus, 231
discovery of the Americas, 147
divine, 271
Divine Wrath, 124
divinity of Christ, 224
divorce, 28
Divorce and Annulment, 27

Dominicans, 240
Duns Scotus, 146, 211, 228, 286, 307
ecclesiastical authority, 126
Eckhart, 86, 197, 221, 228, 240, 281, 283, 284, 288, 317
ecology, 92
educated elite, 305
efficient causality, 199
egalitarianism, 284, 313
Einstein, 76
elemental particles, 76
embrace of being, 200, 201
emergence, 73
Emperor of Rome, 226
emptiness, 265, 267, 308, 311, 314, 317
England, 274
entity, 268
eradication of "self-will", 253
Eriugena, 105, 228, 230, 255, 268, 270, 285, 288, 300, 307, 308
Ernest Becker, 82
espousals, 301
esse in se subsistens, 3, 202, 213, 219, 222, 223, 251
essence, 268
estrangement, 193
eternal objects, 154
Eternal-Now, 253, 259
evolution, 73, 77, 93, 186, 188, 205, 298
ex opere operato, 36, 38, 39, 40, 42, 47, 122, 247, 249
existential finality, 167

existential relationship, 244
experience, 236
extinction, 155
extra ecclesiam nulla salus, 22
faith, 5, 19, 26, 58, 59, 60, 65, 80, 81–82, 83, 113, 114, 115, 116, 117, 118, 126, 132, 134, 146, 147, 202, 264, 265, 275, 277, 290, 311
fall, 195
Father, 19, 20, 77, 113, 116, 141, 157, 158, 159, 166, 178, 192, 193, 197, 202, 223, 225, 226, 227, 243, 244, 245, 253, 257, 259, 260, 302, 309
Fathers, 31, 43, 71, 98
feminist movement, 241
fertile crescent, 232
Fertile Crescent, 310
feudal lords, 243
feudal society, 305
Fidel, 121, 123, 135, 136, 142, 277, 303
Final Cause, 151, 176, 200
forensic pardon, 248
Formal or Exemplary Cause, 200
Forman, 260
Fortuna, 150
Francis of Assisi, 196
Franklin's Tale, 280
free will, 247
functional pantheism, 254, 255

galaxies, 316
Gavin de Beer, 152
genus and specific difference, 92, 137, 181, 268
German Princes, 243
God as Being, 251
God as Creator, 148
God as empirical, 299
God as Mother, 166, 308
God as One, 259, 260
God as person, 135–41
Godhead, 259, 260, 266
God's wrath, 274, 286, 295
Great Schism, 275
Greeks, 60–64, 67–71, 73, 84, 89, 92, 94, 104, 116, 151, 168, 186, 187, 204, 212, 219, 223, 224, 225, 227, 231, 232, 310
Gregory of Nyssa, 134
heathen, 22, 47, 301
Hebrews, 309
Hegel, 148, 152
Heidegger, 258, 265
hell, 290
Hemmerlein, Thomas, 289
Heraclitus, 206
heresy, 241, 242
hierarchy, 35, 247
Hilton, 282
Hindus, 194, 308
Holy Grail, 229, 308
hominid, 94
homoousion, 223
Honorius, 22
Hostility, 248
human consciousness, 72

human nature, 94
Humanae Vitae, 26
hundred years war, 276
I am who am, 251
ideas, 63, 94, 219
illusion, 84, 86, 101, 203, 212, 231, 237, 238, 254, 316, 317
imagination, 237
Imitation of Christ, 288, 289, 291, 301
immanence, 180, 182, 186, 192, 195, 227, 229, 245, 285
immortal soul, 2, 17, 61, 65, 88, 108, 109, 212, 213
immortality, 18, 19, 60, 61, 63, 64, 77, 78, 80, 82, 83, 84, 85, 87, 92, 98, 99, 101, 104, 113, 116, 135, 146, 152, 213, 216, 217, 229, 231
Imperial Christianity, 246
Incarnation, 187
incomprehensibility, 269
indelible seal of the priesthood, 36
India, 232
individual judgment after death, 88
individualism, 213
indulgences, 287
Indwelling God, 254, 285, 286, 288
Infinite Self, 242
infusion of the soul, 108

Inquisition, 228, 241, 242, 247, 284
Intelligent Design, 299, 309
interiority, 153
intuition of being, 207
Islamic, 309
Jaquerie, 278
Jesus, 9, 15, 18, 19, 21, 36, 37, 53, 54, 56, 58, 59, 60, 65, 67, 70, 71, 99, 116, 117, 119, 141, 193, 196, 224, 225, 226, 227, 231, 242, 244, 245, 256, 257, 290, 291, 292, 302
Jewish, 310
Jewish Law annulled, 245
Jews, 128, 244, 278
John of the Cross, 261, 264, 311, 312
John XXII, 242
Judaism, 37, 65, 69, 96, 97, 100, 116, 245, 310
Juliana of Norwich, 282, 288, 294
justification, 248
justified by faith, 248
Kant, 148
Karl Marx, 243
Karl Rahner, 87
Knight's Tale, 280
Ladder of Perfection, 282
laesa majestas, 139
Langland, 276, 280, 282
Leibniz, 224
liberation, 98
Logos, 223, 225, 227, 253, 259, 285, 287

Lollards, 279
love affair, 302
Luther, 247, 282, 287
Lutheran Reform, 247–49
Manichaeism, 96
Marcion, 140
Marcus Aurelius, 71
marriage, 25, 98, 99
Mary's virginity, 99
mask, 196, 230, 270, 308
massacre, 243, 244
matter, 63, 151, 186
matter-energy, 72, 85, 90, 92, 93, 106–7, 110, 111, 113, 114, 120, 149, 169, 177, 180, 183, 184, 185, 192, 194, 195, 196, 203, 216, 217, 219, 229, 232
Mennonites, 243
merit, 290
Mesopotamia, 138
metaphor, 187
Middle Ages, 132, 247
Midlands, 283
Mind of God, 220, 235
mind vs matter, 89
Mithraism, 96
Modern science, 80
monasteries, 305
Monica, 246
Monster-God, 244
moral goodness, 164
morality, 25, 78, 79, 91, 92, 103, 105, 107, 108, 109, 110, 111, 104–12, 112, 116, 125, 126, 132, 138, 147, 157, 160, 161, 163, 164, 170, 176, 196, 213, 231, 287, 313
moral-legal perspective, 245
Moses Maimonides, 65
movings of grace, 301
mystery, 60
mystery religions, 67, 225, 226
mystical experience, 78, 221, 222, 254, 263, 266, 283, 298, 300, 302, 304, 305, 306, 307, 308, 309, 314
mystical perspective, 245
mystical union, 249, 284, 305
mysticism, 281
mystique, 40
Nagárjuna, 314
native peoples, 75
Nausea, 190
Neanderthals, 75
negation, 234, 237
neo-Platonism, 20, 96, 100, 173, 243, 249, 263, 268, 284, 286
Newton, 148
Nicea, 223, 226, 227
nirvana, 194, 196, 300, 304, 314
non-being, 208, 209, 213, 234, 267, 268
non-experience, 209
non-pursuit, 314
nothingness, 183, 189, 204, 205, 207, 211, 212, 234, 237, 238, 255, 257, 265, 267
O'Murchu, Diarmund, 88

Ockham, 228, 256, 276, 286
Omega, 151, 152, 176, 179, 180, 197
omnipotence, 126, 127, 281, 296
On the Theology of Death, 87
One, 68, 258, 302, 310, 312
ontological argument, 224
ontological relationship, 200
Origen, 140, 227
original hostility, 275, 287
Original Sin, 21, 23, 29, 37, 59, 83, 99, 116, 124, 139, 193, 196, 244, 246, 247, 248, 275, 289, 293, 303
Osiris, 69, 231
ostracism, 44, 49
pagan, 96
panentheism, 179–88, 192, 197, 227, 251
Panikkar, 195, 258, 266
Panta rei, 206
pantheism, 154, 179, 181, 226, 231, 242, 266, 269, 270
  functional pantheism, 193, 195, 201
pantheon, 310
Papacy, 276
Parmenides, 206
parousía, 98
participation, 221
participation in being, 179, 180, 182, 227, 250, 252, 254, 288
participation in the Word, 259

Pascal, 231
Paul, 245
peasants' revolts, 243, 278
Pelagians, 21, 247
person, 135, 301
Peter, 246
Peter Brown, 21, 32, 97, 124, 275
phenomenon of being, 233
Philo, 97, 105, 140, 182, 225, 310
philosophía perennis, 251
philosophy, 70
Piers the Ploughman, 276
plague, 276, 279, 286, 287, 303, *See* Black Death
Plato, 18, 19, 20, 21, 30, 61, 62, 64, 65, 66, 68, 70, 71, 80, 92, 97, 116, 117, 135, 146, 174, 204, 225, 226, 231, 235, 285, 310
Platonic Paradigm, 76, 100, 107, 112, 145, 168, 169, 170, 173, 196, 256
Plotinus, 226, 265, 312
poetry, 210, 236
politics, 37, 213, 313
powerless God, 157
predestination, 127, 247
pre-existence of the soul, 263
presence, 210, 211, 218, 237
presence as univocal, 210
primary cause, 182, 294
primordial nature of God, 76, 154
primordiality of non-being, 214, 234, 238

process, 167, 229
processions, 228
Protestant Reformation, 243
Protestants, 279, 289
providence, 108, 121, 126, 131, 137, 150, 242, 246, 277, 281, 293, 294, 299, 317
Psalms, 303
Pseudo-Dionysius, 221, 268, 283
psycho-erotic union with "God,", 301
Ptolomys of Egypt, 310
Pure Act, 178, 186, 215, 219
purpose, 150–56, 160, 164, 188
pusillanimous, 46, 193, 244, 291
Pythagoreans, 62, 97, 231, 310
Qoheleth, 1
quanta, 72, 77, 110, 112, 113, 149, 185, 196
quantum fluctuations, 185
quarks, 77, 149
quiescence, 16, 23, 100, 231, 254, 300, 307, 311, 312
radical detachment, 257, 258, 260, 261, 263, 264, 265, 266, 312
radical egalitarianism, 243, 306
random variation and natural selection, 149
randomness, 150, 188, 190
reformation, 287

relation of dependency, 200, 228, 251
Religion, 80
religious experience, 286
repression, 11, 13, 37, 53, 54, 99, 100, 101, 104, 126
resurrection of the body, 60, 152
revelation, 286
Revelations of Divine Love, 282
Rhine Valley, 240, 243, 289, 306
Rhineland, 281, 289
Rhineland Mystics, 243
Roman Catholicism, 1
Roman Imperial Theocracy, 226
Roman *Pantocrator*, 226
Rome, 310
Rumi, 196
rural communitarianism, 243
Ruysbroeck, 243, 282
sacramental seal, 39
sacraments, 37, 39, 41, 42, 122, 242, 249, 279, 282, 290, 301, 309
sanctifying grace, 145, 301, 309
sanctity as charity, 305
sanitas corporis, 304
Sartre, 189, 233–39
Satan, 71
schizoid culture, 147
scholastic, 135, 136, 146, 178, 180, 183, 195, 199, 211, 223, 228, 251, 261

Scholastic Causality, 199–202
Schopenhauer, 154
scriptures, 279
Second Coming, 151
secondary causes, 142, 182, 294, 300
self, 86, 194
self-esteem, 37, 313
selfishness, 254
Septuagint, 310
sexual renunciation, 97, 98
sexual revolution, 29
Sheik, 140, 192, 309
Simone de Beauvoir, 190
sin, 13, 14, 15, 18, 19, 21, 22, 23, 27, 29, 41, 98, 108, 128, 139, 182, 187, 241, 242, 247, 277, 278, 282, 287, 289, 290, 317
sin as non-being, 255
singularity, 316
skepticism, 280
slavery, 74
slavery of error, 42
song, 234
Song of Solomon, 302
soul, 233, 253, 300, 304
species, 8, 75
spirit, 78, 296
Spirit, 62, 152
spiritual aristocracy, 197, 242, 245
St Jerome, 98
stand-alone existence, 317
Statute of Labourers, 278
Stoics, 97, 225, 310

Strasbourg, 240, 281
strings, 149, 185, 317
sub-atomic particles, 317
sublimation, 100–104
subsistent relations, 252, 259
substance, 203
substrate, 203, 206
Summa Contra Gentiles, 65, 72
sunyata, 314
super-eminence, 132, 136
super-essential, 268
supernatural, 301
supernovas, 77
surrender, 113
survival, 167
Suso, 243
systematization of mystical experience, 304
Tammuz, 69
tat tvam asi, 316
Tattersall, 75
Tauler, 243, 281, 314
techné, 227
Teilhard de Chardin, 75, 95, 153, 154, 165, 176, 230
thanksgiving, 81, 113, 114, 115, 116
theophanies, 230
theophany, 187, 285, 286, 288
Theory of Evolution, 145
theotokoi, 198
Theravada Buddhism, 231
Thomas à Becket, 280
Thomas à Kempis, 289
Thomas Aquinas, 65, 66

thought, 219
transcendence, 73
transubstantiation, 279
Trier, 243
Trinity, 252, 253
Trinity as secondary, 259
trust, 81, 272
unicity, 210
unity of the Godhead, 253
Universal Act of Existence,, 259
universal call to Christian perfection, 305
universal concepts, 146
universals, 80
univocal, 211
upper classes, 226
Valois, 276
Vatican II, 42
vertical dimension, 252
violence, 157

virginity, 21, 23, 24, 31, 97, 99, 130
vital impulse, 75, 206
voluntarism, 147
Whitehead, 76, 92, 93, 110, 153, 154, 155, 158, 165, 167, 172, 174, 175, 179, 184, 188, 200, 230, 261
Whole, 79, 85, 87, 91, 93, 110, 120, 152, 194, 195, 217
William of Ockham, 146
Wittenberg, 247
women, 74
Word., 253
World of Ideas, 145, 155
wretches, 290
Wycliff, 279
Yahweh, 95, 140, 141, 225, 251, 303, 310, 311
Yhwh, 140

www.ingramcontent.com/pod-product-compliance
Lightning Source LLC
Chambersburg PA
CBHW030134170426
43199CB00008B/64